4 Quadrant Dynamic Intelligence

Volume I

The Art and Science
of
Four Quadrant
Thinking

www.erickson.edu

ISBN-978-0-9953329-2-8

Printed in Canada.

The paper used in this book complies with the Permanent Paper Standard issued by the National Standards Organization (Z39.48-1984).

10 9 8 7 6 5 4 3 2 1

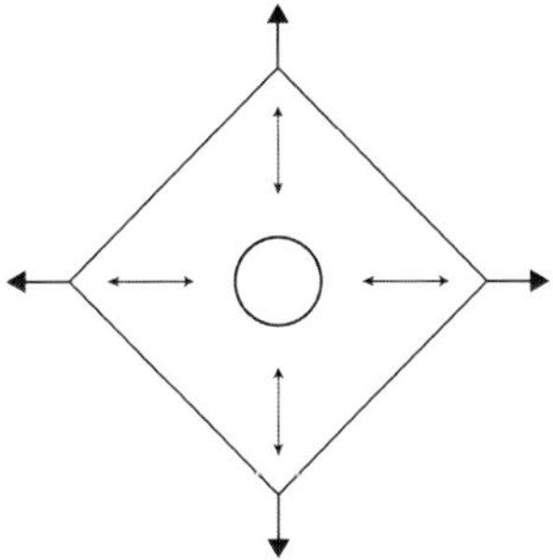

What's Inside?

Four Quadrant Dynamics: An Approach to Mind Exploration

With four quadrant exploration, we are studying the inner creativity system. We are exploring the evolving nature of human consciousness as one whole system of growth, change, and learning. We map the creativity system from outside yet *sense* the *flow* of the system from inside. We expand awareness. Four quadrant drawings assist us.

Our base is always whole system awareness. We use four quadrants to define the natural qualities of whole systems. We explore the dynamics of our own consciousness, thought system by thought system, our 'playgrounds.' We also ask how the wave of humanity's potential can evolve as a whole. Open-ended questioning, deep curiosity, and willingness to be grateful for what we receive allows this approach.

As we ask inward questions with curiosity, we notice how the mind, as a receptivity system, receives information powerfully from key areas: *physical*, *emotional-relational, intentional,* and *meaningful.* We discover how we can explore the content, structure, process, and inner form or flow of these emergent awarenesses. As we ask open-ended questions, we receive ideas — often in quick, visual 'flashes of insight.' We call these sensory 'bits' or flashes 'dynamic ideas' for a variety of reasons. Learn basic practices in Volume I, Parts 1 and 2.

In two volumes, you will discover new doorways into awareness for your own development of mind. You will also learn basic and practical practices you can use in all areas of your life.

Volume I, the book you now hold, is about defining your own 'Playground of Intelligence.' It exercises your ability with four quadrant thinking and with multiple sensory practices.

Volume II, Entering The Playground, takes us to Parts 3 and 4. Part 3 shows key ways to explore and to develop what we now call Formats A, B, C, and D — developmental frameworks for self discovery. These are special learning approaches and breakthroughs that can shift whole systems. These four formats tie very closely to basic discoveries of quantum physics. We move from particle to pattern and build coherency at the larger level. Observing these emerging patterns also ties very closely to the practices of many mystics, and integrate into approaches used in the art and science of solution-focused coaching.[1] Part 4, Integration, expands this further, with an exploration of the nature of inner truth, and how we are able to find it, individual by individual.

Sincere Acknowledgments

Both Volume I and Volume II of ***Four Quadrant Dynamic Intelligence***, results from the combined labor of many persons. Peter Stefanyi, deeply involved with reading each chapter, consistently assisted the overview. Heather Parks, with her love and consistent usage of four quadrant map-making, was responsible for many clarifying text edits. She studied and overviewed all text changes. Kim Leischner, Teodora Kamenova, Rosa Tkacova, and Lawrence McGinnis were also outstanding friends and colleagues in the area of personal reading, questioning, and script-editing.

Dedication

I dedicate this book to humanity's deep urge for development!

> *May I (We, All of Us), composed of eros and of dust,*
> *Beleaguered by the same negation and despair,*
> *Show an affirming flame!"*
>
> — Wilfred Owen

Contents

APPENDICES

Diagrams

Appendices Diagrams

FOREWORD

by Peter Stefanyi

The story started at the train station in Bratislava (Slovakia) where I (Peter) took Marilyn to catch a train to Serbia after the Icelandic volcano shut down air travel over Europe. We arrived at the platform and learned that there was still an hour for the train to arrive. Our conversation soon revolved around archaeology and evolution of the mind and physics with possible connections. Just before the arrival of the train, Marilyn said to me: "Why don't you come to Antalya in two weeks time? There might be courses of interest to you there."

Two weeks later, I became a participant in the Training of Trainers in Antalya, and a few days later I stayed for the course called "Four Quadrant Thinking."

It was an interesting course with lots of provocative ideas and shapes covering the flip-chart, when all of sudden I had an "Aha!" moment. It was a moment that had a profound influence on my future and became the key turning moment for the collaboration on this book.

I was sitting in the class, listening to the content unfolding, when an explanation of a mind process given by Marilyn suddenly caught my attention. A kind of strong 'Déjà vu' feeling occurred. I thought, "I know this process very well. This is, of course, how my mind works when I come up with something totally new and unexpected in physics." I remember myself thinking, "Wow, this is a systemic explanation of the creative process that a scientifically-oriented mind goes through when something totally new is being discovered." That was the turning moment. From that moment on, I was caught by the course and after the course itself, I spent six months reading the handouts again and again, followed by pondering on the meaning of it all. I realized that I had an extraordinary tool in my hands, and I decided to investigate whether it could be used for visualizing realities in a systemic manner. Being a physicist, I decided to discover if it could be used to systematically visualize any reality and stay consistent with basic principles of physics and mathematics.

It did stay consistent, and the more I explored the better it got.

Based on my study of the four quadrant tools, I (Peter) approached Marilyn, and we began to have regular conversations on various aspects of the system. Marilyn once said, "Peter, I have a lot of material on the subject and I want to make it into a book, but somehow it is structurally a bit disorganized and not so easy for people to understand. Would you want to participate in writing a book on the topic?" My answer was a resolute "Yes!" and, at that moment, our collaboration on the book was declared.

There is a joke that every good business consultant makes his or her money by using a two-by-two matrix. Well, it is actually not a joke. Our mind likes a visual of a two-by-two matrix, and explanations based upon using this tool tend to be more explanatory than others and easy to grasp at the same time. These two-by-two matrices usually provide an ad hoc view of some aspect of reality in two dimensions digitalized into four domains. The most advanced ones try to provide an integral view of reality based on three points of view.

However, the four quadrant tools developed by Marilyn had all the benefits of the simple two-by-two matrix and much more on the systems side. They provide a first person look at one's own mind map showing one's internal reality in one whole picture as well as rules for the mind moving along and through the map. This procedure is consistent with the method used in physics where physicists first establish the so-called initial conditions at a certain time, and then use relevant laws of physics to study the evolution of the initial state into the state in its final conditions at a later time. These rules for the movement of the thinking Mind on the internal map, when practiced, give the thinking Mind power to execute, at internal will, various advanced activities and gain awareness of its own state of affairs. This immediately shifts the original state into a new state of the Mind, which can be described by an updated internal map. One of these Mind activities might be focusing on and achieving a goal set in advance. The next type of activity might be when the mind finds a new aspect of a given reality in a creative way, which is just another name for "out of the box thinking." Instinctual appreciation of beauty and symmetry on a full picture of reality gives rise to new aspects as well. Exploration of activity or inactivity when the mind has chosen a course of action leads to better choices and increased motivation for a chosen course of action. Finally, the full exploration of the above described patterns (formats of thinking) leads to freedom of thinking and hence of subsequent doing.

The systemic tools of Dynamic Intelligence, which are based on Four Quadrant Thinking, allow for studying the realm of our internal reality in its entirety and then study what is True for us. Not all of our internal reality might be True for us, some can be false, leading to stress and associated troubles. However, the tools of Four Quadrant Thinking allow us to construct the whole picture of our internal reality and study the fundamental processes that are available to the whole Mind to evolve its current state into a new state. This is like visualizing the beautiful statue of David, hiding in the slab of stone as Michelangelo did. We can visualize and hence bring to awareness the three fundamental processes of internal state evolution. This gives us freedom to see aspects of self and to choose which aspects we need to develop while building an internal reality which is True for us. We give these processes a metaphoric name: the three staircases of Whole Mind evolution. They lead to integration into a state of True Self resonating in harmony with itself on all levels and with all of its context.

What is Inside

The tools of Four Quadrant Thinking allow for self definition, self expansion, self exploration and finally self integration. As well they allow this book about Four Quadrant Dynamic Thinking to be self structured by the tools themselves. The book is naturally divided into four parts which coincide with the main structural topics called the three staircases as well as an integrative fourth part. (See Diagram 1.5: The Three Staircases of Mind Expansion.) Each staircase assists us to construct or enrich specific types of 'playgrounds' for mind development.

The First Staircase

The first staircase of Mind evolution is described in Volume I, Part 1 and it is about Truth development in its balanced form. It is based on the availability of the *Now*, and the perception of the Now rooted in the natural attention focus of the Mind. Overviewing our inner state with mindful observation or thinking processes for state examination, and using simple processes, such as a 'stateline,' are good examples.

Perception is naturally positive, but people get used to linking perception immediately with negative evaluation. Negative evaluation relies on old conclusions about the meaning of perception and the Mind is reliving that old state again and again. This gives rise, paradoxically, to negative experience based on positive perception data. This is like a tree going through the seasons. In an early stage — spring and summer — we conclude "beautiful." At a later stage — leaves gone — we conclude "ugly." Here we get aspects of internal reality which are not True for us.

Learning to perceive the input of positive sensory data with a clear awareness of the process empowers us to freely choose how are we going to evaluate our experiential data. This newly found freedom can change the mood of remembered experiences and hence tilt the odds towards personal optimism as opposed to pessimistic moods linked to previous negative experiences. Once we gain an optimistic outlook, the road to creative plans and relevant futures opens and we regain our intention for movement forward. We have replaced a negative feedback loop with a positive one. The Mind can now find resonance with it's own purpose.

The first staircase is all about our internal reality development either from falsehood of stress or from random glimpses of truth all the way into balanced four quadrant Truth exploration. This Truth is balanced but it does not have to be fully conscious.

The visuals of four quadrants are important as well. The Mind can now freely choose: Either I look at some reality as it is appearing to my currently defined perception, my senses (a VAK map,[2] visual-auditory-kinesthetic), or I split that reality into a four quadrant map of that reality, a four quadrant map. The original VAK map of that reality will be transformed into a four-fold map of that reality. You will then see a four quadrant map with your perceptions of it in the bottom quadrant, your experience of it in the left quadrant, your relevant plans/ideas related to it in the right quadrant, and as well, the resonant deeper meaning of it in the top quadrant.

'Four quadrant thinking' then means we add a sense of open questions to clarify our perceptual filter. These questions — defining and experiencing each quadrant of the key areas of perception — allow our perception to become enriched. We observe the old — add in overview position or Coach Position to the thoughts — and increase the potential for usefulness. This is a very intriguing process, because it links the VAK of some reality with aspect of the mind and creates an integration map of it all. When seeing this map armed with processes and tools from the second and third staircases of the mind, the map can become an effective consultant to SELF.

The Second Staircase

The second staircase described in Volume I, Part 2, is based on positive evaluation of perceived reality, leading to the Value appreciation process. We can notice Value appreciation as a form of Truth expansion. However, this is now a wholly new level of personal mastery rooted in the development of our purposeful ability to take alternating and evolving points of view of the same reality together with changing the scope of our attentional focus at the same time. Five perceptual positions allow you to overview the processes in Volume I, Part 2.[3]

The perceptual positions can start with a simple 1st perceptual position which is an associated 1st person view from inside our Truth perception. We can then move through the 2nd person perceptual position perception of our inner Truth. This is the point of view of someone with us. We can then explore dissociated 3rd perceptual position or an overview viewpoint of this Truth. 3rd position allows us to do 'big picture' thinking so that we can learn to coach our perception, adding positive evaluation and intention to see what we see. We step outside our associated reality for bigger picture appreciation. This continues to 4th perceptual position, which includes time expansion. 5th perceptual position is based on the global view and sensing on our Truth from the eyes of all of Humanity.

The journey all the way up is an interesting one starting with anchored 1st associated perceptual position then gaining freedom to alternate between associated perceptual positions and dissociated perceptual positions and finally ending up paradoxically in an associated 5th perceptual position which supplies global values to the Mind. The scope of our attentional focus is growing on the way from 1st to higher perceptual positions and covers all of space and time when reaching the 5th perceptual position. This process works in the other direction as well, allowing movement from very high abstractions of 5th perceptual position all the way down to the specifics of 1st perceptual position. The processes of this 2nd Staircase works well with both VAK and four quadrant maps, but for learning purposes we use them on VAK maps in Part 2 of this Volume.

The processes are based on the purposeful revisiting of Values as related to inner Truth. Every time a Value is revisited with a positive attitude of learning and progress, the Value grows in absolute terms. That means that 'my Truth' expands out into the wider context. Simply put, it gets stronger.

The Mind gains a whole new ability here: the ability to change perceptual positions with effortless ease and hence, to move up and down different levels of abstractions, allowing it to move out of the box of a given reality and change/declare its own reality fresh and new.

The second staircase ends by the process of creating declarations of Truth. The Mind is learning different ways to define new aspects of personal Truth based on the previous expansion of the Truth function. The Self is reaching out and integrating bits and pieces of dis-owned self and becoming a fuller, more united Self in the process.

The Third Staircase

The third staircase is described in Volume II, Part 3 of this Two-Volume Set, and leads to Truth exploration on the level of creative mindsets. We explore how our thoughts develop the increasing freedom of widening options. It is formed through observing mental patterns (formats) of thinking, related to choosing and achieving a goal, (Format A), extracting something new from a given internal reality, (Format B), appreciating beauty and symmetry in our thought system, (Format C), and exploring the consequences of any action, (Format D).

Format A is naturally an unconscious associative process with the Mind forming a new goal and striving to achieve it with effective, positive focus and attention on the chosen goal. This new goal is of course already a great accomplishment over "no goal at all," or over the tunnel vision of "I have to do this xyz goal." Hence, we can say that this is a first level of out-of-the-box thinking.

Format B requires an unconscious dissociated state to appear and when viewing a four quadrant map from an external vantage point, it allows a new aspect to emerge. This means that the Mind is moved out of its original box of perceptions and conclusions. With this, a second, more comprehensive level of out-of-the-box thinking appears.

Format C arrives with the process of appreciating beauty and symmetry. It forms both associated as well as dissociated states, each alternating with each other. This creates the effect of pulling out unexpected resources into wholeness from unconscious levels of the Mind. This alternation of association and dissociation assists the conscious mind to become conscious of these resources with questions and appreciation. Hence the process of out-of -the-box movement continues with yet more resources appearing.

Finally, *Format D* arrives as a conscious process with open questions that alternate varied associative and dissociative states of the Mind allowing for exploration of a wide range of possibilities for any reality or hypothetical reality.

The tools practiced in Parts 1, 2, and 3, using the three staircases allow the adept to move into Part 4 of this book and to become masterful with life exploration by gaining control over areas of actions, emotions, and thinking. We build this through access to the fourth area of inner visions and deeper meaning connected to high levels of abstractions and the 5th perceptual position. This part is about Truth integration into a balanced picture as well as about embodying integrative Truth on all four levels of existence.

With Part 4, the individual practices holding Truth as physical awareness, feeling it as an emotional state, having a consistent thought on it and finally resonating with the global values and principles that it embodies. The adept gains access to the global view from the eyes of all of Humanity, both to VAK maps and to four quadrant maps, opening global values that serve as overarching organizing principles. However with this level also comes the ability to move down to associated specifics and to choose the type of thinking most suitable for the job at hand in a conscious manner.

Metaphorically speaking, the three staircases are the three paths leading up the mountain of Life towards a fulfilling, meaningful existence with alignment of visions, thoughts, feelings and actions. They allow for purposeful evolution of the Mind in the successive experience of "Now" states based on multiple initial conditions, and hence they form a basis for "Reality-based optimism," personal resonance with ALL awareness, and a shortcut to Spiritual Enlightenment at the same time.

However, the three staircases address another topic as well. This is the topic of out-of-the-box thinking related to exploring paradox. The era of Enlightenment has brought in a sense of scientific realism. We are deeply focused on the scientific approach based on problem solving. The techniques of problem solving are rooted in a mechanistic approach and they imply that a real life situation can be reduced into a solvable problem which has a well defined solution/solutions.

To our amazement we keep noticing that the present day world is becoming more and more interconnected, resulting in increased complexity of phenomena. More discoveries keep arising, always challenging us. Complex not only means complicated, but — more than that — it means being partially imaginary, having a component which is out of our scope and cannot be easily counted on. Nor, at the same time can it be excluded. Complex situations cannot easily be reduced into problems which have well defined solutions. If approached in this mechanistic way the law of unintended consequences sets in sooner or later, bringing in results we did not expect.

A paradox is an example of such a situation. It contains two appealing aspects, but the aspects are contradictory in nature and each cannot be achieved except at the expense of the other. Breathing is a classic example, with Breathing in and Breathing out as the two contradictory processes. Breathing in brings oxygen to the body and Breathing out rids the body of harmful carbon dioxide. If we stay focused too long on any one of them, the negative processes set in and we are forced to move to the other process. Life is full of such paradoxes with multiple contradictory processes.

The tools described with each of the three staircases offer a set of approaches that allow the adept to master topics from simple to fairly complex, especially including paradox handling. The First staircase offers tools to enhance perception NOW, which provides data for all the processes of the Mind. The data form personal auto-biographical memories of the Mind in the area of Experience. When filtered and observed, for personal value, these form areas of Relevance. Paradoxically we not only remember the past, but our plans for the future as well. The fourth area is formed through overview integration and gives Meaning to all of it.

The second staircase builds on top of the data gained by perception. It allows us to focus attention to increasingly large and/or abstract arenas of life or, oppositely, to small and/or specific pictures of interest. These flexible pictures can be viewed from outside or perceived from inside and the dual associated and dissociated tools of the second staircase lead to surprising insights and value appreciation. With every changing perceptual position or level of abstraction we gain a 'new look' at the chosen reality, whether it is a VAK map or a four quadrant map. With this increasing collection of new looks we are actually building an alternative to the original reality as well as to our unconscious ability to handle both of them at the same time. We learn to build our complex and flexible NOW to suit our Life purpose best.

The third staircase offers types of thinking which are suited best for certain classes of topics. Let's examine each in a preliminary way. *Format of thinking A* offers a clear cut road to achieving 'this' goal. This provides a very great accomplishment over an unstructured random Mind walk. *Format of thinking B* offers a structured view of 'this' goal/picture and allows for a new element to arise in a programmed manner. So, 'This' and a new element 'That' appear as a system. Hence, organized creativity comes to us. *Format of thinking C* allows for systemic pondering over 'This OR That.' This allows for totally new avenues forward to appear. Now the Mind begins to see more options in situations, where previously only one option existed. Finally, *Format of thinking D* allows for a structured study of all options around 'This AND/OR That.' This is a basis for conscious paradox-handling. Hence the Mind can freely choose from: 'This,' 'This' with the extra element 'That,' 'This OR That,' and finally "This AND That."

Finally in the process of integration we can build on all three staircases by adding four quadrant structure to our enhanced NOW as well as to choose the type of thinking best suited for the topic at hand. This is a totally new level of skills. Being able to view from outside and to perceive from inside a totally flexible Mind with a NOW structured into four quadrants gives the Mind extraordinary power over itself. It provides flexibility to handle paradoxes of life in a conscious way! The Mind can now choose and measure aspects of internal reality and come to useful conclusions whether the aspect is True or not. So the state, like the 'statue' of True Self can emerge!

> *"In every block of marble I see a statue as plain as though it stood before me, shaped and perfect in attitude and action. I have only to hew away the rough walls that imprison the lovely apparition to reveal it to the other eyes as mine see it."*
>
> — Michelangelo

INTRODUCTION:

Flexibility of Mind

Developing Coach Position: The Observer Within

Let us ponder the purpose of four quadrant explorations to explore the key ingredients of an efficient, effective self-development program.

I once visited the class of a famous meditation teacher, Adyashanti, in a large North American meeting hall. Such an interesting man! What he described caught my attention. He told us all that it took him seventeen years, sitting and looking at a wall while practicing meditation, to 'jump-start' dependable abilities to maintain an overview observer position on the Mind. His aim — like that of many explorers — was to attain inner peace and serenity of mind. In his own words, he used meditation to build what I call an 'effective observational viewpoint' on the 'chattering monkey' of the mind.

He spent his meditation time observing his mind chatter while systematically following his breathing. He described doing this for 15 hours per day. Can you imagine spending 15 hours per day, week after week, staring at the wall while following your breath? Seventeen years looking at a wall is a very long time.

Observational meditation of this type takes a lot of time because people need to develop a complex ability: a strong and flexible observer or 'coach' position while still maintaining intention and focus. The time and energy used for meditation translates gradually into the capacity to maintain Coach Position on multiple levels and types of inner dialogue and inner viewpoints. There are many ways to do this, and the systematic practice you learn in Volumes I and II allows deep, comprehensive integration. I offer more about what is Coach Position in Appendix 1.

Four Quadrant Assistance

What if you could move quite systematically and directly into this level of pondering, exploring, and defining your ground of being? And what if it didn't take 17 years to develop your Coach Position ability but only several? What if simple overview habits developed with diagrams could stabilize your overview ability with various levels and kinds of thinking.

What if you could stabilize your positive emotions, and your comprehensive learning so that you quickly shift your capacity to maintain overview awareness and to empower this development? And what if it was possible to build a growth development system, both associative and dissociative, that can take you into the furthest reaches of your own truth by working *positively* and not just negatively, (watching the endless internal dialogue of comparison and judgment)?

Imagine if you could effectively move yourself into habits of clean overview or Coach Position in such a way that you build a strong heart-mind 'infrastructure' despite life's winds and storms? This is the practical aim of all meditation. Explore the practices in this book to find out if they assist this purpose.

With Coach Position you can explore any whole experience to integrate the larger experience beyond it. Begin to envision smaller wholes as components of others, allowing yourself to *move endlessly outward and endlessly inward.* You can quickly learn to create this system for *visualizing, examining, questioning,* and gradually *expanding* your awareness through such a hologrammatic framework.

As with the famous metaphor of the Russian Doll, four quadrant thinking assists you to do a 'depth review' of any specific idea that is important to you. We can explore from multiple levels and from both inside and outside.

Through Overview Coach Position, you move quickly into integrative system thinking. Along side a strong ability to overview your mind arena, you naturally, develop a positive mind frame. Overview requires seeing all aspects, including your values. You then become able to be true to that aim and understanding. You develop an 'expansion habit system,' much like strong meditators learn. This moves you quickly to high-level integrity of awareness. You begin to apprehend consciousness itself, inexorably moving our human development further. Many exercises in this book will develop your skill with this.

Setting Forth

I invite you to use this book to create a four quadrant 'value awareness body,' and learn to 'tip yourself' towards the strongest point of engaged value awareness needed for a life of ongoing self-discovery as you ponder the inner form of the questing mind. Our expanding awareness mind is always on a quest — through us and through our moment-by-moment perception. Out of the mist, the vibrancy of your inner life — your *wholeness intelligence system* — then emerges.

We have powerful challenges facing us in the 21st century. People everywhere need clear, workable pathways towards personal mastery and inner growth. The ability to build a robust overview Coach Position allows us to develop quickly because it assists all areas of overview awareness.

As your attentional stability grows, you learn to center in the moving mind like standing tall on a surfboard, *even as it continues to move.* You develop balance habits even as you develop and strengthen the 'muscle' of your perceptive systems. Negative inner commentary and cynicism then gets perceived for what it is. These thoughts are noticed briefly and left alone. In this way they gradually fall away from disuse without a lot of struggle. In other words, you learn to discriminate inner truth from noisy internal dialogue.

Working with multifaceted, balanced diagrams, our capacity for Coach Position awareness gets developed as a stable system...and quickly. Full neural linkage to inner value awareness becomes the basis for a relaxed perception system...usually the 'hard part' for humans because of the negative power of the old reflexive emotional system. By thinking from your integrated awareness system, you learn to choose effective, positive aims, and redevelop the emotional system and its purpose, situation by situation.

Through using a four quadrant system, you learn to activate your 'playground attention,' your field of expanded awareness. We call it a 'playground' because with four quadrant thinking we consciously 'form' this awareness. This means the field of wider self-knowledge becomes activated as a resonance system — filled with value. Meanwhile, by developing Coach Position, you learn to actively disengage from convoluted negative self theories and identities, the old opinionated 'mind stuff.'

This learning journey may take about two years, often for some, or less when supported by basic weekly practices. You learn to sense the vibrational awareness of inner resonance. You learn how to build the inner ship of 'truth awareness' that lets you sail beyond the old compulsive identifications, the various self-protective judgment systems that populate our negative thinking and belief structures with internal dialogue.

Being Self

We need to build a ship of consciousness on which to sail into the ocean of truth. You can set sail powerfully, until there is nothing else but the deep recognition of connection with your inner flow of *Being*.

As you continue through this book you will separate different levels of identity thinking. You will learn to differentiate various types of identifications with contents, structures, processes, and the flow of inner form. (You can soon learn to distinguish associative, personal *(small 's') 'self'* thinking from your vast, integrative *Value-Self* exploration, expanding into wholeness comprehension. From Coach Position, all levels of self exploration quickly becomes knowable.)

Each time you practice while maintaining Coach Position, you expand the sails of self-discovery further. You will notice the strong *flow* of expanded awareness. You will recognize how it arises like a wind, how your sails fill, and how you are carried into the wide expanse of inner wisdom.

Exercise: Outer and Inner Viewing

As a small beginning exercise, find a place where you can view a tree and take a moment to perceive its phenomenal uniqueness. Look carefully at it. What makes this tree different from all others? Notice all its specific features: its trunk, bark, branches, and leaves. Now dissociate to overview through time and to imagine it growing from a small seed or acorn through many seasons: spring, summer, fall, and winter. Really pause to imagine its beauty at every stage and through every season: in sun, snow, wind and calm. Now, notice the inner branching design? See the various life conditions that show up in branches and their reach. Any signs of weathering? What events might have bent that branch or twisted the trunk in its own peculiar way? Take some moments to look ahead. How will the tree leap further into its sky? How will each branch bend upward? How will it affect all the forest life around it?

You are expanding what is whole and complete, your current image of the tree, to open wide the inner gift it offers — a positive, wide-range long term overview of self-developing life.

We can 'water our acorn' of growing knowledge and imaginatively see it's further unfolding for any place and any time. All our future knowledge is available to us now for the asking. We can also do the same with others and with all humanity.

PART 1

The Central Staircase of Enhanced Salience

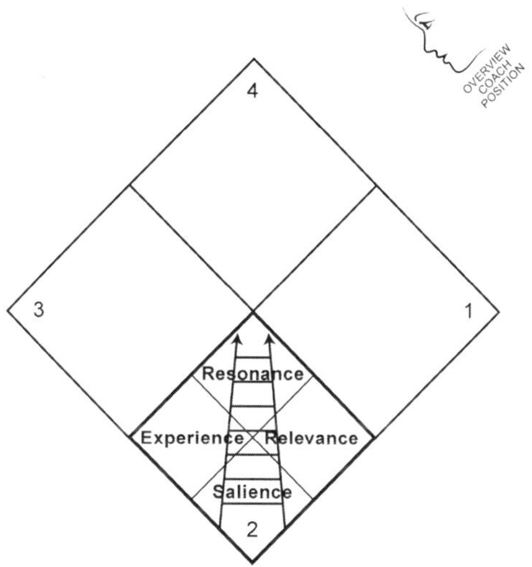

Defining the Playground

CHAPTER 1:

The Power of Four

Exploring the Mind

Let us ask the key question: What is intelligence? How goes the Mind? This is a topic studied by philosophers and poets since the dawn of the human age. Today it is also the realm of neuroscientists who do fMRI scans, interpret them, conjecture, and dialogue about the mind and the brain together. The questions we ask about consciousness itself could fill a library. Consciousness, as deep as the ocean, remains as a simple primary awareness for all of us.

You probably know the story of the 10 blind men and the elephant. Each man blindly touched only one small part of the elephant: ear, foot, trunk, flank, or tail, and declared that an elephant correspondingly resembled either a fan, a pillar, a hose, a wall, or a rope. We laugh, yet this is just like our multifaceted thinking apparatus trying to define *Mind*. It is far too easy to stop too soon, and define the aspects in terms of various *contents* or structures of intellect rather than the vast overall *context* of living awareness we notice with wonder. With a purpose to explore beyond small aspects, whole system awareness suddenly opens and momentarily we may flash on, feel, and intuit, the whole amazing 'elephant of consciousness,' dazzling with intelligence.

We can observe the process and flow of *engaged mind*. With this we can begin an effective exploration with questions about *minding*. When we move from an assumption to a question we go from 'noun' to 'verb' and we get closer to self-discovery.

What then is intelligence? We might define intelligence as the coherent combination of our detailed granular focus with our wider contextual overview built from many 'takes' on our perception. *Intelligence* means activating wholeness of thought and, thereby, the richness of inner meaning... very different than simple *intellect;* which activates a collection of methodologies.

Any exploration of intelligence and of mind-movement leads to a further important question: "How does intelligence grow?" When we observe the *process* of awareness across time we begin to discover and notice the whole system vibrantly self-exploring, as if by itself. We discover that mind is an *emergent* phenomena.

What then *is* mindfulness, the process of simply observing this unfolding intelligence as it opens before us? We might describe both intelligence development and mindfulness as the ability to accentuate and expand awareness through whole system attention. We notice our 'level and kind' of consciousness. We become aware of awareness. A new *level of intelligence* or *integration* begins to form.

You will find this book useful for your own exploration of *minding* as well as mindfulness. We offer a diagramming system that provides an effective compass. If 'minding' is a process, ongoing and moving like an ocean with surging currents and many shores, then you can use the four quadrant dynamic system described and developed in the volumes as a kind of boat. You develop your own effective compass use, and discover your own steering prerogatives. Dynamic intelligence opens with your focus and curiosity.

Diagramming provides a powerful aid to awareness because it allows us to quietly bring in fresh insight and intuitions through the *visual* power of the mind to explore itself. Self-exploration can then reach beyond preset perception and habitual assumptions. Our rule is to keep all diagrams as simple as possible.

Expanding Wholeness Awareness

Whenever we see four ideas or aspects together and visually appreciate their balance, our attention moves to their wholeness. This becomes an immediate doorway to wider awareness. When we see system balance and integrity, we naturally want to explore it further. Exploring for inner balance and wholeness is the foundational ground of four quadrant thinking.

An integral part of being human is the sensing of wholeness, focusing in, and then expanding out. The flower of awareness then opens. Consider a morning walk. Imagine you are walking down a woodland trail and you discover an open, green meadow. In the *first* moment do you not immediately scan the whole space of the meadow to appreciate it *as a whole*? Only in the *second* moment do you begin to look at the details, the specific plants and flowers around you.

Whenever we sense wholeness, we humans instinctively widen our perception out to appreciate it. This, then leads to the desire to explore further. Appreciation of wholeness leads us to see even deeper levels of integrity; we naturally begin to ponder or explore for an even larger system, and probe once again for the next level of system integration. Coherence appreciates.

Paradoxically, it is useful to build an overview map of wholeness. With wholeness as our territory we effectively begin to examine the nature of integrative awareness. Gradually, we begin to relax, construct, and play in our 'playground.'

Four Aspects

Examining for inner truth is an interesting process, because we are looking into the heart of wholeness awareness. Our deepest, natural instinct is to build *coherency*. To do this, we observe both map and ground. Interestingly, we gain magnetic power when we examine at least four aspects. Through widening attention and pondering coherency, something integral begins to emerge within the system. We commute our attention from detail to whole, yet the whole now contains all the details simultaneously. The jagged edge of our mind-maps melt and integrate. Wholeness thinking immediately flowers into further discovery. We pause and deeply appreciate. We become enabled to expand again.

If we stand in the middle of our world, relax and simply *sense*, (a combination of see, hear, feel, and more), we can begin to experience this wherever we are. Pause for a moment and take a deep breath. See and sense expansively in four directions around you, and simultaneously notice your internal world as well. See Diagram 1.1.

Diagram 1.1: Expanding Wholeness Awareness

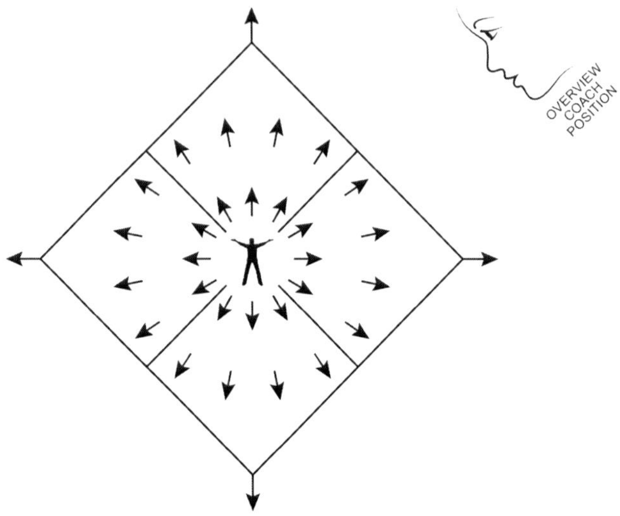

We are describing the essential process of four quadrant thinking here. This becomes the basis of our work. Every mind idea or 'reality' can be expanded, like the thumbnail icons you open on your computer. You will expand four principal areas of a theme and add in a central and peripheral perspective. The Mind observing or experiencing the whole — even as a diagram — becomes an energy system and moves further into enlarged self awareness.

Engage your personal curiosity with this. Four quadrant thinking is based on setting out the initial whole picture of the Mind, as if taking a 'selfie' of the Mind, followed by expanded exploration of Mind as a process. We can then end the initial process with another 'selfie.' This back and forth can continue with further learning in an ongoing way.

Working with 'Fourness' as Viewpoints

Inner development accelerates with the number of viewpoints the mind can handle as an internal system for exploring realities. You can do 'test runs' with each of them experimentally, and discover distinctive and useful 'stick shifts' into mind expansion. Each quadrant of exploration offers a different method to experience insight and inner intelligence.

You are probably asking how does a four quadrant viewpoint lead to expanding wholeness awareness? The major question is: How do we move through all levels and viewpoints? Try it:

- a '*one viewpoint*' system provides only an ideology.
- '*two viewpoint*' systems often challenge each other, creating conflict.
- '*three viewpoint*' systems begin to offer an overview position or Coach Position for exploratory development, but usually require very hard work to maintain balanced overview into mind expansion.
- '*four viewpoint*' systems offer enough viewpoints that we can keep development moving forward — while we balance and learn!

Equate this to the relationship we can hear in an orchestra playing a great classical symphony. We hear the relationships between the instrumental sounds, the players, the symphony conductor, and the musical composition itself. This creates a multiplicity of experiences, much more than four. Similarly, with a four quadrant awareness system we begin to think from at least four distinctive areas at the very same time, which creates expansion — as a meaningful experience — the way the music does. Specifically, we learn how to commute between areas until we can listen and observe *simultaneously*. The music of Mind flows meaningfully as we activate all areas together.

Think of a player, a four quadrant game board, an 'outer game,' and an 'inner game.' Again, this multifaceted overview of Mind in process can assist the same expansion into wholeness experience. Now, visualize a playground with playing fields, and pathways as well as various playground structures, and then a compendium of potential games and tournaments.

Who do you become — with either 'game board' or 'playground' — as a player in relationship to the structures and processes you have established? How do you establish your purpose and your strategy? Again, at least four key distinctions, as complimentary facets of a deeply unitary system are before us. We quickly discover how to develop the 'muscle' of awareness using a four quadrant mind map.

What is the four quadrant advantage? When you learn to do true systemic thinking of this nature, the capacity to establish a profound purpose unfolds at the center of the whole system. The braid of intention creates a unifying vision. You learn to think *as the system,* and, through sensing it well, you gradually learn to *become* the whole system while staying awake to it. The whole system opens and grows purposefully. This is the heart of mystic awareness.

The key to four quadrant intentionality is keeping all four aspects in our attention and awakening them all simultaneously, honouring how each aspect is relevant. We can shift between all aspects of our awareness, but honour each aspect for genuine self-development. Each interlinks and complements the principles and practices of all. We discover beauty and perfection in process.

Four Quadrant Diagrams

Creating meaningful four quadrant visualizations from which you gradually build your inner mapping system solves two major difficulties for most people. Firstly, you don't need to try to dissolve years of negative thought; focusing on old thought systems tends to make them stronger. Secondly, you can learn to think *integratively*, using a balanced structure to ask profound inner questions. This moves you beyond simplistic positivism.

Four quadrant pictures and diagrams allow us to perceive both *inwardly,* the inner integration of your ideas — and *outwardly* — the outer balance of your ideas. We go far when we work with the power of perception.

- You learn to develop a double observer position.
- You learn to use mind maps as powerful recipes for asking inner questions.
- You become able to move and see beyond specific thought systems, and even beyond the thinking process itself, into the space of awareness. Metaphorically we might call this 'quantum awareness,' linking and enlarging many aspects.

Seeing elements that complement each other also provides a way to appreciate the creative process. We can ask: “How do each of these aspects contribute to the whole? How do they relate? Are the relationships fully balanced?”

These questions, using four-part thinking, also assist us to up-level and integrate our *comprehension*. We are able to create flexibility while maintaining balance within the flowing currents of self-exploration.

Let us summarize how four quadrant diagrams particularly inspire holistic understanding: You facilitate your ability to view any wholeness system as a grouping of ideas holding complementary relationships. Once you look for this, you can see it. You develop a whole new mind.

Practicing Association and Dissociation

What do we mean by a double Observer Position[4]? Sensing and viewing, as if from *inside* any system, we become *associative*, zooming in and appreciating our experience with refined feeling. Moving outside, we become able to dissociate and overview. When explored as a pair from both inside and outside, the experience offers a coherent space for self-observation. Every self-exploration is like a dance with a delightful, unknown partner.

Let's diagram a simple example of association and dissociation with Diagram 1.2. Try it with an immediate experience.

Diagram 1.2: Inside and Outside Viewing: Associative and Dissociative

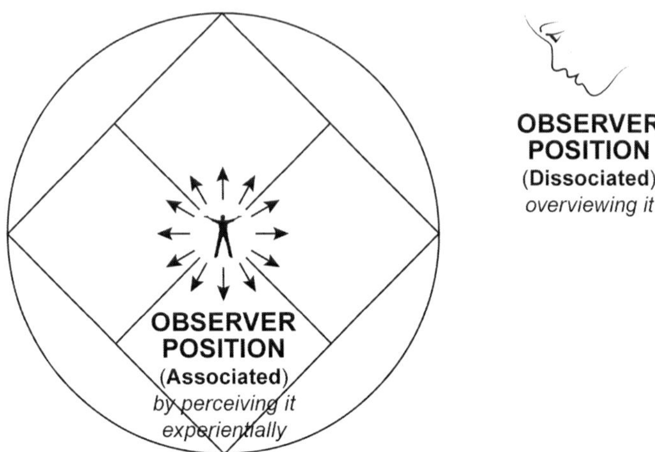

A graphic example of associative and dissociative Coach Positions will bring this to life for you: Let's start with an *associative* experience. Imagine you are wandering through a busy carnival with lots of exciting rides and attractions. As if you could, dive into such a scene to smell fresh buttered popcorn and carnival hot dogs. Perhaps you can hear a calliope playing carnival music. In the background, you might hear the sound of laughter and kids squealing as they ride the wheels. You see others step up to ride the roller coaster and you now walk over and fall into the line to jump into it too. Behind you, many people excitedly begin waiting in the queue.

The line moves and you are finally to the ticket booth. You pay your money and take your seat in the first car. The attendant closes the metal bar across your chest and you now feel its tight grip and anticipate the moment when the roller coaster leaves its dock and climbs the first big hill.

Feel yourself relaxing in the car as it begins. A summer breeze is blowing through your hair. You notice all conversations stop as the coaster moves up, dragged by a big clattering pulley. *Associate* to *feel* the full sensory range of this experience! Expand your view across the fairground.

Now, switch to a *dissociated* view from across the fence 30 meters away. From here, you can see that very *You* who is sitting in the first car of the roller coaster. You can see your hair being gently ruffled by the breeze. Notice, you can also observe how you physically prepare yourself as the roller coaster begins its slow climb up the first long ramp. Notice that, from over here, far outside, you can still hear the powerful pulley clattering as it gradually moves the small train up the hill, and you can watch that *You,* over in the ride, who gazes out across the busy carnival, and downward to the people below. Watch that *You* in the car who clearly enjoys the panorama as the small train moves higher, and even higher, right to the top.

Now switch back to the *associated* experience at the top of the coaster's climb! Be there! *You* are now at the very top. Feel it! *You* are in the first car looking about, and suddenly you can *now* look straight down to what appears to be an almost vertical drop. *You* feel *your* body straining at the restraint bar. *You* notice that you would fall straight down without it. This second of 'pause' seems endless. Now, in a flash the small train beneath you leaps into motion — straight downward. Down! Down! Down! People around you scream. Away you go! Feel it! Grab the bar. *Association*!

Notice the vast difference in experience between dissociated overview and the participative experience of association. Each offers an important contribution to awareness.

We all know how to shift the mind by shifting our association pattern. Doing this consciously allows us to stay conscious of our range of habits. The real challenge is *learning to step in or out at choice.* Discover how to do this, moving from 'thumbnail picture or icon' to vast participatory expansion. This allows four quadrant thinking to become deeply meaningful. Practice again with Exercise I at the end of the chapter.

Comprehension Through Diagrams

Comprehension is a very interesting word. What happens when you 'comprehend' something? You integrate ideas by 'pre-hending'[5] their relationship. We can use scaling to assist this. When we *comprehend*, we can gradually scale up the level of comprehension from one to ten, or from low to high. We gradually move the level of comprehension upscale. This means that we move beyond the narrow aspects, or the surface aspects, of our idea. We move beyond *our mind of the moment*, and we observe integratively from *our larger intuitive mind*. We learn to explore ideas as potentials. We can gradually weave this wider, more *comprehensive* sensing and feeling into everything we do.

Comprehension means we learn both to *associate* and *dissociate* separately with all the different aspects of our 'thinking' process. Call this larger observation process *pondering*. We can even step out to *contemplate* all sequences of thought and feeling. Our roller coaster of attention can change rapidly taking different points of view, yet we can still *comprehend* them all. We can use metaphor to integrate our logic system into this larger perception. For example, we can move out like a rocket into the stratosphere of awareness, perhaps climb upwards into the warm atmosphere of value. We can also sink like a submarine moving deeply into a depth probe as we begin to explore various 'currents of mind.' We learn to take a neutral Coach Position on all the different aspects as they emerge.

Holography

Take a moment to examine a holographic image, perhaps on your credit card. A holograph is created through a special form of photography, using a process that bounces light off of metal plates so that when an image is developed it is not only multi-dimensional but has some other rather startling qualities: the unique property of these images is that any part or fragment, no matter how small, provides a complete miniaturized version of the original plate showing successively smaller versions — *in all three dimensions*. The image can be viewed from many angles and with each change of angle the image also changes. A holograph is a way to imagine — and to see — infinity!

In the same way, all parts of the natural world from large to small, are interconnected and interpenetrate to form the whole. At first, any one 'picture' only gives us 'inklings.' This is like the beauty of fractal patterns showing the deep intelligence inside non-linear yet mathematically integral patterns. We can see these inner patterns of informational and mathematical intelligence linking all together like a Russian doll, one inside the other, yet each unique. See Diagram 1.3.

Diagram 1.3: The Nature of a Holographic Image

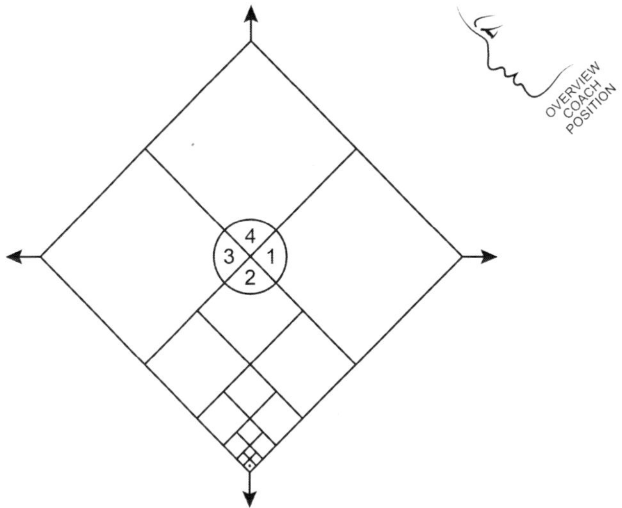

What is really fascinating about holographic photography is that when you break off a piece of the image and put it under a light, you can see the entire original visual image again. It may be slightly less distinct, yet it still contains the whole picture in every particle. If you break yet another part off the smaller component and examine it under a light, once again, amazingly, you see the whole. It will be fuzzier, but still represent a complete picture of the original. You can continue to 'map smaller' till you reach very tiny, indistinct particles. Think of the fractal mathematics of the ocean's shorelines with each continent; a mathematical pattern emerges from the largest to the smallest aspects, repeating at every level. This is also like our human DNA map; the whole model of each human appearing in every cell.

Four quadrant exploration assists self-exploration through the power of our own holographic imagination, assisted by a simple map. It provides a method for developing flexible access to inner knowledge, not only as mathematical design but as *intelligence* design; giving us easy access to multiple, comprehensive understandings that build and integrate through time. Again, intelligence is not simple intellect but includes inner sensing and feeling, as well as viewing, to develop. It requires presence, curiosity, and heart-mind connection. Honing our intelligence, we gradually begin to ask potent system-mapping questions and, as we ask inwardly, we see more. We move from the observation of one 'particular' after another, to the simultaneous *flow* between rich fields of integrated understanding. Our perception becomes educated. We begin to explore the multiplicity of inner connections in our 'hologram' of wisdom.

We gradually create a system of inner mind-heart linkage by building knowledge of the inner mind and its 'workings' that is naturally *comprehensive.* We create multiple levels or facets to our experience, and we develop our ability to comprehend it *usefully.* Through careful mapping, questioning, and delving further, our larger self-awareness becomes accessible.

The Beauty of Wholeness

Because the conscious mind itself is narrow, only relating to about four 'bits' of information at one time[6] we need to keep our 'first-steps' maps very simple, as shown throughout this book. Yet when you gradually overlay each map to see them as a system, the diagrams in this book and in our appendix will assist you to develop your own methods of self-exploration and plunge deeply into the sea of discovery.

When you develop four quadrant thinking as a habit, you will begin to fall in love with the profound and yet practical thinking you can pursue with comprehensive systems of four. You learn to appreciate your 'thumbnail' conscious mind as a useful doorway to the infinite. You learn deeply as you organize questions with diagrams and small graphs.

Understanding means to 'stand under'! When you start working with deep multifaceted awareness using four quadrant charts, you move beyond emotional quagmires and simplistic assumptions about what

Self is. You learn to 'stand under' your own integrity. You develop the ability to think, question, ponder, and self-explore towards the much wider comprehension of your life, and to become more focused, yet balanced with both your inner and outer self-observation. You energize your own growth.

Step by step, you can explore this for yourself. When you hear this description of comprehensive 'larger ideas,' take a moment to wonder what profound whole system awareness really means to you? We open inner perception by looking for the beauty of wholeness. What we put our attention on we open further.

Let me summarize some key aspects we will work with. We are exploring the Mind and 'minding' by working with four quadrant models both dissociatively and associatively. Four quadrant modeling[7] provides a simple, stable method for developing flexible access to wider perspectives. Originally it is easy to be attached to our habitual perceptions and to the false appearances that they present. We may be attached to our personal emotions, perhaps pride, anger, and emotional craving, exaggerating these associations and their importance. We may have the notion that things and people exist as only self-sufficient entities. Using four quadrant approaches, these old perceptions open into larger, inter-connected awareness systems of which they are all a tiny part.

Clarify Your Aims

I invite you to use this book to focus on connecting with and developing your own deep intelligence system, the framework of your Mind. With this, you will be able to take away many different results from this book and build upon your own abilities at different levels:

- in terms of the various *content* areas in your life using two distinct perspectives. You will be able to look at the Mind from various points of view. You move from a static "selfie" picture of the Mind to explore many dynamic processes of *minding.* You develop a 'Mind compass' of the basic elements of minding itself. You discover minute 'minding habits' as well as how you can take Coach Position Mind;

- in terms of the *structures* of the mind ranging from the microscopic mind compass, through state enhancement tools, to expansion processes allowing value appreciation. All different types of thought comprehension structures lead to increased freedom of the Mind;
- discovering inner *processes* of exploring along the most fundamental expansion dimensions of the Mind; and
- shining a light on essential, natural *forms* and *flows* of the Mind.

See more about the flow, process, structure, and content of ideas in Appendix 3 of this volume.

Diagram 1.4: Content, Structure, Process, and Form for Mind Exploration

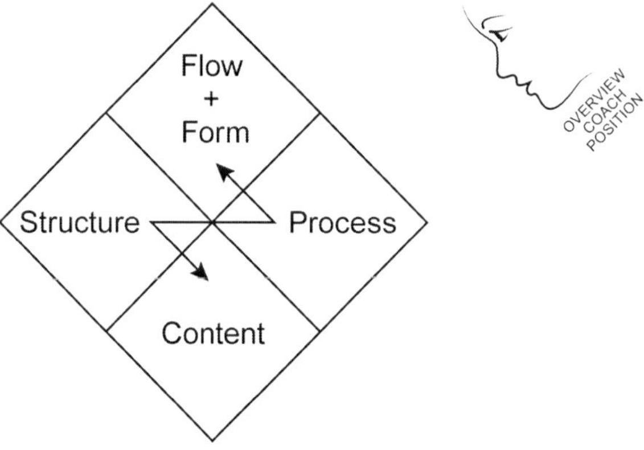

Volumes I and II are structured into four parts along a four quadrant pattern as seen in Diagram 1.4.

Through the two volumes, we will work with three basic metaphoric staircases for mind expansion as seen in Diagram 1.5.

Central Staircase: The central staircase of enhanced salience is all about the direct experiential evolution of mind states. The remaining chapters of Part 1 are dedicated to this central staircase.

Left Staircase: The left staircase is related to evolutionary development through Relational Development and Value Appreciation. We open this door using expansion processes, alternating between association and dissociation. All of Part 2 relates to various aspects of Value Appreciation.

Right Staircase: Finally, the right staircase is devoted to increasing Freedom of Thinking with an intentional capacity. It is centered around four key evolutionary systems of thought called the four Formats, Formats A, B, C, and D. Part 3 in Volume II outlines these Formats and how they work.

The Integration Point: Part 4 in Volume II is devoted to the power of truthful integration. The three staircases meet in the integration area of the top quadrant. We look towards a holographic continuous evolution of the mind with increasing inner knowledge, awareness, and freedom of the mind. We work towards developing a neutral, ever-expanding overview, as well as harmony and balance. We develop a stable dual Coach Position, or in different terms, the realm of practical enlightenment.

We start Part 1 with a map over to the mind, exploring possible ways to look at the Mind. We will dive into the associative experiential side of 'minding' as a process, as well as the dissociative impartial look at the Mind from outside. Step by step, you learn four quadrant processing systems. In other words, you explore taking the 'step' (the verb) and developing the 'platform' (the noun) that each step leads to. You *associate* to try, and *dissociate* to overview. Overview our three 'startout' areas in Diagram 1.5.

Diagram 1.5: Three Staircases of Mind Expansion

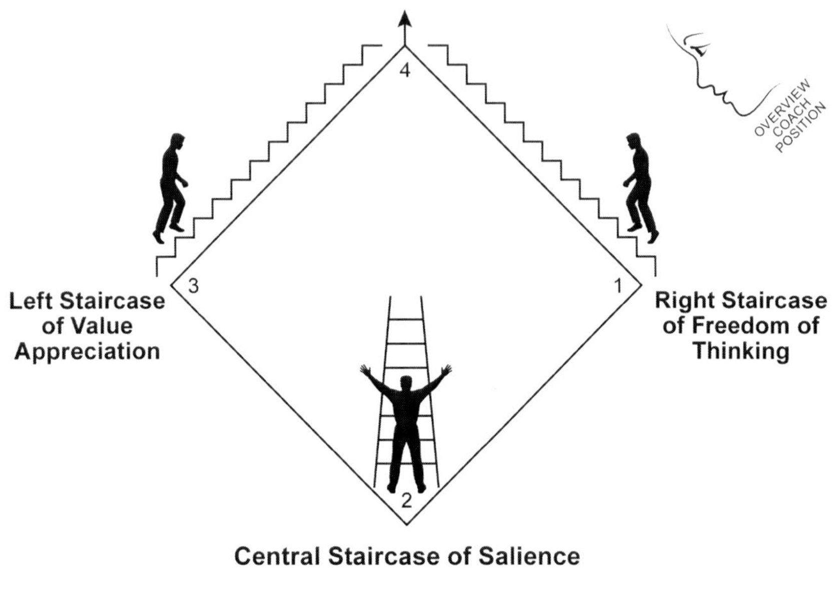

Association — Dissociation Exercise 1

Try the association-dissociation exploration with a simple two-minute experience of your own, perhaps a weekend walk or exercise, perhaps taking a shower and washing your hair, dressing or simply doing some chores in your home space. Find a recent event and recall it thoroughly.

- Start with physical association. Review your event carefully, 're-feeling' it.
- Move in and out, associated then dissociated, feeling from inside, then viewing from outside, seeing from closer or further away.
- Notice the various perspectives that interest you. You are developing an important mind 'muscle' as you practice.
- Now do another practice with an area of engagement that provides a physical challenge for you, like diving off the high diving board at the pool, trekking in the hills, or learning some dance steps. Give yourself about 30 seconds in each position associated or dissociated. Once again, allow yourself full presence from each viewpoint. Gradually, allow the full scene to unfold from various viewpoints. What do you discover with your perception?

CHAPTER 2:

Why the Diamond Shape in Exploring Intelligence?

The Benefits of Using Diagrams to 'Draw the Mind'

Notice that, with all diagrams, we necessarily reference *comprehensive* ideas. This is very simplistic and obvious in the same way we use letters on a page to code a word. As we declare a 'map' for mind exploration, each picture becomes a magnifying glass. A map or symbol is a thumbnail of condensed consciousness. As on your cell phone, it needs your focused 'click' to open it up.

A four quadrant picture can be particularly useful for mind explorers. It may seem like a peculiar practice — to 'draw the mind' — however a picture offers us great insights. To think about 'minding,' we must both explore inside, and also overview from outside an overview scope or Coach Position — which allows us to enrich all aspects of our exploration. Comprehending through the *linkages* opens *All*, like the 'rubbing' of the lamp for the Genie in the bottle.

It is particularly useful when we code our diagrams to show *complementary* ideas. What does complementary mean? The qualities of any complement, as often seen in a quandary, are two-fold:

1. You cannot have one aspect without the other; and
2. You cannot easily associate with both at the same time.

This becomes a beautiful, integrative paradox when viewed from an overview scope. Seeing such a beautiful, complementary structure means that viewing any thought system 'from the outside' now immediately reminds us of the wider thought system containing both. With this, we can comprehend — and sense — much more about what we are observing as a growing living system. The linkage system opens 'the flow' like a stream in a stream bed. The stream flows in the stream bed, but the flow also creates new beds. We start to think more holistically. Complementary thought systems often seem like polarities or paradoxes. Wonderful abilities develop when you view them as *Wholes.*

Complementary systems provide a framework for balanced explorations moving between inside and outside. They are like the beating heart or the movement between the expansion and the contraction of the breath.

The larger four quadrant 'container' shows a dance, which takes us far beyond noticing the individual dancers. We view the complexity and inner meaning that is contained in the mind system *beyond* each element. (This is metaphorically mirrored by the connectome in the brain, the 'white matter,' which provides linkage for all neurons into systems and pathways.)

By drawing 'the mind' as a whole system, complementary relationships can effectively be seen as moving systems. By mapping *All*, we move from mind to Mind. Similarly, we move from coach position to Coach Position. We begin to comprehend beyond the logical time/results frameworks we have built for 'all practical purposes.' We can briefly envision the dazzling inner order of *All*, which moves far beyond the specifics we are examining, so that we expand into the larger field structure, and comprehend our deeper purpose. We comprehend our 'boat of purpose' as it sails through timescapes on the ocean of self-knowledge.

Let us summarize. When we map a wholeness system we can observe as if from outside. Four quadrant Mind diagrams, like all diagrams, are usage-based, designed to be practicable and practical. With diagrams we can stand outside any idea and summarize it. Yet they are also like living expressions, showing something that is both whole, as if complete, yet available for growing and changing at the very same time.

With diagrams of the Mind we can also *enter into* the idea. We then can expand and develop the idea from the inside: scaling it, envisioning it at various stages, stepping out to observe from stage to stage and then associating in and feeling it again. This allows you to develop your self-awareness far *beyond* the ideas you make real in day to day moments.

A hologrammatic diagram is particularly interesting because you can use this to raise the comprehension level inside your thought system on a scale from one to ten even in the details of a complex experience.

Mind diagrams offer doorways for engaging our broader self knowledge. If you can try it on, take it off, and then try it differently, you come to know it, *beyond fixation.* For example, you may be attached to various perspectives of habitual thinking. You may have adopted judgments and various old emotions about the goodness or badness of something. Using a Mind diagram to expand your viewpoint on this habitual perception immediately enriches your awareness!

You can also use a map to diagram the simplifications that create fears and other disabling thoughts, and then use this to see how they become less relevant within a system of wider comprehension. Dissociation and association can work together like dance partners, each giving another aspect of the dance! Seeing various complementary aspects of a system all together allows us to engage and sense the entire system.

By simply working with a comprehensive picture, our own deeper knowing system responds and begins to give us both the inner knowledge and the balanced perspectives we seek. First we need to see the ocean, then we can dive into the ocean, and finally we can become the ocean as a whole!

The Energetic Orientation to Four Quadrants: The Diamond's Tip

Working with different geometric shapes in diagrams produces different inner processes for the Mind and it is useful to notice what shapes tend to inspire you as you start this exploration. You can use these shapes as mind diagrams to explore your profound questions and to invite insights.

There are many useful foundational shapes with which we can think. For example, we can use a circle, an isometric triangle, an equal-sided cross, a diamond, a spiral, and so forth. We can also use movement or expansion shapes such as branching trees or a 'moving' arrow.

Some fundamental geometric forms such as circles, squares and triangles offer special ingredients to all inner exploration and visualization. Each can be used to build comprehensive maps — playgrounds — that assist us to think in totally different ways. Because they are balanced, they easily get partitioned into diagrams. Each offers variable viewpoints for expanding thought. Each offers its own unique discovery system into deeper knowing. From the mind's eye, each shape becomes a symbol that can invoke a powerful dynamic process within us. (See Appendix 4, The Symbols and Shapes Exploration Exercise.)

In every culture worldwide, a spiral, *made with one line*, signifies salient newness and unfolding discovery. A cross, *two lines*, tends to be a symbol for balanced connection and for deepening relationship. An equal-sided triangle, *three lines*, signifies the process of climbing higher towards a goal. A four-sided square, *four lines*, signifies solidity, something that is foundational and changeless, like a brick.

Notice, a 'point,' such as a period on this page is also a fundamental form and also has interesting properties. For example, it can be expanded into a circle, then into an even wider space — as if with no lines at all — to represent expansive unity or wholeness. With this inner potential motion, we can ask: "What is the *point*?" and explore our own ideas, both inward and outward, following the expanding or contracting symbol. We can find the pattern, the hologram, that takes us into the heart of one area of 'in-form-motion' as a kind of deep understanding. It then becomes information in our 'known' world. The tiniest bit connects to the largest. The largest bit connects to the tiniest.[8]

Shaping Thought

For many aspects of life, foundational 'fourness' diagrams are often created like simple 'brick' diagrams. These are particularly common in the world of ideas because they are so easy to make. We see them everywhere from billboards and signs to the 'boxes' in newspaper advertising.

Consultants with the aim to impress their customers use two-by-two systems that are 'solid' — like a brick. These often seem very captivating, and many two-by-two systems have been developed for simplistic business thinking. Consultants also frequently use them to define and to segment our 'personalities' into categorically rigid systems.

With four quadrant thinking we now adapt this foundational shape very differently to create a dynamic flow of awareness. We move it onto its tip and so we define a 'fourness playground.' Through overview and purpose, we create — and observe — a moving system.

We are natural system thinkers. Through association-dissociation practice we can learn to take our exploration much further than we think possible. The unconscious mind loves anything that is balanced, beautiful, and shows integral complexity. This is the 'stream bed' for the volatile, uncertain, complex, and ambiguous ideas that we do observe. And, we can effectively shape what we see.

Once you define a 'mind playground' as a particular balanced yet moving relational network, your unconscious mind — your deeper knowing system — will naturally start to use it for exploration. It will expand to develop the various structures of the thought system you are exploring. Your shape now becomes like a room or space for the mind. We tend to 'step in' to 'try it on' and test it like we would test any building or construction. This means that you can associate in and *feel* what you are actively defining. You can gradually explore with comprehensive interpenetration, sensing the various areas separately and together. Through association practice you can learn to use this skill for self-discovery.

Shapes for Exploring the Mind

Thirty-five years ago when I first started drawing charts to explore the mind, I mainly used squares and boxes. A fourness system allows enough structural 'framing' to explore a deep and comprehensive idea system. A block or box has a very particular quality — it's solid and foundational. In fact, anyone who has worked with squares and thinks about them metaphorically will notice that working with square blocks is like constructing a building. Blocks are foundations that don't move much, but they are great for 'on-the-ground' visualizations just like the 'solid' constructions of architecture. Or, consider Minecraft™, the favorite Internet game of many youngsters in the first few decades of our 21st century.

A 'squared off' box-like diagram tends to create strongly structured thinking. This, of course, is useful when you need to get grounded. Yet a foundational square is not always a particularly good framework for exploratory processing. It particularly hinders creativity simply because a brick-like square moves slowwwwwly!

This points to a key difficulty with squared-off diagrams as a base for processing ideas. *Squares tend to produce the idea of the 'already finished,'* and this tends to stop further movement as well as to inhibit all questions. Before I started using the diamond shape to assist overview thinking, I sometimes looked at ideas as 'givens.' Square frameworks can do that.

The association of boxes and squares with the 'already done' is a big hinderance for exploration's purpose. Powerpoint diagrams are an example of this. They often show words or diagrams in a box. We see a frame with bulleted ideas inside, which creates an air of completion and authority. One sees them almost like *things; solid bricks of reality.* It is easy for us humans to do that as we attempt to stay down-to-earth, grounded, and 'real,' accepting what has been 'blocked out' already. We see the boxed idea as defined and framed (bulleted and 'particled' as a particular thing). It is easy to think of 'solid results' as a 'given' in exactly this way. The world (and words) pulls at us to focus outside, not inside.

In contrast, if you observe the way the mind moves moment-by-moment, you always notice a wave-like whirlwind of activity. When we create a model of 'minding,' we want to explore *flow* and *process*. Our profound mind is sheer process, sheer motion, just as is the universe, from quarks to galaxies. On every level, from the most abstract and inclusive to the most sensory and specific, the mind is always in motion. For exploring moving mind, with lines on paper we need metaphors and diagrams that take us into the moving process. If we show our system to be like a brick, we tend to stop with only the physical foundation.

Diamond Awareness

How do you make a flat, two-dimensional diagram become a useful symbol with strong, dynamic potential? How do we define a system to be *process* in *potential* and begin to experience with this *process potential*? We need to be able to overview multiple moving aspects in a simple way.

In this book, I use the diamond shape as this shaping metaphor for our process of *Mind as wholeness* yet always in motion. Notice that it is a standard foundational square, the symbol of 'solid reality' *but it is tilted onto one tip*. It is a square yet *it is as if it is in the process of moving*.

What makes this shape so appropriate? Follow now: What realization does a diamond shape support? With a diamond, when we invite a four-sided shape to stand on its end, it becomes dynamic, fluid, and moving. As it spins and pirouettes it reaches and expands into the space beyond its four edges. A diamond has four 'tipping points' to propel fresh 'view-points.' It assists us to take both an associative and a dissociative point of view of the Mind. We can now move effectively yet stay connected to inner solidity and wholeness. A diamond shape easily represents that *movement*.

Diagram 2.1: Diamond Awareness: Wholeness in Motion

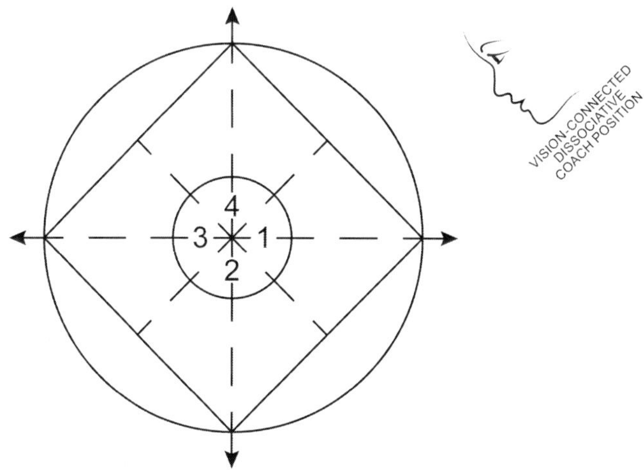

See the *point* in a diamond shape. Notice how compelling it is, as the centrifuge for movement. With this, we really do ask that key question: "What is the point?"

For any geometric diagram it is useful to notice that a tipped square is easily seen as a *moving* square, the oxymoron of the resonant quality of the 'changeless change' and the 'choiceless choice.' It tilts us into the fundamental paradox of the mind, moving us to a complete system filled with complementary oxymorons, like wave and particle. When we explore one, the other disappears from view. We experience *the eternal principles of the solid and changeless that paradoxically always includes change. Within our diamond, both are together at the same time.*

Diagram 2.2: The Mind: A System of Complements and Oxymorons

By its nature, it can always include:

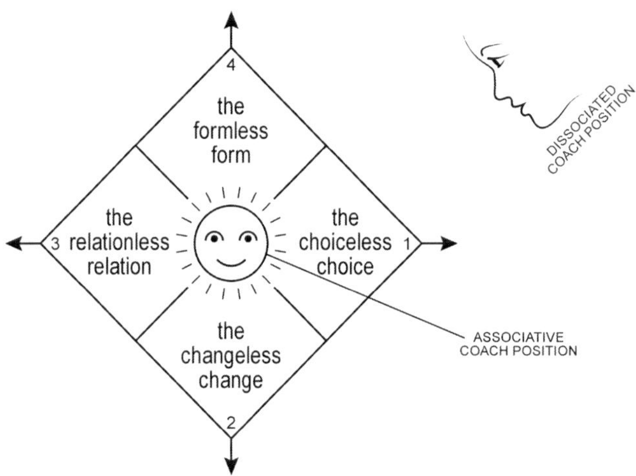

Paradoxically, then, the diamond shape brings foundation and movement together; similar to other aspects of our human habitat, body and action, noun and verb. *Our mind seems always the same, and yet it is endlessly moving!* Human life, all life, is energy! To build that energy into momentum needs plan and motion, visual expansion-scope and kinesthetic balance-scope. It needs the dancer and the dance.

The diamond shape links us into the creative aim of moving beyond our habitual or '*solid*' mental habits. With fourness systems, the diamond's four tips pull us towards paradoxical oppositions, a counterpoint of complementary relationships; yet, within the counterpoint, the conscious observation that makes real or 'collapses' our attention in one area of another, all stays together in a meaningful wave of linked connection. Viewing all aspects together assists to access vibrant and meaningful perceptions. We then adorn our moving image with playful aspects, and with arrows and symbols of movement. With these we open the questing mind just as we can easily do with open-ended questions. You can diagram your 'values mind' as a *moving* values foundation that grows with questions and insights from the inside out.

With diamond awareness you stay balanced in your thinking, maintaining movement. The observer becomes the surfer, balancing on the surfboard of overview, always moving into the interplay of fresh comprehension. All aspects can unfold timelessly as you ask open-ended pondering questions. New awareness emerges. Wonderful!

Personally, I have used this diamond framework for self-discovery, finding multiple facets of my life. It has kept me awake and exploring, with many aspects of 'Quantum playground development' throughout the past 35 years.

Beyond Static 'Believing' to Moving Intelligence

Right now, our world is full of hopeful *believers* often with 'boxed in' or 'squared-off' mindsets. People often yearn for foundational reality systems: solid systems, equivalent to towns and cities, policies, and institutions. They want 'given ideologies' to tie things down like a set of simple procedures. They think they want a mind that is all squares and bricks, solid and complete. Yet, 'solid' does not sustain us, or feed inner growth. *To plan the game is itself the game if we are to find our inner world of self-development*! We are always working with Mind in motion.

Commitment to the moving mind assists us to shape our thinking and to explore moving intelligence. The diamond form divides into four smaller diamonds and can be divided again, ever smaller and smaller, in a hologrammatic way. We can explore multiple details yet stay with the whole. We can stay expansive, as with a Russian Doll. The shape holds enough foundational form to build with, yet allows us to move between thought systems. We find that all systems naturally intermingle. The diamond provides an excellent framework to explore the holistic principles of the flowing mind with its natural relationships, simple to complex, yet also to assist the thinker to undertake the engaged thinking process. We stay with the amazing gifts of living, moving vision. Maximum intelligence emerges.

Diagram 2.3: Holography in All Directions at Once

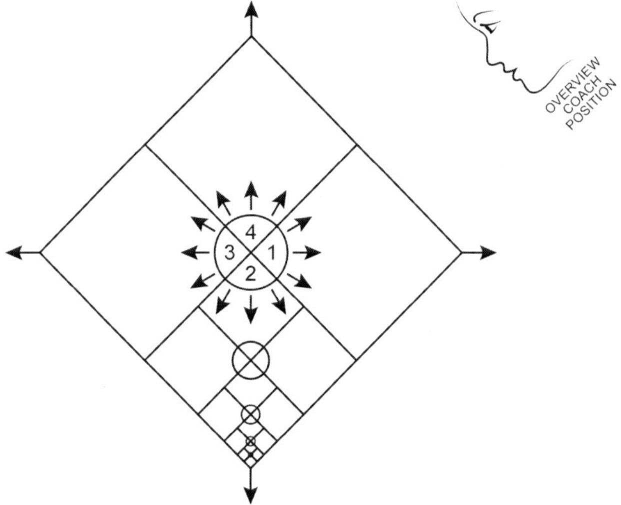

In regards to all quadrant diagrams in the book, we suggest the following: We refer to quadrant one and assign a number one (1) to the right-hand quadrant, two (2) to the lower quadrant, three (3) to the left-hand quadrant, and four (4) to the upper quadrant. We will use the numerical references consistently throughout the book for ease of discussion irrespective of the various aspects and systems described.

You will find this framework in use throughout Volumes I and II, sometimes surrounded by a circle to indicate a context of expansive hologrammatic wholeness as well. This numbering system does not suggest any process for using or explaining our mind — just for differentiating the quadrants — a simple referral system.

A four quadrant model for 'minding' is particularly useful. We can associate in and try it on. We can dissociate out and develop our overview abilities. Everything interpenetrates everything else. Aspects connect holistically. When we associate into our physicalized ideas we similarly build our brain connectors as neuron highways for the nervous system of present moment physical awareness. When we dissociate out, we develop the overview of expansive possibility. Various Mind diagrams assist us to do both easily. We 'tip' from one exploration to another and the learning becomes as rich as we can imagine.

CHAPTER 3:

Beginning the Great Climb

Do a Small Sensory Exercise:

- *First*: First feel the body physically. *Feel* your inner *beingness.* This moves attention through the doorways of your senses. Notice what 'being here' means for you now, in the most associative way possible. Take a moment and attend sensorially from throat to toes.
- *Second*: Reach out. *Sense* your 'belongingness' in the quality of your strongest, long-term relationships. For a moment, warmly sense the people you love in your life as well as your relationship to plants, animals, and even the earth itself. This is relational, present tense awareness.
- *Third*: Notice your life aims and how your quest towards specific *choices* is relevant for your developmental life. For a moment, activate your own visions of valued futures and notice that another aspect of your inner awareness immediately gets engaged that takes you into entirely different mind territory.
- *Fourth*: Finally, notice *wholeness.* Expand your awareness including all of these aspects together. Notice, you can actually hold the paradox of wholeness while being aware of contrastive elements, including all the aspects you have just explored. Notice the expansive quality of this. Physicalize this for a moment: Hold your hands high, palms up, and sense 'all together'! Now, *sense* the entire paradox as a whole, including all these separate awareness systems co-developing at the very same time!

Basic Dimensions of the Mind

Our aim in Part 1 is to begin to explore some central processes and practices that naturally lead to mind evolution. We identify four fundamental processes of the mind which enables it to evolve through observable mindscapes.

To be able to start we postulate the basic dimensions of the mind as follows:

The first dimension is *physical.* We need to develop the physical promise of our lives. We can engage and love life by refining physical and sensory awareness.

The second dimension is *relational.* We need to develop the relational promise of our lives. We learn to engage and love life through developing emotional and relational awareness. We evolve as we appreciate our joint values and value each other's growth.

The third dimension is *creative.* We discover ways to develop the creative promise of our lives. We need to engage and think about our lives through developing and evolving the creative capacities that we discover as we start to grow.

The fourth dimension, the expansion of *life meaning and integration*, continues our creative evolution forward, as we integrate all the former areas into an evolutionary system for self development.

Children discover the first three dimensions as basic survival skills. Their purpose is to survive and grow strong, and they learn through advancing all these areas. They eagerly learn them all! Teenagers continue this, testing and developing themselves to discover their own special ways to link what they learn into a basic 'life skills' package. With these as their base, they can start their lives on their own.

Children and teens are focused learners, practicing how to survive. Adults, however, have another purpose. Their aim is deeper and wider, opening the fourth channel. They want to make their life *meaningful.* As adults, we can move much further since we sense the call of destiny. Individually, we exist like a single acorn in the forest, yet our individual development evolves all. This may be a purpose that is even unknown to us, yet the deep urge to rise up beyond our 'private and personal' history is a genuine one. On some level, every one of us wants our life to be a true contribution. We look towards our legacy.

Exploring the Brain System

With our mind's evolution as a focus, it is also useful to overview the human brain itself, which loosely *corresponds* and *evolves* as a reflection of our evolving mind system. We can view these evolving dimensions as parallels, a natural map-across between mind system and brain system.

Have you delved into the wealth of brain research since the advent of fMRI brain explorations since 1997, and especially since the beginning of the 21st century? There is much to explore. You might easily feel overwhelmed by the complexity of the human brain system and the amazing data coming from recent brain research. For this reason, in the next section, we now present a layman's introduction into the subject, a simplified evolutionary metaphor of a few core brain functionalities.

Contexts for Brain Development: Your Brain-Aims

What do we discover when we start to study the brain? We discover various levels and kinds of thinking tasks from four separate and distinct *contexts* for our development. This means that as we explore brain evolution, we can begin to think about mind evolution and wonder, integratively, towards our next steps as a species.

In terms of brain-specific sensory systems, we can quickly summarize these basic areas of human brain development currently called the triune brain system.[9] We can observe how brain habits relate to the historical development of the human nervous system over a 100-million-year time period.

- First, starting from the brain's center, we find our *reticular brain stem*, which for humans still successfully protects physical survival. It has remained much the same since the era of the dinosaurs, 100 million years ago. It consistently reminds us of our bodily survival needs, for example: thirst, hunger, sex, and sleep, displaying the most physical dimensions of mind.
- Second, we find our *limbic system or paleomammalian complex*, which for 50 million years has been more than 98% the same

between humans and other higher mammals. Often called the emotional brain system, this interconnected group of structures in large part provides the motivational center for the brains connectivity focus. This includes value motivation towards family and community. It is designed for relational intelligence to support the survival of the familly.

The limbic emotional system is also the center of stress motivation. The amygdalae, two small pea-like structures near the center of the limbic system — and linked to the reticular system — trigger harm warnings and will release fight or flight stress hormones instantly, as a response to any suspected danger.

- Third from the core, we find the *cerebral cortex*, which for the last 3 million years has developed the distinctly *human* quality of our thinking. This left and right brain system ties to verbal and visual logic and integrative deeper meaning. It integrates and organizes our visual neocortex and its amazing ability to create dissociated 'inner movies' of potential future choices. It is incredibly complex, and organizes all attention for system thinking and creative intelligence. The cortex offers powerful evolutionary design features including complex differentiations between left and right hemispheres. It functions holistically, creating a vast flow of information between all connected areas.

Diagram 3.1: Overview Diagram of Brain Systems

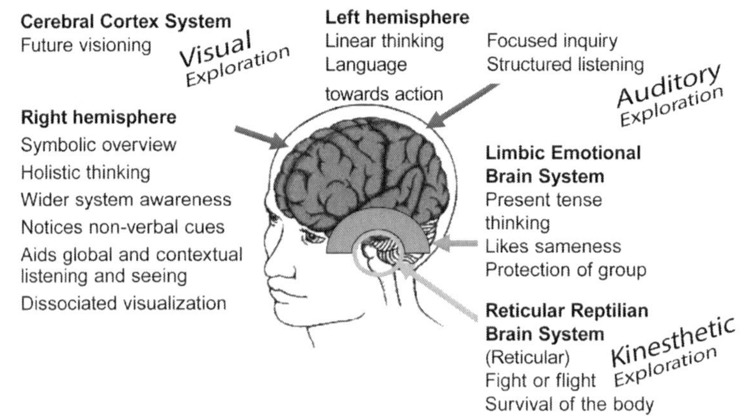

Discoveries about right and left brain divergence support the visual orientation of this work to develop evolutionary and emergent human potential. Left brain-right brain non-laterization show very different functions for the two hemispheres, with the right brain's overview and holistic visualization function being the dominant function. The right brain system can support multiple overview perspectives and queries. The left brain, the more detailed verbal side, focuses on normalized daily requirements and action steps. The left brain supports established processes to get things done, and listens strongly to established internal dialogue commentary about safety and emotional concerns. It follows the right brain's overview, developing practices, procedures, and opinions once a direction is set. The right brain's task is exploratory; it overviews toward the future.

Both right brain and left brain systems are linked to the limbic system, the ancient emotional system. However, the corpus callosum, the connecting structure between them, often acts to inhibit comprehensive linkages between the two sides. Without the right brain system intervening with meaningful overview, the habitual running commentary of the left brain system tends to prevail and activate routine attention patterns.

Since its job is to detail the needs of daily life, the left brain is much more responsive to negative messages and neurotransmissions from the amygdalae, the limbic system's warning center. It replays the details, usually old 'tape recordings' of right-wrong comparisons, and listens to these messages. It is highly responsive to any perceived threats and concerns. Stress from old messages impairs working memory and effective decision making.

The right brain system, though dominant, only freely shares its larger contextual overview and 'bigger dreams' when there is the experience of relaxation, safety, and opportunity. Visualization, imagery, open-ended questions, curiosity, and deep interest in creative development encourage this and stabilize it. Inner requests, declarations of purpose, and practice can build the connective capacity for all areas to support mindful overview and link holistically to clear action steps.

Whole system visioning rebuilds human intelligence. You will find that practicing the exercises in this book moves you beyond old emotional fear habits. The practices are designed to build strong connectors across the corpus callosum 'divide,' between left brain and right brain. Connection and linkage assist visual overview, and this produces the experience of inner strength, resilience, and flexibility.

Perception

Notice that our cerebral cortex right brain-left brain system offers the potential for powerful perception, potentially combining both overview and detail. There is a wonderful picture of the 'aims' of the intake areas of our nervous system found in many physiology textbooks. Perhaps you have formerly viewed the picture of a 'brain face' like the one shown in Diagram 3.2, which details a large percentage of the neocortex and the frontal lobes of the brain dedicated to eyes, mouth, ears, and fingertips.

Diagram 3.2: The 'Brain Face'

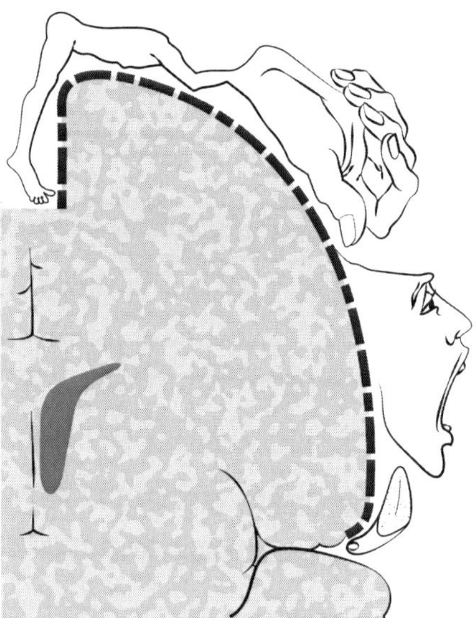

The picture shows how much the brain system is emphatically engaged with the visual, auditory, and kinesthetic intake of *salient* sensory information. It is designed for wide perception. Our brain dedicates a huge amount of prime territory to these intake areas and channels. In fact, much of our frontal lobes function for the effective *intake*, *storage*, and *retrieval* of sensory survival information. Our use of language, only about 200,000 years old, has started to co-opt to this function, since much of our internal dialogue filtering process tends to be repetitive of old messages. Only with practice do we develop overview and multi-faceted perception into a more integrative visual-value narrative that supports clear presence and connected sensory awareness. With curiosity and interest we grow the garden of perception to become richly multi-dimensional.

The Mind System Tour: The Four Central Intelligences

Relating to the triune brain system, with the reticular brain stem (physical), the limbic system (emotional), as well as the key contrasting left-brain and right-brian capacities, we have postulated the corresponding four dimensions of the mind: they are 'physical,' 'relational-emotional,' 'intentional' (thinking), and 'meaningful.'

As humans, we naturally see these facets through our human metaphors and we want to become strong in all. We want to develop our mind system and enlarge our creative engagement with life. Yet, to grow our lives in these four key areas requires different kinds of life engagements which may seem paradoxically opposite to each other.

Notice we are speaking of brain and mind holographically here. We are postulating that each process of mind development has provoked and encouraged key functions of brain development, and these all provide discovery channels and templates for our evolving life. In the next section, we specifically center on the integrative inner work that we — as a species — are doing through these channels. We will explore mind development practice with a fourness system, which I like to call the four central intelligences.

What are the four intelligences? First, let us oversee their functions. With inner resquest, our brain's perceptive systems amplify the following processes and discovery systems:

- First, salient *perceptual intake*, visual, auditory, kinesthetic, smells, tastes, muscles (proprioceptive), and internal feelings, all available, moment by moment;
- Second, the retrieval and linkage of successful social and relational abilities and habits. We collect *useful reference experiences,* moment by moment;
- Third, through anticipating valuable futures and 'next steps' visions, we learn to choose and maintain our *relevant life priorities*; and
- Fourth, even without noticing this, we hone and integrate these capacities as a *model* or example of 'our best.' We are the species that *aspires to more*; and that responds to inspiration, both *internally* — from our own questions and visions — and *externally*, from the needs and requests of others. We are the species that gropes and reaches forward to explore every potential, valuable crucible for our own development that we can find.

What does this mean? Naturally, the great climb of evolutionary intelligence maps directly from our brain's development to the inspirational, integrative processes of our Mind System. You will notice that the first three systems provide direct pathways for inspirational, perceptual explorations. I have coded these first three evolutionary 'brain-aims' with the terms: *salience*, *experience*, and *relevance.*

Salience, *experience*, and *relevance* describe three key 'springboards to learning' that instigate these evolving directions of inner growth. Like dancer and dance, the systems grow as partners.

The fourth system, *resonance*, involves their *integration.* We humans have a design function to continually advance our human capacity in each area *and as a whole.* Together the first three functions support this fourth area, which emerges on its own, and it is felt and seen as a kind of *inner and outer harmony.* We gradually organize a holistic awareness system propelling long-term evolution both for individual and group. We can sense resonance vibrationally as a kind of functional inner knowing, or love of life. We also experience this as *cultural* emergence.

We can map these processes as basic dimensions of the mind, experiencing them as fundamental mindscapes. We can also view this system of four basic intelligences on a simplified four quadrant map. However, notice that each of these four mind processes are deeply connected and continuously bring new elements to all four dimensions.

Diagram 3.3: Staircases Up and Out — Four Survival Packages to Four Central Intelligences: The Four Directions of Whole Mind Growth

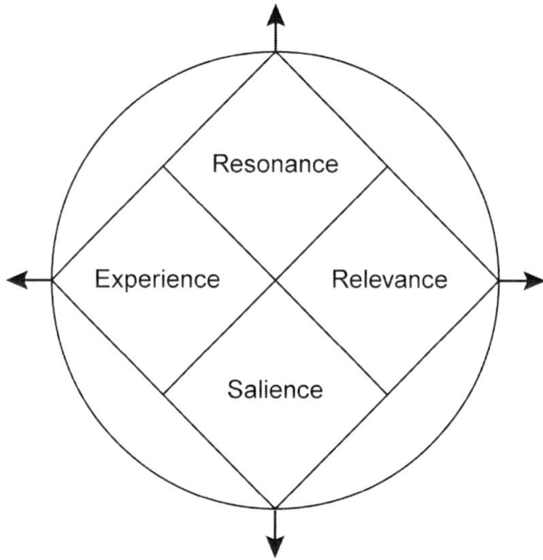

Diagram 3.3 shows this interlinked system. Again, these can be explored as four basic intelligence systems. We can experience these first, as fundamental mindscapes — and then as key centers for our learning processes. To evolve as humanity, we find four distinct natural functions and developmental directions of brain/mind evolution.

Evolving Your Human Mind

- First, you are developing *physical* intelligence, shown as quadrant two interlinking many nervous system functions starting with the ancient reticular and limbic, or paleomammalian brain systems but now combining much, much more. To do this, you need to fully taste and explore your salient moments. What do you love about being a human being?

- Second, you are developing *emotional-relational* intelligence and the ability to respond strongly to relationship and communal cohesion. This relational system functions as a stairway for value development, interlinking all humanity. What do you love about your family and your culture? About being a human being?
- Third, you are developing *creative* and visionary intelligence. This also includes musical, mathematical, and aesthetic intelligence. This continues to integrate your overview ability to visualize next steps and futures with your vast cerebral function indicated by quadrant one. Our creative aim organizes and activates our large cerebral cortex with both its right and left hemispheres but most specifically with our right brain system, capable of vast overview.
- With strong perceptive practice, vast numbers of linkages start to engage across the corpus callosum, the linkage system between the left and right hemispheres. The perception exercises which follow in the next chapters are designed to enable this communication between the hemispheres providing a pictoral 'language' to assist strong, non-verbal interconnection. This linkage then continues through all systems as we ask open-ended, expansive planning questions. We flash on our various purposes and envision opportunities. Neuron fields interlink. On a larger level, the aim for greater choice and freedom interlinks all humanity and needs effective visual overview communication. What do you love about your ability to envision and choose your next directions and steps?
- Fourth, you are developing a *resonance* system — a kind of inner truth center — we call *integrity* intelligence, quadrant four. This creates a matrix for integrative evolutionary awareness, gradually joining all systems together. *Resonance* is a useful word. If you think about the way a guitar string or a Tibetan bowl resonates, amplifying and expanding the quality of the sound, you notice that a kind of 'echo effect' gives power and inner meaning to all our experience. We can hear the differ-

ence between a deeply integrated and resonant sound and a less integrated sound or tone. We *resonate* with our own inner coherence or integrity — our 'well-sounded' qualities — and can learn to attend to this integrity. We can become deeply aware of our own inner knowledge and core truths. What are you aware of when you experience your inner integrity? How do you experience the reach towards inner harmony?

The Great Climb

We can briefly overview this great climb by exploring the connective process. How does humanity move from the four elements of our 'basic brain package' to the creative freedom of whole-mind growth?

Each key area requires different 'engagement processes,' providing the creative tension each human being faces as they explore how to develop their life on a personal level. We might also call these the first steps on the four staircases of human evolution. Each human being faces these four challenging areas differently, yet we must each face them to develop our personal courage to grow our life no matter the challenge.

For example: What do you need to grow each area? How does the process of inner development proceed for you? Each step has two phases: First, we envision what we want. This is our 'landing platform' so to speak. Next, we notice what we *need* to do or learn to develop if we want to engage in this way? This starts our next step.

- To grow the physical dimension, what do we need? Very simply, we daily need to maintain balanced health and physical well-being. We need to give engaged attention to the body as its own self-expressive system.
- To grow our relational-emotional life, what do we need? If you examine your life in multiple circumstances, scaling the value of all, one key factor will stand out for you: *the maintenance of positive emotions!* Plainly put, we can only build our emotional-relational intelligence by investing in and maintaining warm appreciation, inward and out.

- To grow our capacity for the intentional mind, we need *focus on relevance*, do we not? In fact, we need to focus again and again until our capacity to discern what is truly relevant to us, both long-term and short-term, becomes a well-developed inner skill. What we put our attention on, we get more of.
- And, to grow our capacity to creatively explore what is meaningful, we clearly need to develop *inner congruence*, the capacity to stay with our strongest expression of inner purpose. Does this not activate self-discovery for you?

Notice we find, again, a four-ness system for inner evolution. We *need* attention to the *process* itself. Again, each area is different. One needs focus. The next, congruent awareness. The third, maintenance of positive emotions. The fourth, health development. We always see verb and noun moving together in the 'sentence' of human development! We see how a 'step' and a 'platform' reveal themselves with each key exploration on the life development staricase. When we work with all areas together, everything amplifies.

All of these require tiny steps, daily. The first step for each of us is to explore our vision and purpose for each area. We do this as children whenever we play. We ask, first, what do we want in this area of play?

Diagram 3.4: Staircases in Four Direction

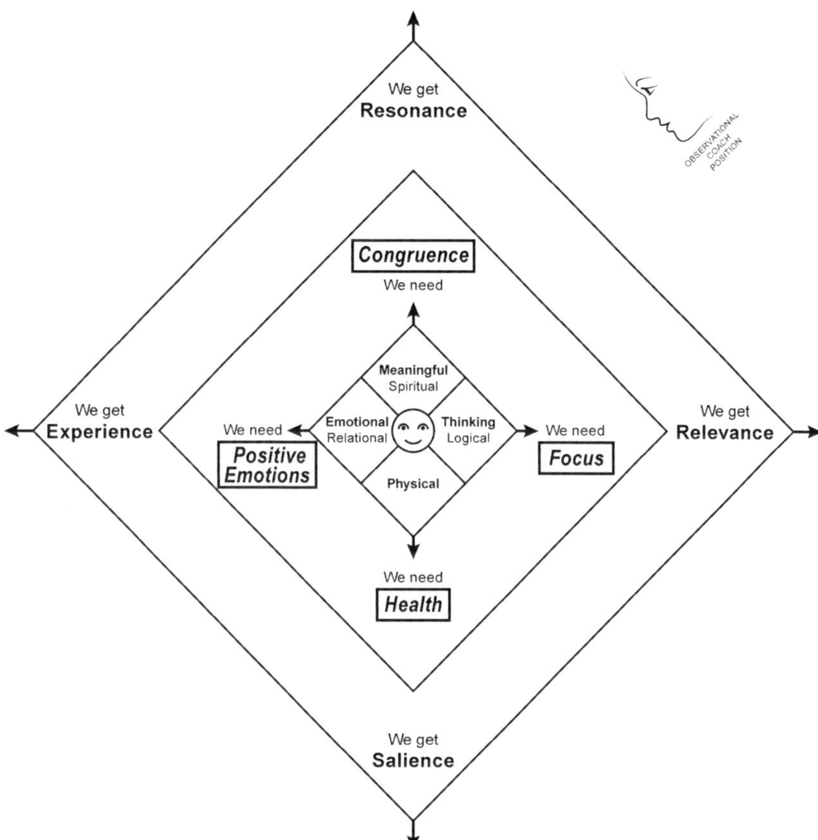

Expanding all four together allows our mind-garden to grow. We develop the enhanced interconnected pathways that link us to this expanded awareness. We engage in four kinds of self-development to expand these four areas, and as children we eagerly set about to build skills in all of them.

Brain System to Mind Evolution: The Great Climb. Discovering the Staircases of Awareness

We humans are 'called forward' by the urge to explore and develop these four powerful dimensions. It is useful to think about our developmental steps as a kind of upward climb because our integrative learning is necessarily incremental. Each area of focus corresponds with and organizes the brain-mind climb in its own way showing us specific types of 'stairs' for learning and integration through the brain and nervous system. Yet, results can happen fast!

As we focus on the integral learning in any area, we experience enhanced awareness and an immediate shift to strong inner certitude. We notice excitement and congruence. We are 'on track' in our life. With practice, we begin to organize our lives with these integrative intelligences.

If we organize to expand and balance in all four areas throughout our lives, we also tend to become happy. If we step back to view our development, we can also begin to see the long game; our part in humanity's development as a whole. We become partners in human evolutionary emergence, and our lives immediately show it.

How do we develop each area?

1. *Salience* attention, quadrant two, gets honed when we *appreciate* life physically through the development of our physical aptitudes. As we refine our distinctions we expand this sensory intelligence. We engage with it through the different sensory channels: visual, auditory, kinesthetic, olfactory, and gustatory. We see it, hear it, feel it, smell it, and taste it. The appreciation of multifaceted sensory intake, *salience,* allows us to evolve towards deeper awareness through refining these areas.
2. *Social Experiential* intelligence, quadrant three, gets developed as we emphasize communal support and community practice. *Experience* is a comprehensive word that simply means that you have tested and integrated specific areas of practical, societal, and relational learning into your life. For example, effective communities, as with all effective relationships, require kindness and patience. We need to evolve these relational capabilities. This also assists us to build true system awareness and world partnership.
3. *Relevance* attention, quadrant one, can be measured through developing and scaling up goal effectiveness. The capacity for goal refinement, for prioritizing, for studying relevance, and for

creatively discriminating best choices allows us to gradually — both individually and as humanity — move towards the flexibility we need as a developing world community. We enhance our creativity in designing unique, yet relevant, human goals.

4. *Resonance* attention, the fourth function, has to do with appreciating inner inspiration, congruence and integration within all these systems, and then *sensing* the combined *integral awareness* as a kind of certitude or '*truth*' *function*. We consistently move towards our inspirational expansion, braiding into a holistic, central awareness beyond all unique strands of development.

   Developing this fourth intelligence means that we evolve our capacity to integrate and co-engage all areas. We learn to attend holistically and expand the symphonic 'echo' into multiple areas of our life. We can ride the wave of this integrative, expanding intelligence as it leads to the emergence of masterful new abilities and qualities, again and again. Our personal conscious mind gradually becomes a servant to this wider integrative function, our crucible for development. This creates an emergent *resonance*.

   We are continuously sensing and expanding this *resonance* as human purpose. This also connects directly to our capacity to maintain overview or Coach Position awareness on all of life. As we develop and maintain principles for living that hone inner resonance, our capacity for joyful engagement — even with very hard work — gets stronger and stronger.

We are like mountain climbers exploring how to climb a great peak. The great Hindu sages practiced yoga paths that describe these key methods of ascent:

- We can approach evolution through expanding body awareness itself, (metaphorically like Hatha Yoga, the *yoga of physical flexibility*).
- We can approach evolution through expanding relational discernment, (metaphorically like Bhakti Yoga, the *yoga of love*).

- And, we can ascend by expanding creativity and mental acuity, opening pathways to greater system awareness, (metaphorically like Jana Yoga, the *yoga of mind development*).

The best and quickest ascent happens when we practice all together. As we approach the higher levels of our climb, we experience our desire for the final evolutionary ascent as a compelling *magnetism*. Again, metaphorically, this is like the practice of Kriya Yoga, the '*great yoga*.' We interlink and combine all approaches towards integrative awareness for 'peak' engagement.[10]

We step beyond the basic 'brain packages' we are given: the reptilian reticular physical, sensory, survival package, and the relational, mammalian, limbic, experiential family package developed to fight for and protect the family and the group. We even step beyond the fundamentals of our creative, aspirational development, and our capacity for envisioning futures. As we explore our evolutionary potential, we start to *resonate* with our unique human purpose. We sense this as 'being on track.' We start to integrate all of these areas into our wider journey of expanded purpose and vision. We begin to glimpse this as a very specific human journey. Yet, paradoxically, a journey that in some ways is simply to develop humanity itself.

Growing the Four Intelligences

To start your own four quadrant self-mapping process, distinguish and test each specific area for yourself, step-by-step. You might organize this as a small research project as you read. Even by just observing these intelligence functions, you can note your own habits. You will find various experiential tendencies with each area, perhaps to open them up, or perhaps to close them down. Whatever we put attention on, we evolve. Where do you put most attention? Where do you build your most valuable 'thinking spaces' or playgrounds? What else can provide deepening, overview, and emergent growth?

Once we develop a relevant four quadrant mind map — for example with a personal habit system we wish to examine — we can use the four quadrant overview space to move beyond our habitual thought systems and examine from the four domains of the mind. With each quadrant we can examine by first overviewing it from the outside while sensing it from the inside. We can see both the *platform* and the emergent '*next step*' together, then begin our *move*. We can overview all together for balance in all four directions.

Through the two volumes, we will give you processes with the four quadrants to develop your own practice for choice and change. Some you will discover are like 'elevators' and 'accordions.' For example, chapters 7 and 9 are designed to move you quickly to integrative exercises so you can blaze a path for future use. Other processes — practice builders — are designed so you become enabled to build clear stepping stones or habits you can step on consistently to climb the mountain of courageous self-development with a self-examined life.

Our Mind dimensions — as 'playgrounds' — are consistently reflected in our 'starting out' habits for value and vision awareness. Once you distinguish each area, you can refine, practice, and link systems with certainty and power. We are always starting out. Each 'next step' emerges.

Exploring *Salience*, *Experience*, *Relevance*, and *Resonance* together as complimentary awareness habits opens your various mind playgrounds to inner development. For each capability you can easily scale your own strength and vision from one to ten; one being 'just a curiosity,' ten, a 'developed skill.' Gradually, you distinguish relevant areas for attention and expand the power of your reach. This means you build a strong Coach Position and overview awareness on all growth areas so that together they become your creativity springboard. You begin to see them evolve together as you practice, providing a resonant inner compass to your own guidance system.

How does this work? It is like a great soup recipe! Each intelligence coordinate around its own 'stretch' zone, yet still needs 'stretch' in the other three zones as well. With the physical area, when we accelerate health and well-being, then exploring '*salience*' — our capacity for rich perception — becomes a next step. But to do this, we also need the experience of positive emotions and relational expansion. To expand, our creative and strategic logical abilities takes true focus, and this is also what we need to build positive emotions and salient habits of effective perception. Developing each area assists the others to also develop.

For the next chapters of Part 1, you will be moving along this central staircase. In later chapters, you will gradually unfold other advanced processes of mind evolution which we call the Left and Right Staircases.

The principles of holography we described and modelled with Diagram 1.3 can help you view the thumbnail 'pictures' and 'mindscapes' that you can explore for yourself using diagrams, journalling, and self-coaching. Now, as you explore Volume I, start to build your inner staircases. Move forward and provide yourself some very expansive overview 'thumbnails' of the physical arena of being human. 'Physical' particularly points to those areas where we most often become lost, totally associative with body and thoughts. Adding a four quadrant system allows you to regain your larger perspective on the rich, multifaceted offerings you experience in any 'now' of habitual associative awareness. This will assist you to grow multiple sensory distinctions and abilities; the foundation of self-discovery.

Now, using this broader map of the habits of physical association, magnify and 'open the thumbnail' to explore your bottom quadrant, viewing, tasting, and testing your own 'inner' system of four quadrants. The process of holographical exploration can go on indefinitely, from area to area.[11]

Diagram 3.5: The Central Staircase of Enhanced Awareness: Developing Quadrant Two

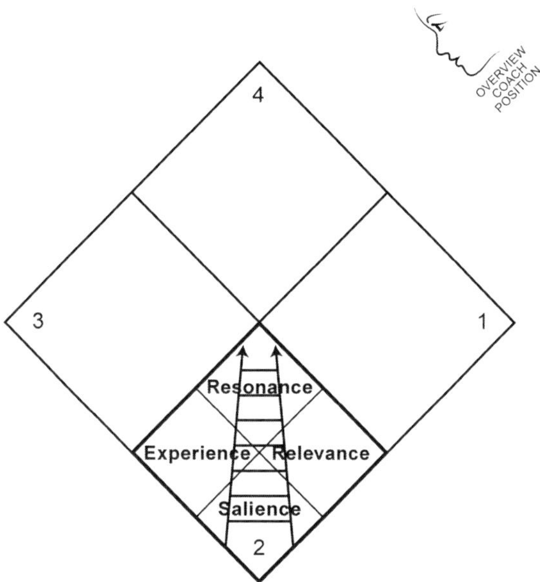

CHAPTER 4:

The Central Staircase: Exploring Perceptual Growth

The Dimension of Salience: Quadrant Two

Let's first begin with sub-quadrant two and explore our natural *physical* awareness system, the arena of salience perception. This is a useful beginning point because practice is as close as feeling the warmth in your hands and hearing the range of sounds around you. Moreover, it is a source of all external raw data for all other processes of the Mind.

The word *salient* refers to the natural richness of 'on-the-ground' physiological awareness as we manifest our physical 'intake' capabilities and widen key life-manifesting sensory distinctions. What are some skillful ways you can *see* more profoundly, *hear* more profoundly, *feel*, *taste*, and *smell* more profoundly?

You can learn to build a strong Coach Position on various kinds of perception by differentiating, integrating, and observing your intake awareness systems *as a whole*. These key areas of attention interlink your 'inner' and 'outer' physical worlds. You can explore your inner 'physicality' and your external 'sensory' world together. You explore orchestrally by noticing from overview, then entering each of the senses as unique perceptual doorways.

Opening to *salient* exploration means the enrichment of your inner and outer life. You need to pause to taste the moment, and only in the moment do you learn to expand the senses.

This moment is different from any before it! Pause to experience. Notice that all varieties of physical perceptions immediately emerge. We engage and expand the senses and suddenly we see things or hear them in a unique and marvellous way.

Wake Up and Smell the Roses!

Our sensory intake channels include our visual, auditory, kinesthetic (tactile and proprioceptive), olfactory, gustatory processes, and more. Only you can become aware of the richness of these perception systems — your physical playing field — by expanding your awareness systematically through all these areas separately. For momentary practice you might want to begin with sight, then sound, then tactile feelings, smells and tastes. What happens? Usually people experience their awareness both widening out to sense the environment and, at the same time, deepening into *presence*.

How do these sensory systems intertwine for you? Your habits will be unique, and you can get to know them. It is also useful to interlink together all the systems that you personally know *well* to other sensory areas that are less travelled. To do this, you need to *discern* them and then *map* them. You need to *flex* them and then *appreciate* them!

Diagram 4.1: Arenas for Growth and Learning: Exploring Relevance, Salience, Experience, and Resonance as Integrative Thinking Systems

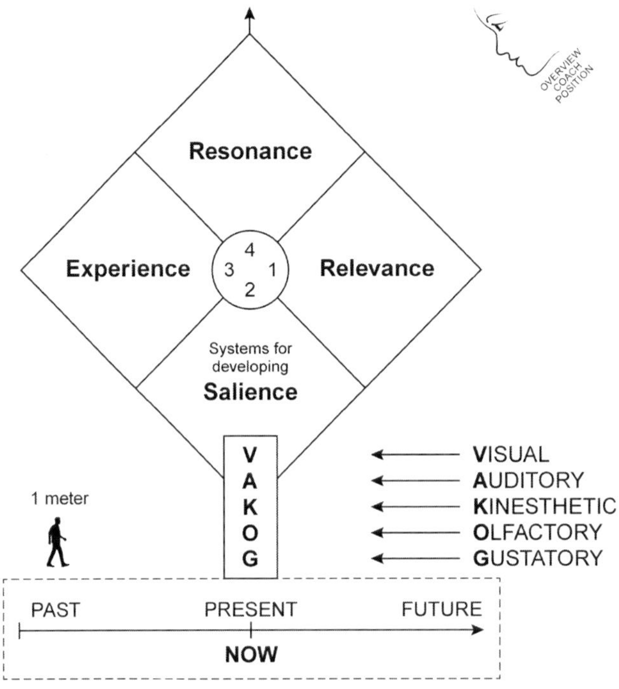

With the timeline shown under Diagram 4.1, you will notice that both *salience* and *resonance* are areas of awareness we metaphorically 'step into,' yet *only with present moment experience.* Notice how, when they become integrative, we naturally expand our energy and presence. These are learning areas for all of us. Adults find joyous life appreciation as they learn to 'pause in presence.' With them, we build our human capabilities to their next level. Children dive into this physical learning game with great gusto.

Salient sensory development requires 'on-the-ground' awareness of all aspects of body perception: visual, auditory, and kinesthetic. Kinesthetic awareness includes skin and muscle perception as well as olfactory or 'smell' and gustatory or 'taste' awareness. With attention, we accelerate the sensory differentiation and integration of our perceptual life. With the focus of a conductor with an orchestra, you can immediately realize how to expand and deepen your awareness of each moment's sensorial uptake: sight, sound, external body, internal feeling, external feeling, smell, and taste.

Our working memory expands beyond 'our limits' as we strengthen our combined sensory perceptions. With our overview scanning capacity, we can learn to move effectively between these multiple areas of consciousness to empower them as doorways to inner strength. This means that old rigidities of view dissolve, and consciousness expands.

A four quadrant system can be an immediate reminder to explore and expand balance in all these systems. You can recreate your capability, with overview, so that you can move down into each specific sensory arena *and also can shift out again quickly.* You learn to open the accordion of awareness as a linked system. Enrich your working salience system! You can practice exploring and realizing all of these systems with a simple walk in a park.

Physical and Sensory Salience as a Whole

We are like an orchestra with many instruments. In one moment, we can scan all areas of our sensory experience, then perceptually 'enter into' what we're looking at, what we're listening to, and what we're feeling, smelling, or tasting. These concrete 'intake doorways' are naturally very rich, and our inner capacity to make sensory distinctions widens as we focus on each of them separately.

Physically, we are always experiencing one moment of time, even as we rummage through old memories. You can find a rich, sensory memory, then use it like a springboard, opening into powerful, synthesia distinctions right now.

We have all had amazing experiences of engaged salience. Have you not — from time to time — suddenly found yourself 'awakened' into a special moment that jolts the senses into surprised and revitalized life awareness? It is especially interesting to move deeply into specific areas of perception that have been there all along. You suddenly look through 'different' eyes to see with, or listen through 'different' ears to hear with, so that the moment — and the perception — is completely fresh.

When we see the world afresh it is as if we become the creative eyes and ears of the Universe. For example, on one occasion while visiting a Japanese garden, I was looking at some moss and stones that were artfully arranged, and suddenly it was as if I was 10,000 meters up above a forest, looking at mountains with cliff faces and thousands of little trees. Of course, it was actually the moss and rocks, yet it was as if I was looking at a whole small world, a microcosm of forest life right there before my eyes. It was a fascinating vision to see that moss in that new way. I simply allowed myself to have a wildly divergent point of view, a unique perception. And I could see 50 different shades of green in that 'forest.' I could view the energetic qualities of growing green life, all amazingly connected into one breathtaking, salient moment! We can also do the same in art galleries. We can do it with drawings, shapes, and coalescing forms; adding in our own creative, integrative perceptual filter to have the world dance before us.

Visual, auditory, and kinesthetic salience can be studied and expanded through a lifetime as we meet teachers and experiences that open these doors. In this chaper, we will briefly give a few exercises for each and leave a few ideas for expanding auditory experiences to whet the appetite.

Auditory Salience: Four Quadrant Music

How about auditory *salience*? Study moments of 'being with' music that you love. You will learn a lot when you overview your music appreciation system at the 5,000-meter level, by overviewing various energized listening moments through time. You can find 'on-the-ground' examples of specific enjoyment areas by listening to some favourite music now.

Notice the ways you can hear the integrative sounds of music. For example, you can combine the themes of a whole orchestra into one, or can dive into the separate, yet distinct nuances of the ongoing musical stream, paying attention to different instruments as they interact together.

Personally, I like to combine visual and auditory together. Some brilliant music is organized in four quadrant patterns. Try listening to some highly ordered four-part music. Often you can find four repeating sections slightly vary and enhance the musical experience like a Russian Doll system. They can also be viewed as moving mandalas, expanding from the center point.

You might consider the musical form of a canon, such as Pachelbel's Canon, repeating and holding a four-part pattern with a structure that shows various levels of developing complexity. Similarly, a Baroque melody repeats four 'beats' to a bar with four depth changes to develop base and melody line. The melody develops our focus on a 'musical purpose' or intention, using counterpoint as an attractor field. And, at the very same time, we can visually attend to all aspects together by metaphorically watching them, then (dissociatively) painting them into a mindstream with different colors for each sound.

A person can dive into any classical music experience by expanding attention while following the artist's intent, noticing the intertwining musical themes. Enlarged awareness emerges through the flowing matrix of musical intention combined with musical value. You might start with Baroque music, which often shows multiple themes mixing together.

Music, in all its manifestations, is a wonderful doorway! Repeating patterns of rich tonal symmetries open different aspects of our awareness because they model our natural mind movement patterns of *contraction, expansion, exploration*, and *coherence*. There might be variations and interweaving themes organizing and building the sound in new directions. Yet all themes cohere to create a higher level of integrative musical awareness, which opens capacities for expanded awareness like the center of a rose.

Diagram 4.2: Mind Patterns: Exploration, Contraction, Expansion, and Coherence

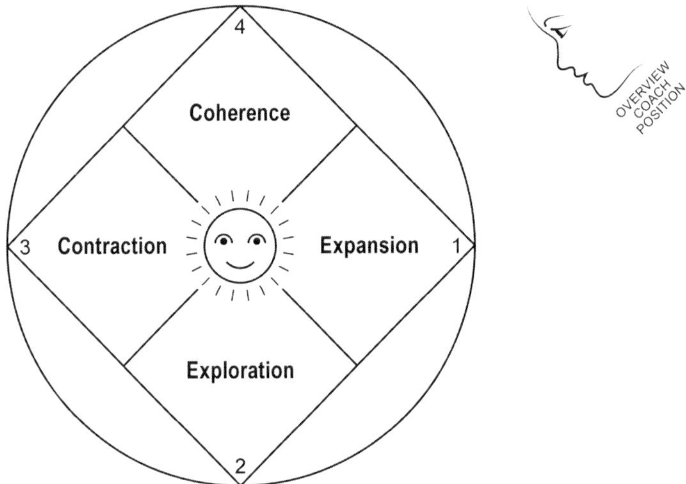

Explore Auditory Salience Through Musical Systems

If you listen with the ear and eye of a musician, perhaps with a classical piece such as Mozart concerto, you're going to notice various ways the musician has *visualized*, then built these integrative arrangements. Mozart, for example, organized his music *visually* using his own inner 'mandalic' pictures to build wholeness systems. The musician usually intertwined several four-part structures together. His sounds also reflect a conversation between inner and outer musical strategies. He visually combined different orders of sound with inner melody expansion patterns.

When he originally described his music, Mozart explained that he 'saw' all the sounds as colored symbols. He both visualized and heard the resonant interplay.[12] Try this as a listener — at least a few times — with different types of music, for even one sitting. The salient awareness of musical exploration takes us naturally on a journey into deeper awareness. We experience multifaceted richness.

Musical systems develop our learning pathways. Look for four-beat melodies that repeat a specific patterned emergence with different ramifications, reflections, and tonal qualities. You dive into deeply meaningful learning. You notice the widening of awareness through all your sensory channels.

Explore four quadrant thinking with all kinds of musical genres. As you listen to many genres, including hip-hop, reggae, and rap, you will hear many variations on balanced expansion, often in systems of four. Notice how a strong systematic musical beginning really opens your basic awareness of levels and kinds of musical structure. With any strong coherent melody, there will be developed themes repeating in different ways, often four to eight times... with variations.

When you read Part 3, to be found in Volume II, you will explore four quadrant 'mind-building formats.' You will then be able to notice that many music patterns also echo Formats A, B, C, and D, our four natural, and fundamental four quadrant processing systems. Salient music provides rich 'playground' training and you start to hear — and see — the rich patterning. Take some time to explore this.

Exercise I: Explore Visual Salience Through Images

Visual *salience*, like my example of the Japanese Garden 'moss forest,' can become available anytime we open our eyes. One great expansion exercise is to play with the distinctions of a good photographer.

Photographers Process

Pretend you are taking a picture of the room you are in right now as if you were a photographer. What visual interests call your attention? What 'snapshots' would you take?

- What light and shade patterns catch your attention?
- Are you attracted more to color or to form? More to texture or to shape?
- What specific objects immediately stand out against the background? What makes special features interesting for you?
- What design aspects attract you?
- Do you zoom in on detail, or expand out to the big picture?
- Upon what do you focus most easily — people or things?

You are naturally organizing your perception by what attracts you. What is visually beautiful for you, engaging for you, or shows pleasing aesthetic integration?

Snap these 'shots,' (by declaration), as you review your room. Close your eyes and make a click sound to emphatically photograph the three most 'interesting' features in your 'exhibition area.' Choose them carefully, as if preparing to submit them to an art gallery. Now, how do you see the room or space differently?

Exercise II: Explore Kinesthetic Salience Through Smell and Touch

Physical awareness through touch is amplified when you briefly remove the other senses:

Kinesthetic Salience Process

Here is an interesting exercise for you to do: Study and expand your awareness with a fifteen-minute exploration in which you walk through your garden or a park area blindfolded. Use your nose to smell at least ten different plants: leaf, stem, and trunk. Use your fingertips to touch whatever texture is of interest.

Feel the quality of each leaf or flower surface, comparing it to the plant before it. Smell it. Touch the variations in stem and tree bark, noting what makes each unique. You will enjoy this process!

Salience often seems like the easiest area for beginners to build clear distinctions linking concrete perception with abstract appreciation. Yet with exploration and exercise, all quadrants can be separated, explored, valued and reassembled in new ways. Continue to develop these distinctions.

The Dimension of Relevance: Quadrant One

Let us turn our attention to quadrant one as described in diagrams 3.4 and 3.5. With this we move our attention to a very different area of the mind system and focus on questions of personal prioritization and personal choice.

Relevance is the key value that directs quadrant one attention. We move from *having* salience to *doing* what is relevant to us. *Relevance* questions link us to our prioritizing abilities, and distinguishes the skills and actions that create effective results. The focus on relevance assists us to link our results to a planned future. We develop our capacity to focus well.

Notice that with relevance, we enter into a radically different mind theatre than with salience perception. We move to the realm of creation. Yet, for both, we are able to build the capacity for awareness *expansion.* With the goals in your life, what do you tend to *do* to maximize *relevance* distinctions?

The horizontal dimensions of past actions and future capabilities — quadrants three and one — necessarily assist each other in constant interplay. With quadrant one and quadrant three together, we move to the realms of 'thought design,' creating possibilities. To some, this may have the 'smoke and mirrors' quality of magical dreams. With our quest for relevance, we open a 'satellite dish' to emerging ideas. We design with multiple flashes of new and prior thought, and stabilize with declaration and promise. We explore the process of building a future, step by step.

The thought about what *has* happened is quickly followed by the thought — what *might* happen? What I now know I can do is followed by what I might *now* be able to do. The forest of our intention is seeded first by our developed *experience,* our quadrant three focus; and only then cultivated by *relevant* quadrant one focus, noticing our next steps. From Observational Coach Position, we can watch this interplay in our Mind as we make a choice.

Our life is like a glider rising higher on the hot air of our *relevant* dreams, yet moving through the atmosphere of possibility by the skillful guidance of the hands of *experience. Relevance* is about expanding what is most important to us now in our life-building projects. We're joyful when we make our developed experience (quadrant three) *relevant* to our future aims (quadrant one) because we can integrate our experience, our work, our plans, and our aims as a powerful part of building our lives forward.

To celebrate our moments with joy, we also link relevance back to quadrant two, salient physical awareness. Do we not make our salient moments relevant to future elements of our life? Through focusing on what is relevant, do we not want to build value now? Building our capacity to expand awareness moment by moment is always relevant to us. We then make it meaningful (quadrant four).

For example, for someone becoming a classical musician, being able to hear music the way Mozart heard music (and then thinking in expansive four quadrant formats) becomes *relevant* to writing great music, does it not? We relate sensory depth to a specific experiential skill set and then we take the time to build it. Combining multiple ways to focus as a *tool set*, we develop the distinctive capacity to accomplish *relevant* results.

From Coach Position, we can learn to expand relevance through all areas of our life's operations. Look at the following Diagram 4.3, which shows building the capacity for relevant choices. It points to the process of stretching the *horizontal* focus of our awareness beyond commonly marked time frameworks we might normally use so that our matrix of time and value holds a life awareness system of deep and wide relevance.

Diagram 4.3: Exploring Relevant Choices: The Horizontal and Vertical Dimensions Together.

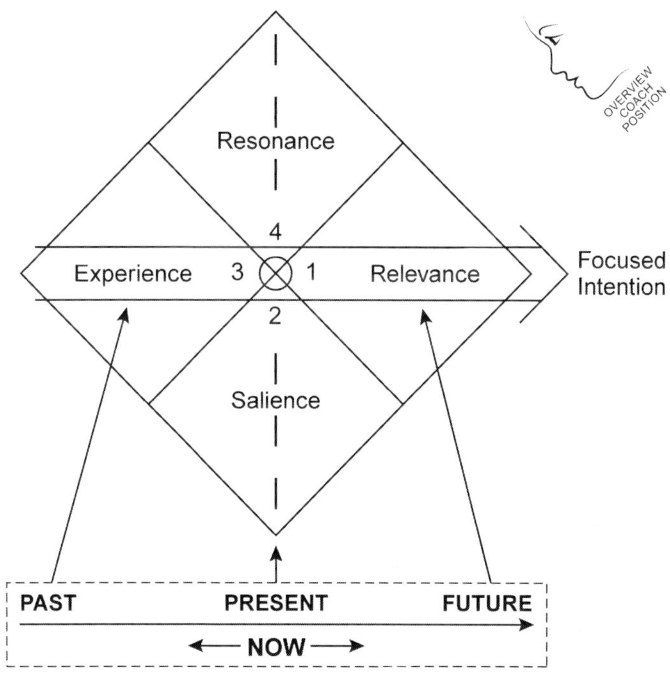

Being, Doing and Having a Life

Our 'moments' of relevance always point to a specific time scope, which is set by the engagement boundaries relevant to our projects. There may be many of them as we overview towards our best future. Each boundary adjustment resets both our timeframe and our identity as a project planner. Compare that to the map of salience where we step into one salient moment at a time. See the timeline below Diagram 4.3. Directionality, mapped with arrows, indicates the four quadrant system as a time-map potentializer, available *now.*

Our '*experience*' awareness, by habit, links us to our already-built (past) capabilities, while our relevance focus pertains to the ways we design future possibilities. Examining past experience alone tends to link us to our either-or emotional system. "I like it" versus "I dislike it" often shows up as our key experiential processing system. Yet, linking each to each, *we can learn to follow the thread of all our deeper learning by inner request. We learn to move forward and to overview the whole connected thread.*

We can let our deep beyond-conscious integrative ability choose the learnings for us. This happens best when we take Coach Position to overview the richest and widest time-range we can muster, and explore our learnings from combining past, present, and potential future positions so that we truly become curious about what is most *relevant* to us today.

Build Coach Position on Relevance

Our focus on *relevance* builds energetic, creative, 'intentional mind.' From Coach Position, you can practice inviting your intuitive process *to balance across your inner timeline system* using your 'larger intention' as a guidepost *for* creating your most relevant time scope for *now.* Then, while making any choice, you can ask inwardly to engage relevant past experience, braiding the whole system together.

For example, if you are a hockey player on the ice scoring a goal, you are *doing* what is relevant to a future you are creating, yet you are physically and emotionally referencing and engaging many moments of former experience to design immediate strategies for *this* moment. Our focus on mastery enriches the engagement in all areas: what we *have*, what we *do*, and what we *be*.

Explore your *relevance* focus. How do you engage relevance well? What habits do you have? What happens when you specifically *add in an Overview Coach Position*? How can you learn to braid your life together into a richly patterned whole.

You can use *relevance* focus to develop your inner strategy questions about future direction, while from Coach Position you ponder 'all of it' in the moment. In this way, you trigger unique, surprising questions as you examine what is most relevant to your purpose. Coach Position overview links your strongest intention to your most curious, insightful questions. Fear-based thinking gets sidetracked while optimistic, realistic, creative intuition gets cultivated.

Relevance focus works well as a spark to fire up questions of inner purpose. With a strong Coach Position on all of it you learn to light the inner fire as a whole system. You can do this even if the conscious mind just 'holds the frame.' Then, even when we focus from 'past' or 'future,' our whole four quadrant mind system is genuinely coordinating — at Coach Position level — as a smoothly operating life mastery system! This means we are able to taste our current moment deeply, even as all awareness systems converge. Our deep creativity stays alive and open. We can relax and receive. See again diagram 4.3.

The Dimension of Experience: Quadrant Three

The arena of *experience* references both the memorable and the well-practiced skills of conscious working memory available in the moment. This includes all the smoothly operative habit systems we consciously depend on as our life capabilities.

This area may seem extremely self evident, yet is useful to overview briefly because these habits are the matrix that holds together everything that we consider most 'ourselves.' This includes our knowledge systems, even the 'basics,' such as the languages we speak. It includes the sociability systems we develop, and the interactional habits we create to exchange with others. Call these your 'connectivity patterns.' As well, it includes our baseline of physical habits. All are smoothly operative, interconnected systems we *have* and *do*, and that we seldom think about. We have developed skillful physical habits, walking, dancing, eating, speaking, and being sociable, as everyday occurrences. We skillfully drive to the meetings where we demonstrate our sociability and leadership expressiveness. All represent arenas of well-functioning integrated, cultural abilities, our *experience* of well-organized human interplay.

Diagram 4.4: Exploring Essential Habits Building

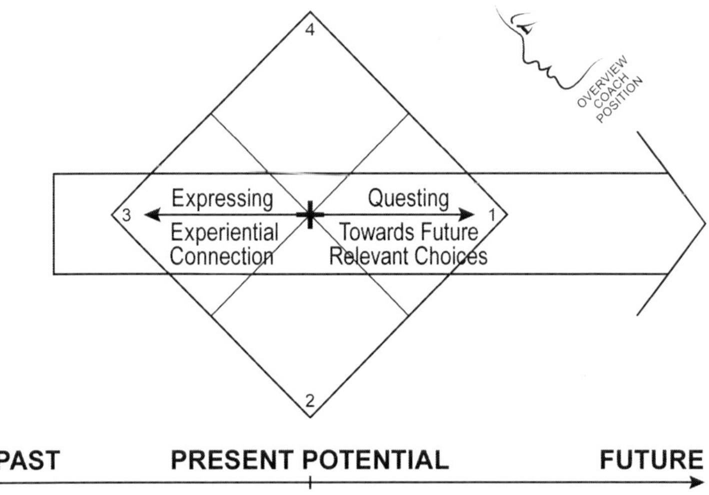

Expressing and *Questing* look like separate elements.

Past and Future Combined

With the experience dimension, we move horizontally between evaluating our *experience* to date, and the process of questing towards future choices. Current neuroscience shows that both memories of past and future are all linked together in the same area of the brain. Past and future images are always studied together as we make choices.

Diagram 4.5: Instigating and Exploring Futures

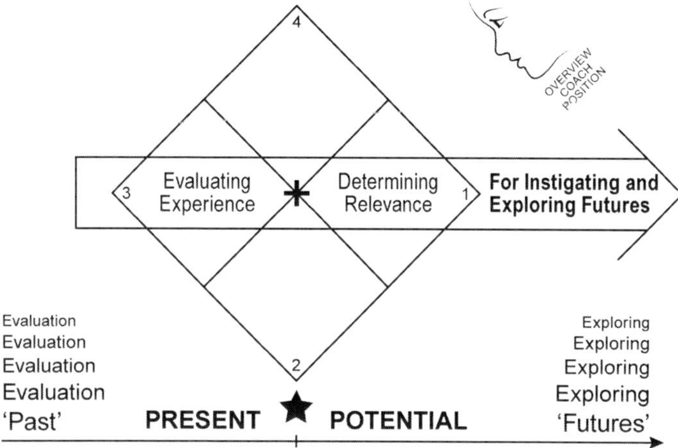

As we evaluate our experience, we are always checking relevance.

Notice this for yourself when you think of a potential choice. Don't you naturally integrate former *experience*? We use *comparative* questions to explore our inner commentary, feelings, or images of these choices, and to determine what are the *relevant* actions and next steps.

This carry-over emotional habit of our brain-system, relating past, present, and future all at once, is very important for expanding coherent relationships. From Coach Position, we can build unconditional positive regard with a spouse, a workplace team, a community, a nation, and even for all persons in the world. Looking out from our wisdom system, we can experience all relational choices together as a base for good decisions.

Relational experience is the fundamental area for comparative evaluation. As humans, we do many activities together: we share experiences, we hang out together, we joke, we strategize, and we discuss. We earnestly evaluate our best ways to interact with each other, relating our joint experience with our relevant aims. All of this can be used to create a baseline of security and safety as we develop our next steps.

Time-Marked Evaluations

The horizontal axis of experience and relevance takes us to the very specific realms of well-established thought systems that are '*time-marked*.' Our evaluation habits are time-marked. We compare our experiences with each other over time. Time-marked evaluation, even when used with positive scaling, is always *comparative*. Again, no matter our criteria, our old emotional systems references either-or, and better or worse.

Most evaluations tend to be cause-effect oriented because they follow old emotional brain system habits with simplistic either-or decisions. Our mammal ancestors with their simple survival patterns — fight, freeze, or flee — needed to make immediate clear-cut choices. If we met the sabre-toothed tiger on 'that trail,' we stopped new learning about it for a while. For us, now walking on 'that trail' was dangerous; as if the trail 'caused' the tiger.

Intellectually, we can realize that life is truly effect, effect, effect (chicken-egg-chicken-egg-chicken,etc), but the ancient habit to look for causes (and to make fearsome linkages) has tended to prevail, and all the world's cultures include many fear-based cultural habits in their repertoire. We need habits, but we need to see how the habits we build aim towards development, not just survival.

Historians label and relate eras, times, phenomena, decades, to 'generations' — such as the Millennials — and their specific cultural habits. This builds mindframe identifications and cultural movements. Clearly, however, these divisions are arbitrary — people are being born all the time. We need to pay attention to these reductions. 'Eras' and 'generations' are mainly being created by the writers themselves. The question is where do the 'brackets' of separation and cause-effect generalizations become useful? Where can we begin to create new developmental 'brackets?'

Stepping back, we can see the total arbitrary nature of these time-scoped divisions. The tribal and status-oriented separations need careful re-examination. There are always 'inner brackets' inside the 'outer brackets' of personal, linguistic, and socio-cultural categories. Yet, what we always discover is singular moments of *experience* and choice. The 'stream' of 'identity experience' is an illusion. It is always 'take one – memory one' in our inner movie theatre.

We need to check 'personal memory.' We need to notice where does one useful memory stop and another begin. We feel the body now. We experience self only now! Stop and notice the conscious mind as a 'thinking machine.' Widen your context of awareness beyond this. Notice that your 'thoughts' disappear immediately as you gain resonant connection with your wider context.

We consistently need to overview our experience to 'make sense' of it because our conscious mind tends to connect to the old either-or emotional system and makes these arbitrary linkages. Our old memories usually lack an enlarged positive context. We can widen our experience across space and time to include all of us and our humanity as part of a wider awareness that opens a much bigger scope for thought and imagination.

Only we, individually, can truly make our own human evolution a personal discovery system. Only we ourselves can take effective Coach Position on our multifaceted interactive cultural/emotional system as a means to orient to deeper awareness and inner growth. We can do this from our purposeful awareness now. We can also do this by learning how to notice how to link our brain habits into a four quadrant framework. With four quadrant thinking we can design truly empowering processes to develop categories for thinking that allow a coherent mind matrix of core distinctions.

With practice, we can learn to set an empowering wider context on all our *experience*. We can quickly learn to regard old protective evaluation habits as temporary and ask our deeper knowing system for guidance. Create the widest context for your experiential life that you can develop! Link this to the most relevant choices you can make! With pondering and exploration we learn to creatively steer our own lives, towards a purpose that fosters us.

Resonance Awareness, Your Integrity System: Quadrant Four

For building the awareness of our *inner resonance*, quadrant four, we align with the inner *integration* of all our four quadrants of purpose. We appreciate them together as an integrated, harmonic 'Russian Doll' of awareness. We engage a symphonic system.

Are we not happy when we are able to describe the salience of our moments and can positively empower our life through these moments? As well, are we not pleased to be able to make this experience *relevant* to what we will be doing next? *With all three levels in coherent play* we easily move to engage the fourth level, the experience of inner *resonance*. This is the integrative level of inner truth. As we overview our life, we receive and experience this integration entirely from our deeper knowing, our beyond-conscious realm.

Resonance opens as we observe, listen, and accept the mind matrix with all its levels and contributions. Resonance occurs especially as we let our unconscious mind learn to do the dance of contextual overview and integration, while the conscious mind observes it all with interest rather than judgment! Realizing and responding to your inner resonance level allows you to grow your values and develop your integrity awareness... even as you consciously enjoy your inner 'garden of awareness.'

We really discover inner *resonance* when we move our attention to appreciating all *inner meaningfulness* — right now. When we relax and ask questions inwardly we can notice the integrity of the moment. We are truly asking: "How does this unfolding moment — my learnings todays — resonate with my larger life? Does this life — as a whole — deeply agree with my values and my commitments?" Appreciating what is meaningful allows us to be *here* now.

We only lightly touch the topic of resonance here in Part 1. Bringing all elements together, integrating a higher level awareness to amplify deeper *resonance* is the focus of Volume II, Part 4. You will find that building resonant systems is the undercurrent topic of Volume I, Part 2, with exercises for enhancing value awareness. Moving into Volume II, Part 3 we then focus on developing the freedom for conscious flexibility of thinking.

Resonant Heart Awareness — Exercise I

Take a moment now to practice whole system awareness for yourself. You can do this physically by breathing *as if through* your heart. For a moment, notice it beating and even visualize this heartbeat. Then, sense your heart as center for all four awareness systems, physical, emotional, intentional, and meaningful. Feel it.

Breathing provides a vehicle for widening the awareness of your intake channels: your hearing, sight, sound, taste, and smell. Run your attention through them all as you slowly breathe 'from the heart' for several minutes. Allow all aspects to integrate — heartfully — as you breathe.

Expand your awareness of *Self* through every sensory portal, 360°, and link — as if you could — out to the whole universe. Sense, feel and resonate with this larger awareness. Move to overview and from Overview Coach Position take a snapshot of this symbolically, however it may look for you.

Now, again, breathe 'through the heart' with an expanded sensing of *presence*. You can view Diagram 4.6 to playfully key in a visual framework for this.

Diagram 4.6: 'All Together' Awareness

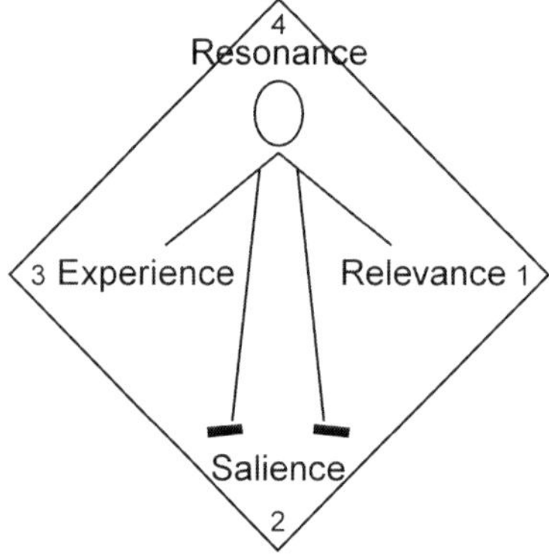

Your Garden of Awareness — Exercise II

As if you could, briefly visualize your life awareness as if it were a garden, a walled garden with four doorways, physical, relational, intentional, and meaningful. Serenely walk in through any doorway and seat yourself in the very center. Visualize this as a vortex, a dazzling creation point. Feel it as the very centerpoint of your own life awareness, combining all salience, experience, relevance, and resonant life. Experience yourself in the center of all this potential.

Relax, breathe, and immerse in the serenity of being at the center of your life, becoming aware of all the channels of perception through the body. Notice all four doorways to your garden as ancient, evolutionary doors, easily touched and opened wide from where you sit.

Sitting at centerpoint, experience simple presence, the awareness of symphonic deep concurrence and aliveness inside and out. Notice the deep vibration of presence.

Expand into the widest overview, the meaningful coherence of the whole. Relax. You are home.

With the next few practices, you will be using four quadrant 'space' as a framework for self-exploration. You can use the two Four Directions Exercises in this next chapter to explore how to build meaningful pathways to your own experience of inner truth.

Using these easy practices explore four important areas through which you can *grow* advanced consciousness capacities that move you up the Central Staircase. This will develop your freedom with *Having*, *Doing*, and ultimately *Being* your strongest Self. Discover how to take your awareness 'on a daily walk' out to each apex of your own unique four quadrant system. You can also use this as a way to instigate visionary project thinking.

CHAPTER 5:

The Four Directions Exercises: A Four Quadrant Meditation

Four Quadrant Pondering and Inner Flow

What will you learn by asking visionary questions inward? The *Four Directions Exercises* work with the quality of the questions you ask and this, in return, gives you the quality of the responses that you find. With the *Four Directions Exercises* next, you let go of your conscious queries about any specific question and just learn to listen for and respond to messages from your own inner knowing. You learn to tune your inner 'satellite dish' to deeper responses daily or nightly, and point towards the area of maximum effectiveness. Call this *dynamic pondering*! You are saying to yourself: "Okay, I'm just going to trust that my own deep truth awareness will bring me the key directions I need. It will show me what I need to move through and develop next steps."

What does an effective four quadrant pondering system give us? It is great value to know how to really ponder a question inwardly, with open curiosity and a willingness to explore. Only then do we pass through the sacred doors that link us into dynamic visualization and inner flow states.

Pondering Powerfully

The *Four Directions Exercises* in this chapter work well with your most value-focused, open-ended inquiries as you ask them inwardly in an open-hearted way. Explore what pondering means to you. We develop our ability to expand Coach Position, first overviewing our mind garden, then jumping into a specific vision or query to explore it deeply. We can begin to ask questions powerfully when we ponder well.

The *Four Directions Exercises* show you much about your own access to inner self-knowledge. To ponder effectively you learn to elevate and widen your focus. You also learn to pay attention through all the four quadrants of your experiential inner and outer worlds, and to stay with your pondering process long enough to dive deep into specific areas.

The aim is to approach your deeper questions. You gradually learn to practice, measure, and scale up awareness so that you perceive these core questions from all sides. You begin rich, developmental inquiry so that even as you explore the system, it develops *you.* You begin to deeply trust your own inner depth!

We are participants in a constantly restructuring living system. The mind of the whole is always much bigger than the sum of its parts. We have access to our larger mind-garden at any time; we need only ask questions that are organized towards comprehensive discovery, especially with our creative aims. With the following exercises, we are doing all of this.

The mind is like a treasure chest filled with inner jewels. These are particularly available through quadrant one, which instigates our inner creative vision. This means that we will go to quadrant one first in the night exploration. We then shine on all these 'jewels of discovery' with quadrant two, by requesting ideas for specific action and completion steps. We then continue with quadrant three, also useful for sensing best practice and best fit for others. We link them all together with quadrant four, like a deeply jewelled and value-laden crown of inner wisdom. Using the *Four Directions Exercises*, we learn to trust the full integrity of our own beyond conscious deeper knowing.

When we 'set' our space as a whole thinking space, all four systems will integrate together around our questions as a treasure chest of available knowledge and wisdom. We then access this inner truth as visionary ideas about our quest and our questions.

Style One: The Four Directions Floor Exercise

We have several practices for doing this. The first Four Directions Exercise you might try is a floor exercise where you physically move around on a four quadrant floor pattern, perhaps a two-meter floor area. In other words, each quadrant represents the step-by-step unfolding of a physicalized thinking space. Here you diagram four types of inner development, scaling from 1, at the center, to 10, at the edge. This becomes your personal gameboard. Each of the 'floor quadrants' then corresponds to the key areas of inner and outer inquiry we explored in the last several chapters; physical, relational, intentional and meaningful and the four intelligences you are maximizing through these. For example, you may be examining your physical energy with questions such as "How might I really start to build habits to maximize my physical vitality?" Or, perhaps you have key inter-relational questions or questions about core areas of your work development. The aim of this exercise is to assist you to activate exploration with creative questions in each area.

By linking to a key question and physically exploring each area on the game board with our questions, we energize an effective pondering system. You will likely get strong visualization with each key area when you ask questions truly relevant to your own learning and growth in each area. (See Diagram 5.1.)

The exercise can be started by sitting on a stool in the middle of the space. Organize the four quadrants as a large working area around the body marked by small papers or post-its at the center and at each corner apex. In this way, you can visualize four lines around you, each 90° apart, scaled from level 1 to level 10.

Diagram 5.1: The Floor Exercise Steps

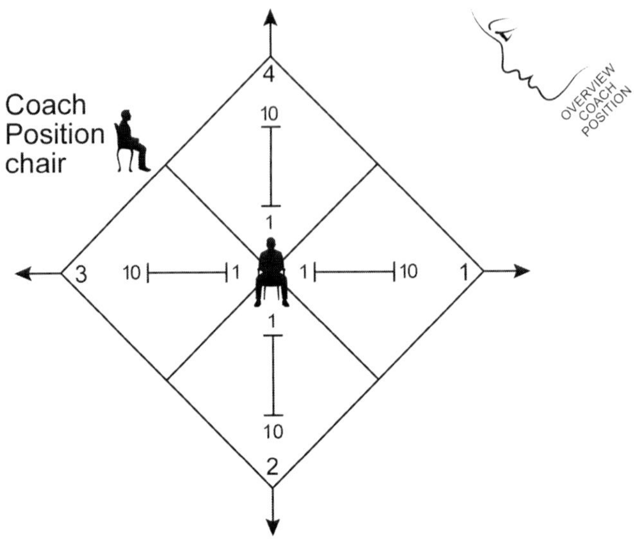

Setting a game board in this way, and using the body as your access system as you move through it, can quickly assist the arrival of useful, systemic information. Such a floor plan makes it simple to visualize four key 'state lines' where we can ponder our inner 'information' through physical association. Practice this even one time — and ever after you will know how to mentally associate the four quadrants to a floor plan as a basic self-learning strategy.

Reflect on the Quadrants in Four Directions:

Quadrant one, the intention-creation arena, can be used to represent the arena of dreaming, hopes, and planning, and the accompanying thoughts, metaphors, pictures, feelings, and words you have built to amplify the *intentional* aim of your core questions. Perhaps journal questions about key areas for life development over the next three to five years might be useful here. It might be used as a launch pad to explore your deeper purpose. The *relevance* of the questions you ask here at step one, determines the power of your result. This focus also connects you to your deeper creative process and your intuitive power. Ask an open-ended question that energizes your inner connection to purpose and vision.

Quadrant two, the physical arena, can be used to represent sensory data available in the world, especially data which might assist your result. What information needs to be seen, heard, and felt for you to understand and fulfill your aim effectively? What is available now in the world of practical, experiential exploration that you might want to receive from current sources?

Quadrant three, the relationship area, can be used to represent historical practice, experience, and valuable ideas that may have 'accumulated' in the world as available knowledge from others. What has been learned and found to work by others through history? What do others offer that you might want to receive and learn from?

Quadrant four may be used to ask for deeper knowledge and inner guidance. Here you are exploring to how all the aspects integrate into your own inner life, and into the current moment. What is currently unfolding as a brand new, developmental meaning in your life? What spiritual, meaningful discovery is energetically coalescing from your request? What wisdom and what life principles are available? What is your inner guidance.

The Four Directions Floor Exercise Setup

Please do the exercise *physically*. First, begin with an open question that is truly relevant to you about a project or about your life.

Sit on a stool and visualize a four quadrant diamond around you. Consider the corners and quadrants as if each separately representing all levels available to you of the inner *physicality*, *relationship*, *intention*, and *meaning* pertinent to your question. As you explore this space you will be examining *physical*, *emotional-relational*, *intentional*, and *meaningful* aspects of your question.

Set the center of each quadrant section as level 1 and each apex as level 10. Inwardly request that level 10, the apex of each quadrant, indicates full and complete satisfaction with this key area. The aim is to perceive and understand more about the larger context of your question, as well as to get your answer. Place two stools where you can easily move to them, one at center of the system and one on the outside, where you can see all of it. You can mark the corners with sticky notes or small objects if you choose. You will be frequently sitting in the middle.

For each quadrant 'line,' you are separately asking:

- To move further, what are the relevant intentions that I need? (Quadrant 1)
- To move further, what do I need to understand as the physical action steps here? (Quadrant 2)
- To move further, what is truly my deep relational experience here? (Quadrant 3)
- To move further, what is most meaningful here? What resonates? (Quadrant 4)

You can ask these questions (or variation on them) in any order and walk on any of the lines as you choose. It is useful to explore all of them at least *once*.

The Exercise Steps

Slowly and meaningfully step out from level 1 to level 10 on your stateline with your chosen question. Ask inwardly to see and know what is comprehensive in *this* specific area. As you walk slowly down this line with your one open-ended question, feel your body with each step, sensing inwardly. Watch your thoughts as you move step by step, pondering your question.

Do the same slow walk from center to each of the four apexes, one by one, holding a paper journal or a recorder to record your thoughts as you proceed through each mindscape. As you do so, place all attention on the body and its clear apprehension. Notice your visioning, feeling, and messaging systems. Watch for vision flashes. Notice body feelings, find values and insights.

Walk (or back-up) slowly towards each apex as you choose, with your question in mind, noticing the quality of each step on the scale. You are doing a powerful focusing practice to assist you to access useful inner knowledge about each of these four key arenas of awareness. Pay close attention to the body feelings with every step you take, and describe your physical, emotional and inner dialogue responses to your recorder. You might also walk with a partner who scribes for you.

Between each walk, step aside to the stool on the outside, which represents Coach Position. Consciously take this position as a way to step outside your whole system. If working with a partner, take time to discuss and debrief the experience of each line. What was the value of each exploration? What was the value of all the four statelines you have just engaged? How do they 'add up' to give you greater understanding of your question and its answers? How was the whole exercise of value to you?

Style Two: The Four Directions Night Exercise

Another very useful version of this exercise, which I have used for 30 years, is the *Four Directions Night Exercise.* Here we work with our sleep time to connect inwardly to a specific purpose so that it becomes sustainable in an ongoing way. A night request is a very effective way to build your linkage to inner intelligence. Let me explain how this exercise works and then invite you to try it!

With the *Four Directions Night Exercise* you have a simple methodology to connect inwardly to your deepest and widest aims on a *regular* nightly basis. With the exercise, you develop a clear methodology for four quadrant exploring, learning to maximize learning and integration through your sleeping period. The process builds powerful inner self-discovery and learning habits.

The four areas are exactly the same as described earlier, yet now your beyond-conscious mind 'directs the journey' each night as you sleep. Moving clockwise through each area during your sleep cycle, you learn how to move your important questions towards a creative result using your inner 'dream guide.'

The exercise can best be used to work with one major question each night. We need to request inwardly just before sleep, visualizing all four areas together with ourself at the center. It is useful for examining big challenges. It always works with the quality of the question you ask and this, in turn, gives you the quality of the response that you find.

Have you ever been stressed about a problem and found it hard to fall asleep? With the *Four Directions Night Exercise*, you let go of your conscious queries about the problem and just give in to your developmental intuition, your beyond-conscious mind. You say to yourself: "Okay, I'm just going to trust that my beyond-conscious mind will bring me what I need to truly explore the hard part." Then, simply do the steps described in the framework which follows next.

The Four Directions Night Exercise Steps

Plan to do this exercise just prior to closing your eyes as you lie down for your regular night's sleep. The Four Directions *Night* Exercise begins when we physicalize a specific inner question or request. We create a 'thinking space' using our natural, physical sleeping arrangement 'on the bed.'

The easiest use of 'four directions' questions is to make an evening request just prior to sleep. You privately ask inwardly for knowledge and guidance. Do this with deep appreciation for whatever you will receive.

Lying down to sleep, the next step is visualizing the four quadrant system itself, while sensing it, *as if around you.* We get a very rich connection into the four quadrants of any coalescing aim by taking a few moments to vividly picture the four quadrants *as if around our body* as it lies in its regular sleeping spot.

Diagram 5.2: The Four Directions Night Exercise: Imagine Lying in Your Four Quadrant Bed...

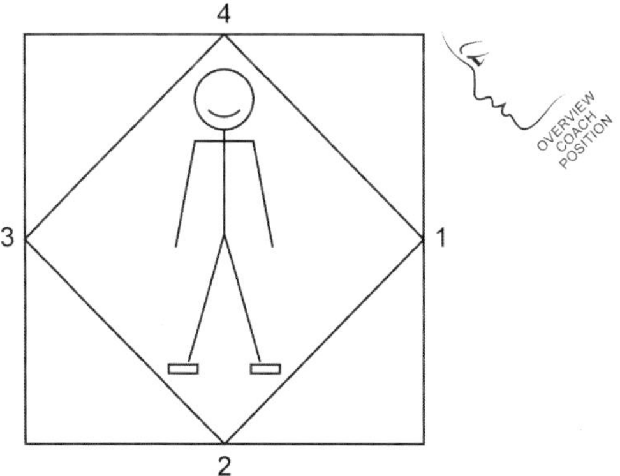

Briefly note that you are *laying in the creative centerpoint of the universe.* This, in some Hindu systems, is called '*the Bindu.*' You can view the full four quadrant spectrum around you like a clock, visualizing your head in quadrant four. (See Diagram 5.2, the four quadrant 'bed.')

You can always observe yourself from Coach Position, outside the personal system, even as you physically lie down in the centerpoint.

Take two minutes at night to start your exercise with focus and vision. As you lay down for sleep, recognize the space (your sleeping place) as your map, and visualize all four areas, seeing them around you like sections of a clock. In preparing the Four Directions *Night* process, take time to clearly represent all four areas to yourself, appreciating the power and the beauty of having access to each area. The process begins when you point your nose to your left, into quadrant one, towards your goal, while you inwardly request to explore one specific, important question this night.

Point your face towards quadrant one to express your aim. The process is one of exploration only. Ask your question as 'consciously' as possible, and make your request for insight clear and direct. Be sure you are inwardly voicing a specific request in an open-ended way. Everyone develops their own detailed process with this. One of many options is to specify the data, the inner meaning, and the level of inner truth that you wish to access. *Ask for more of what is required, more understanding, as well as more learning or more insight...* and more will come. For example, ask to scale up insight and visualize your scale moving up. Appreciate the gift of this inner connection and response. Thank your inner guide.

Then, still lying on your bed, visualize each of the other three 'directions' and request that your core 'truth function' connect into all four of these quadrants during the sleep process. Mentally review all four directions quickly with your question. You are asking that during the sleep process, your deeper knowing system will review what is intentionally required to do your aim and, what is physically, emotionally and relationally required to do your aim. This assists you to learn the meaningful connections you will need to make. You can rest the whole night while all aspects are explored and integrated.

Visualize the 'hour hand' of your clock moving fully around from 12 to 12, seeing all areas of access becoming totally available as the clock moves to each. Link this movement to the visualization of your normal sleep time on the clock.

Discover your results when you awaken in the morning. The next day, usually right away on awakening, you will receive some immediate responses, often a flood of meaningful ideas and interconnected areas of larger awareness. Make sure you have something to write with on hand right beside you, so you can capture areas of clarity in the visions and ideas you get. Then do what is necessary to build on this.

The Request and Response Process in the Morning

Immediately begin writing down your received answers upon first waking. Again, allow yourself to move your attention, at least briefly, into all four quadrants integrating what has gone before.

Start to write from the assumption of having received the answers you wish, and immediately write what comes to mind. In other words, write *as if* the answers have been delivered and you just need to put them down on paper. When you are finished, let your document 'cool' for a while before examining it, and only then explore the value of the messages that you have just written to yourself. Explore with gratitude for whatever you receive!

This is an exercise to do not once, but many times. It can also be done during meditation periods. I have personally used it to write six books, awakening from my questions to write each morning. Enjoy letting your unconscious mind do your inner work for you. Dynamic intelligence now guides your life.

PART 2

The Left Staircase of Value Appreciation

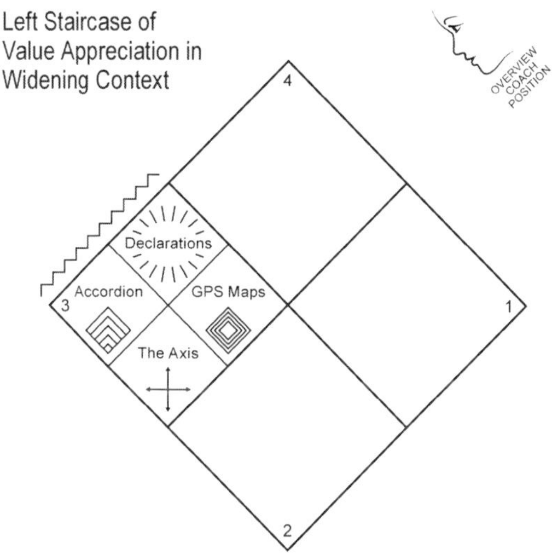

CHAPTER 6:

The Mind Compass and Its Vertical Dimension

In the following chapters of Part 2, we will use physical metaphors to explore areas of inner development and comprehension, noticing that using them we can sense inner truth, growth, and viability in quite a developmental way. This next part of the book gives some specific four quadrant amplification exercises. Exercises can be found at the end of each chapter.

We can inspect the functioning of our Mind and find the following strategies of it's functioning. We realized in Part 1 that there is a horizontal dimension of the Mind which includes our intentional focus and which is closely linked to our time-based identity Ideas. This dimension plays on the interaction between Experience and Relevance.

Similarly we always can find the *vertical dimension* to the Mind, which is easiest to explore with shifts of our value attention and focus. The scope of our attention includes all aspects of our meaningful value placement, inside and Outside. If this is directed towards the outside world, it sets the parameter from which we receive information via sensory perception.

All ideas in the focus of our attention will be evaluated either positively or negatively based on the viability of our intention. Directing our attention shifts everything. As we do so, we can set the span of the corresponding vertical dimension. Metaphorically, you might see this as the as-if altitude above the 'present moment' ground. We postulate this 'altitude' of overview as *levels of abstraction*, the *value states* and *spaces* of the Mind.

The horizontal dimension is secondary to this, since 'memory' is like an elastic band, and its size adjusts to the size of the vertical dimension to form a symmetric picture. Hence the Mind 'size' determining the scope of our 'Now' is open to our determination. On a scale of many microscopic 'Nows' the horizontal axis is formed by continuous interplay of *Evaluation* and *Intention*, giving us the various time spans of our memory systems.

The vertical scale, in contrast, is formed by the interplay of *Perception* and *Attention*, producing our Space-of-Mind states or Altitude. With the 'Altitude' scale, we are viewing and feeling the abstraction levels of our current perception, and noticing the attention of the Mind. The two sets — horizontal and vertical viewing and feeling — interplay to form an as-if macroscopic to microscopic *Mind Compass*.

Diagram 6.1: The Mind Compass and Its Two Axes

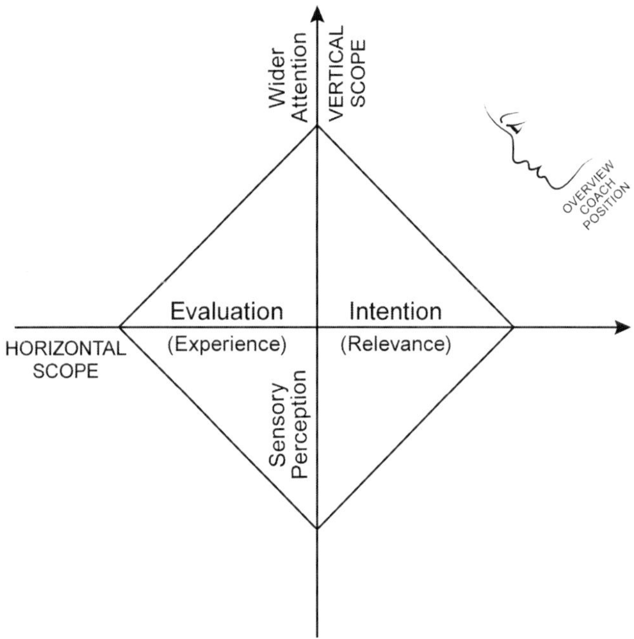

The Process of Vertical Expansion

Let us explore the vertical dimension further because this is the area where most people have the least practice in shifting focus and ability. When we practice moving down or expanding up on a metaphoric 'elevator of mind,' what exactly are we exploring? What do you notice as you narrow or expand your abstraction-perception lens of awareness?

The *vertical axis* as a scale from very specific to very abstract, moves us from *sensory-specific perception to 'big picture,' expanded, abstract attention.* Sensory specific perception is like a bubble inside a larger bubble. This easily adjusts down or up and in or out and moves like breathing as we perceive our lives from various points of view and different thought systems. Use a metaphor, 1 meter to 15,000 meters, to signify this expansive capacity.

Big picture 'vertical' *attentional* capacities holds big picture awareness in the same way that a painter holds a paintbrush. This creates a huge palette of possibilities, available right now. You can use your questions to organize the detailed brush strokes of your perception as well as the wide contextual applications of overview attention. What detailed brush strokes do you enjoy practicing? What vast expansion of vision and value do you soar with? How might you want to associate into your realm of vision to briefly try it?

'Moving up' means less and less detail in our pictures, yet our value-vision playground becomes clearer nevertheless. All positive overview inspires expansion, choice, and change in the mind gardens we develop —just by putting our attention here. We open up our intuitive inner sensing as we expand our sensory value awareness. We seed the integrative visions of our life possibilities. We discover more about ourselves as we open our awareness and stretch into open value. Moving up, we *expand* the Mind's capacity, experiencing the meaningful awareness of core values we can activate now. Take some time to explore with the exercises at the chapter's end.

Remember, while exploring the vertical axis, that *attention* is always a present-tense phenomenon. Both moment by moment perception and attention to the spacious awareness of value are always available now. We are exploring a value-reality system and it is phenomenologically tangible. Yet, paradoxically, vertically, we can always move into and associate to other 'moments of *now*,' and expand up with these as well.

Notice that the qualities of attention which go with higher, vertical levels naturally enrich your decision-making capacity. Your brain easily integrates every positive vision and value review that you do as a real time 'actuality.' These can include all the moments of your life, and the 'lives' as well. With the vertical dimension, you can make every moment *meaningful*!

A 'Lofty' Idea! Moving Up the Left Staircase in Associated Coach Position

You can always sense the major elements of input from the world at a chosen perimeter/altitude and sort it into physical, emotional, thinking and deeper meaning areas. In this way, you develop a balanced *associated Coach Position* (see Diagram 6.2). You can go back and forth between dissociated overview and associated exploration (and associated Coach Position) at every level you might want to explore.

I invite you to use this chapter to develop your capacity to expand attention upward with various awareness stretches. You will need to take some time to develop your own inner experience of your own vertical levels and abilities. You will have opportunities for practice with both this chapter and the next. Imagine the 'altitudes' in Diagram 6.2 as if real. How do you view your 'life' from these points of view?

Diagram 6.2: The Integrative Vertical Dimension of Attention

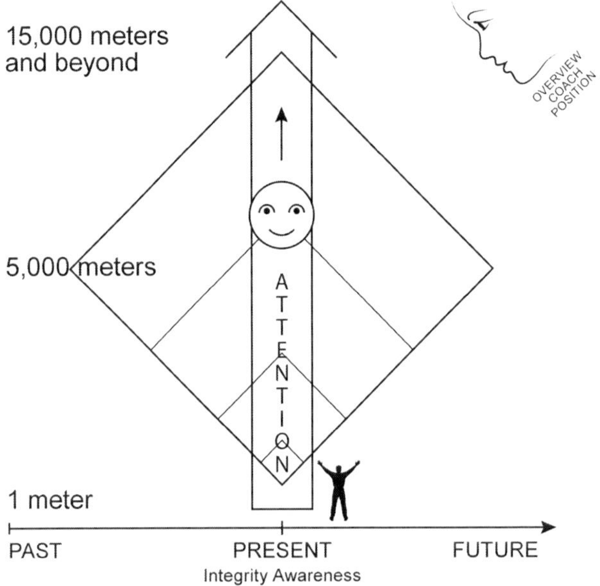

Notice that with all 'learning to learn' processes, it is useful to start 'high.' In other words, build your focus and your goals with a lofty aim. You are learning to expand beyond the habitual conscious mind-habits through which you normally operate. Metaphorically, the work we focus on in this Volume is from the '5,000 to 15,000-meter level.' Playground development begins with vast overview imagination and value awareness. Try the 'Lofty Ideas Exercise' at the end of the chapter. Use this to practice vertical expansion.

Use 'Vertical Viewing' to Energize Inner Purpose

You build your competencies afresh in your mind's eye when you see the self who congruently meets and masters key challenges. It is useful to hold a dissociated Coach Position on these images of the highly competent self. Hence, it is effective to move up or down the elevator of the Mind and observe from a dissociated Coach Position at various levels of altitude-attention focus.

With personal vision 'previews,' we naturally build the inner skills to engage the needed neurological brain-body linkages to start finding solutions to real-world challenges. These visions will easily transfer into on-the-ground practical abilities as we gain the courage to try them out.

It takes as few as 21 'previews' or small 1- to 2-second visual movies from Coach Position — where we see self in action demonstrating high-level capabilities and integrative values — to transfer these abilities effectively into the long-term physical system *so they actually become real-world habits.* For our inner habit systems, the values and behaviors we carefully preview soon become linked in the brain to represent our real abilities. This is especially true with effective communication habits. You will soon find yourself with the strong inner capabilities you envision as you watch these inner movies. You gradually realign your emotional capabilities to match.

Dissociated Viewing and Associated Exploring

Fear vanishes when you can see something working in your mind's eye. A dissociated visual experience is particularly useful because you can visualize yourself achieving strong abilities. When you request the beyond-conscious mind to see how you might handle a specific situation well, you can then start to access your 'creativity system'... an endless stream of 'effectiveness examples,' alternative examples which you can open like a video library. As coaches have learned, this field opens easily simply by requesting it. A wonderful question is simply 'what else'? More choices will generally appear by request.

You can watch yourself in dissociated internal movies of 'self-competence,' perhaps only a one or two second 'commercial' with yourself as the 'star.' You can explore with space frameworks or time contexts. In this way you receive new approaches and suggestions from your beyond conscious mind.

As you move way upwards on the Elevator of Mind in dissociated Coach Position, you may notice that the camera position develops a new 'sense ability.' With associative practice, you can feel values related to your vision at any level. You can even request value integration related to your vision and receive it, combining Associative and Dissociative Coach Positions.

Moving Up the Staircases, Combining Associated and Dissociated Coach Position

Now we bring the two distinct points of view together in a mutual dance of alternating perceptual positions. With visions of self-development using dissociated Coach Position, you are constructing 'meaning and value previews' as a kind of shorthand to your own life and purpose expansion.

The dissociated visions become connected to your values as you link into the fresh awareness of your calling and your inspiration. You can do that at various vertical altitudes on your metaphoric 'elevator of mind.'

However, the strongest way you can do most exercises in this work is through re-linking from dissociated Coach Position to associated Coach Position at every level of altitude. In this way, all the profound vibrational levels of overview awareness now become interlinked into your life through the mind-brain system.

For each expanded level of awareness you build an associated Coach Position by sensing your 'value presence' moment by moment. You can envision that 'self' — dissociated Coach Position — and then step in to that vibrational level — with associated Coach Position once again. You can specifically scale your vibration/resonance on the vertical dimension with spiritual, creative, relational, and physical self-development practice. You can playfully open each life area and explore separately at altitude levels from 1 to 15,000 meters, from very specific and focused to very expanded and extended.

With each level, you can see, sense, expand, and declare your own best practices. You can then use your interlinked four quadrant map for maintaining this inner balance in multiple life circumstances. You are building a Mind Matrix of your expanded and integrated reality system. You now can usefully explore a combination of associated and dissociated Coach Positions on a four quadrant expansion map using the metaphor of changing altitude with all the key areas of life development you care to discover.

Comprehending all systems together you gradually develop the self-awareness to move beyond your own current challenges. Using a variety of 'levels,' you can sense the breadth of your values and talents to engage the integrative meanings and the life potentials you want to maximize. Allow the vertical dimension to become your doorway to higher consciousness by linking sensed values (associated Coach Position) to your visions of life development. See the Lofty Ideas Exercise at chapter's end.

Moving Up to High Altitude on the Left Staircase: Value Appreciation

What happens to the mind as we develop such wide value linkages? A picture to the mind is like a real experience. With three or four viewings and perhaps several alternative choices studied, our confidence starts to soar. We can now imagine ourselves 'beyond the details,' seeing the self operating effective in formerly scary or confusing situations. We start to experience expanded presence.

A great example of this skill was shown by Mahatma Gandhi in the early 20th-century India, mastering the inner strength to face the British Army. He constantly engaged a high-level vision of a peaceful, value-oriented Indian culture, and linked this into his own inner sensing of a congruent and comprehensive purpose. He moved high — into his integrative values — and linked these to detailed plans. In this way, he created clear and specific step-by-step strategies for the Indian people to stand up to the British military.

With each confrontation with the British Army, a massive, weapon-intensive combat system, Gandhi's first aim was the possibility of India's greater development, yet he also looked beyond that to all humanity. His strong commitment to non-violence allowed him to stand firm with many confrontations, and he consistently demonstrated this capacity to all of India's people. He set a powerful example and people followed. This tiny man weighed only 95 pounds, yet with his visionary purpose he single-handedly defeated the British Empire.

Learn to Move Up to 'High Altitudes'

Enrich your maps with high-level visions of vivid, relevant possibilities. As you move upwards on the Elevator of Mind in Overview Coach Position, you may notice that this can also assist you to associate to a renewal of strong 'sense ability' so that you deeply feel the values related to your vision. As you keep moving up and out, your 'as-if' mapping of value states will continue to develop. You will gradually find you are merging all elements — uniting both associated feeling of values and dissociated seeing of pictures. You arrive into your value-vision awareness — a borderless expanse of simple consciousness, enabled to sense all.

The size of such united and integrated consciousness systems we first build around any project tends to become the size we maintain moving forward. As you continue, this becomes the Mind Matrix and energy level of your inner system that your detailed maps will later engage. If you build simple maps with a clear value-vision context, this becomes an integrity system that you continue to develop. The size and the energy of your life now becomes linked to your perception of internal value. *You grow to fit the size of mind you amplify; the one you declare relevant at the start.* By expanding your value system you *presence* all of it as *simultaneously expanded.* The visions of choice and change you revisit and empower then become magnetic.

By using a four quadrant system as a map, you are holding these visions in a value shape that is easily integrated. You have discovered how to keep your visual maps and shapes as 'idea holders.' The longer we keep something in the forefront, the easier to connect this system of value and vision to all levels of behavior and future choice.

You now take ownership of the process of building long-term change. You always have the opportunity to test diagrammed frameworks directly. Use 'just suppose' or 'as-if' questions from '1 meter to 15,000 meters' for studying — and feeling — real-world applications of value coherency. Each test builds your connection further. We learn best when we begin with a specific aim or goal, and we test for value as we begin. We also learn a lot when we visualize ourselves 'at our best' at each level and with each step as we explore forward.

By practicing this method you learn how to create a mind-magnet. In this way, you enable yourself to continue deep value choices and decisions around your key projects. Old negative emotions gradually diminish and fall away like an old skin and new positive emotions emerge and magnify.

The Lofty Ideas Exercise

To start this exercise, make a list of at least three projects, large and small. Do the exercise with all of them. Do each one separately for cumulative practice.

If you think about your life, you will notice that most key areas are embedded with specific projects. We are 'project owners,' both with our families, our friends, our work, our learnings, our health, and our hobbies. Each of these areas will have a vision attached — *if you look for it.* Ask: *What is the vision beyond the vision?* Each of these emerging visions will have values attached — developing perhaps like an acorn or seed. Ask: *What are the core values here?* You can fertilize these seeds to grow the satisfaction that you feel as each project unfolds. Use Diagram 6.2 to assist you and determine what levels you tend to look at each project from? How can you grow — and feel — the values?

Take a project of your choice and try it on in associated Coach Position. Then move into dissociated Coach Position and move up in dissociated Coach Position while viewing your project. Find a location of overview, and with this 'high-enough' altitude, sense the values. Now, move skyward in dissociated Coach Position and then sense for values again. Explore several projects from both 'lofty levels' and 'lower levels' of awareness, noting the difference in vibration.

Explore relevant high-level visions and values for several projects: What values do you commit to for each project? Do your overview visions, your plans, and your specific month-by-month or day-by-day time frames work well together?

Ponder specific 'next steps' with each project while maintaining your strongest vision and values for it. How does the lofty view assist your commitment and your motivation?

When you look from the various 'meters of awareness,' as with Diagram 6.2, you will get many ideas how to proceed further with your key aims, because the inner congruence required will assist to bring you the more specific visions you need. You are linking your vision, your values, and your future together into *habits*, so that you initiate and continue your projects with long term congruent actions.

The Values Elevator Exercise: Start High with Your Elevator

Start by experiencing your life in associated Coach Position. Next, move up to 15,000 meters in dissociated Coach Position to take on *Humanity's overview* as if you could. Allow this viewpoint to converge to associated Coach Position with *Value* as your eyes, ears, and deep feelings. As you look towards the far future, you are both exploring and physically testing — with your feelings — what a human being can become.

Perhaps you also questions and check for Congruence. For example, perhaps you ask yourself what various human values and capacities you want to unfold and make more real in the world. The aim is to truly sense these values physically. Do this for your own future life yet also for all Humanity... as if you could.

Use your inner elevator to go very high, moving up to 'cosmic levels' where you imaginatively create vision and value experiences. Then float lower, exploring downwards, making sure you are finding more and more specific pictures. Descend all the way to 'one-meter,' 'on-the-ground' action thinking, touring various personal 'reality systems' along the way.

Because the 'gravity' of our emotional/physical lives tends to land us in the one-meter level fairly often, you might find it useful to map this descent by 3,000 meter levels, quite slowly. This is an interesting exploration. You are building an elevator you can use ever after.

Start first by exploring the '10,000 to 15,000-meter level' expansive values 'up in the ozone.' Here you can link vision and values into a strong 'awareness matrix' that can assist you to maintain Coach Position and overview of your own value system. Then, maintaining this overview, lower your viewpoint by approximately

3,000 meters at a time, noting your avenues of growth and practice. Look over systems that are 'time-marked,' yearly, monthly, and daily like your scheduler. Float down into the details how these events will unfold.

As soon as you reach the 'personal level,' it is useful to see your 'landing ground.' Watch your 'star self' find the real-world solutions to potential difficulties. You might float down to the action level, where you can hover on an updraft, briefly reviewing your next daily plans at the 10-meter point, seeing yourself accomplishing some key goals coming up soon in your week or day. What did this downward exploration open for you?

CHAPTER 7:

Metaphors for Expanding the Mind-Brain System

Learning to Use the Left Staircase of Awareness and the 'Elevator' of Mind

Is it effective to use physical metaphors for complex abstract ideas? My experience is that these can be phenomenally useful if we use four quadrant systems *declaratively.* We create 'visual declarations,' then 'step inside' to associatively perceive them, or outside to integratively view them. We can use them like practice wheels on our inner bicycle — until a system of balance belongs to us.

Sometimes we discuss staircases, talking about step-by-step practice over time. In this chapter and the next, we will explore metaphorical ascent into abstraction as if using the speed of an elevator. The Mind will respond with integrative visuals.

The Journey — Fast Approaches to Developmental Integration

The human soul is on a journey exploring boundless possibility. For our journey, it is of limited value to have the capacity for purposeful inquiry and deep value thinking for only certain situations and 'levels' of mind. We also need to be able to shift abstraction level quickly and think *situationally* as required.

We need to be able to use abstract visual metaphors to widen, and to steer attention, as well as to build a receptivity system. As we build our attentional scope, we often receive 'flashes' of coherent ideas at the deepest level of our awareness. Later on, starting with Chapter 8, we will move our attentional value much, much wider using the associative accordion.

In this and in a later chapter, we will use and practice with two speed-change metaphors: the metaphor of Google Maps™[13] for the quality of speedy expansion led by dissociated viewing, and the metaphor of the accordion, useful to explore quick expansion through associative perceiving. We will also use smaller 'tool metaphors' such as the compass as well as elevators and parachutes. Each speed-change metaphor assists in integrating next-level association, (Google Maps™), and dissociation (the accordion), but each starts the process in a radically different way. Each of course, also requires its opposite. We only learn when we truly alternate between association and dissocation.

We are like pianists, moving back and forth between trying and overviewing a new piece of music. The composer and musician, Igor Fyodorovich Stravinsky, wrote a complex but beautiful concerto of music and set it before his orchestra to learn to play over a period of weeks. After a fortnight, the orchestra leader approached him and said, "Mr. Stravinsky, I am sorry, but we must tell you that your new concerto is unplayable." "I do know that," said Stravinsky. *"What I am looking for is the sound your orchestra will make when you attempt to play it!."* Practicing 'shifting levels' and connecting value levels is much like this approach. We also need to guide the mind through the ins and outs of surprise learning. We need strong Coach Position to allow us to dive in.

Your inner groundwork as a 'life-musician' has been done by humans over hundreds of centuries before you. Our human life has a life of its own: *You are much further along than you think!* Become, like Stravinsky, able to overview various areas of your own 'concertos of thought' and aim to practice with whatever overview — and association — you muster.

Practical Explorations of Mind Mapping

Do you know Google Maps™ or other GPS systems? You can use your brain just like a Google Maps system™: moving from large overview to detailed awareness, zooming out and zooming in, from big picture to detail, and from abstract to specific. This kind of shift is easy to do. Imagine your own zoom lens, like a Coach Position wide-angled viewpoint expanding up into value comprehensive overview in dissociated Coach Position or zooming down into small, associative, 'here and now,' on-the-ground awareness — associated Coach Position.

You will soon discover how you can always choose your own starting point. Choice is inherent in our inner human form. For the purpose of practice, I have developed exercises throughout this book, where you experience this. Shifting levels of overview quickly from abstract to specific is both an art and a science, yet most people need a practical methodology to quickly move from the 'ozone level' of expansion down to the 'earth' of practical application. Such a shift sometimes seems to people like a loss of meaning, but it need not be. Moving quickly in the 'elevator of mind,' while still maintaining full value connection takes focus. Use this chapter to develop this practice.

With practice, we notice we are able to balance, think, and grow into all levels of mind. Singular consciousness can rise up naturally into integrative awareness. This allows rich insight to flash, connecting vision with value awareness. We recognize the deeper value and meaning through our ability to sense and feel it. Like using an 'elevator,' we move up and down in our awareness between concrete and abstract. We see, feel, and create a wider inner capacity for life.

Let us play with this system for a moment. As you probably have learned, with Google Maps™ or other GPS systems, you can enjoy a global view of any journey upon request. Imagine a global journey and specify Paris as your touchdown target. You can fly up from your current location in the world, then 'speed around the planet' as visually seen through the program to arrive to Paris at 15,000 meters. As a viewer from a dissociated Coach Position, you can then float down towards the city to 5,000 meters, close enough to see your target. Finally, you might sail in at 100 meters into the 'old city' area of Paris, touching down at the 'one-meter' level. You can move from dissociated Coach Position into associative Coach Position and examine the Notre-Dame cathedral, and even 'walk in' to explore all the open rooms and corners. You can do this associatively on your computer right now. *The next step is to learn to do this with your own mind* — and with your own inner 'abstraction levels.'

A simple way to practice moving the mind into values as if into 'rooms' of the mind is to practice again by using the physical altitude idea. This time, we want to build more detail at various levels. Exploring your own thought systems at all these various levels of value is extremely interesting. Notice the different 'stations' where you can get off at a completely different levels of integrative awareness moving from dissociated Coach Position into associated Coach Position and back. You can do this using the 'height specific' metaphors, we began with in the last chapter, while broadening your awareness into abstract perception and viewing from a dissociated Coach Position. You can also do this with timeframes, past, present and future, widening awareness outward 'horizontally' at the very same time. Color and brightness shifts can assist.

I invite you to use this visualization practice for value exploration even towards non-local mindful awareness. You can even learn to move up to complete non-dual fields of value and then dive down again into various unique personal explorations, knitting the two together effectively. With practice you also develop ongoing Coach Position overview and can keep noticing the 'level' from which you are thinking. In this way, both associated and dissociated Coach Positions becomes your natural home.

In Diagram 7.1, I am using 'meters' as the metaphoric frame to develop a matrix from specific on-the-ground thinking to stratospheric, expanded value awareness across time. Diagram 7.2 provides a simple template for how you might use an 'elevator' to navigate and move between various levels and kinds of awareness.

Diagram 7.1: GPS 'Google Map' Thinking

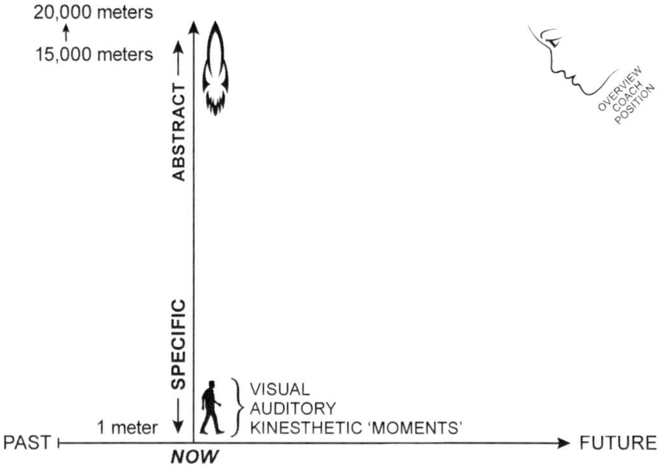

Diagram 7.2: GPS Details: The Scope of Overview. Scaling from Tiny to Infinite Awareness

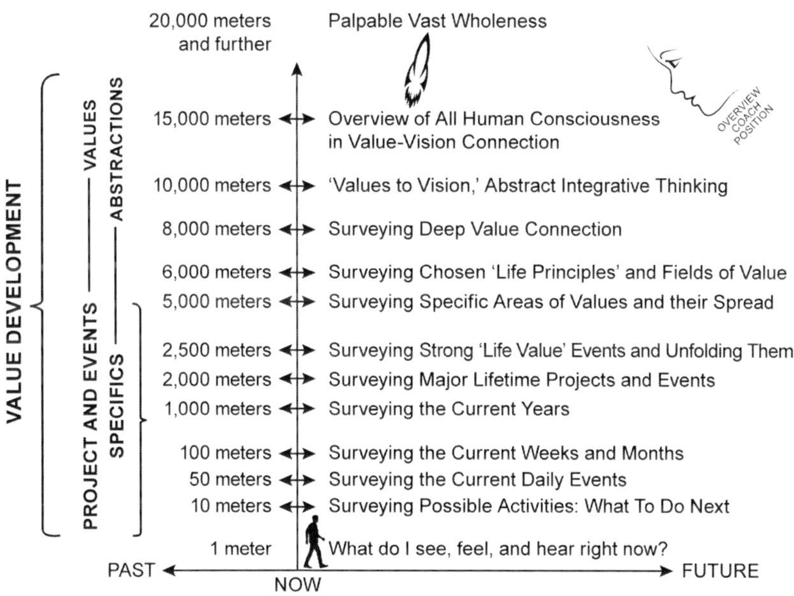

You are welcome to test this template or to otherwise define your own metaphoric inner map as 'levels' of awareness. Practice briefly with Diagram 7.2 and choose a personal talent of deep interest. Explore this value area from local (very local), 1 meter, to non-local, 20 thousand meters, and beyond. What well-loved value might you explore in this way?

As you go *up* your elevator, you will notice a palpable shift in inner vibration and life pulse. This happens naturally as we experience our expansion into the space of life value. We often feel this like profound relaxation. We move from tight to expanded, singular intellect, to wide relaxed intelligence. From both inner and outer Coach Positions, we learn to recognize this palpable shift.

With four quadrant maps, we can easily work from the highest, very abstract level — palpable, vast wholeness and mystical vision, (the 20-thousand-meter level of awareness and beyond) — all the way down to the very specific 'one-meter level' of specifics. One-meter thinking describes eye-level, associated, on-the-ground thinking and feeling: a detail level that allows us to plan for events that require engaged, sensory, action steps today.[14]

With a comprehensive, yet useful template like this one, you can learn the ability to shift up and down in a quick, yet detailed way. The key idea is to practice with your own topics. With one key area of abilities and choices that you have, wonder how you can see the future from different levels of abstraction. Explore specifically with your upcoming plans.

Practice with your 'elevator of mind' for a while, then move to Coach Position on the range of ideas you are exploring. This means that you can see specific elements of upcoming moments while still maintaining comprehensive, abstract value and vision awareness at the same time. With practice, you develop an active and powerful Coach Position for all the planning levels relevant to you.

Explore this further with various areas of your life. For example, practice around a simple theme like a walk in a park. For our walk in the park we can start by noticing a specific park and location where we love to walk. In our minds eye, we can then 'step in' and begin feeling each step, smelling the grass, and seeing the properties of the specific leaves and flowers. We can move up, overviewing the area where we walk, then higher to the arena of 'park activities' and to our feeling-filled ideas of recreation, past, present, and future. We can even rise up to the abstract space of expansive palpable pleasure about recreation, and even further to the experience of wholeness and beauty — non-personal and non-local. Holding in mind our commitment to future generations being able to share this as well, we can spread it across time; past, present, and future. We feel the joy of life.

Notice that your capacity for overview, combining value and vision can contract from macroscopic expansion down into momentary, even microscopic individual events. You can move from universal timeless awareness to the particulars of your plans for the next few minutes.

Note, once again, that this vertical scale our overview attention expands out exponentially in all directions at once: from personal, physical, and specific to universal, meaningful, and abstract. With diagrams 7.1 and 7.2 notice that you can view a vertical scale and a timeline together.

As human beings, we are necessarily project owners with many levels and kinds of goals in the works. We speak for our personal life, our family life, our community, our nation and, at the very same time, we speak for all humanity. *Mastery means finding the most effective size and level from which to think for each specific type of project you are doing. You combine your range of interest with the overview capacity to keep each area of focus positive and in control.*

With practice, three skills emerge:

1. First, you develop a 'high-level' capacity to dissociate and overview, seeing yourself living your values and vision. You look from "Coach Position" and choose the appropriate level to view from.
2. Second, you develop the ability to step in, associate, and deeply experience the relevant levels.
3. Third, you link the appropriate level of the journey to the task at hand.

You develop matrix mind-skills as you learn how to move between multiple levels and aspects of your projects while maintaining overview and comprehensive coherence. You learn to bring Coach Position into your life, from the largest overview of life development to the very concrete, sensory, and local 'on-the-ground' thinking needed for making your breakfast. You can learn to consider and notice what insights and new expressions emerge by maintaining your elevator while shifting levels.

Why Use 'Mind GPS'?

Effective four quadrant practice, moving up, down, in, and out, assists people to shift beyond areas of habitually wasted attention. We bring warm values thinking — like flowing light — down into the life details where they are most needed. You learn to move easily between all the relevant levels of your own life, keeping your focus positive and comprehensive while maintaining Coach Position at every level!

When navigating life's projects, it's common for a person's old memory habits to interfere with his or her own natural higher-awareness flow. For example people sometimes find themselves accidentally associating into ancient, negative thought systems that once became linked to voice tones and facial postures. They accidently imagine old situational 'discomforts' as they sort through aspects of a project. With a Coach

Position elevator, combined with overview and the capacity to move up to a higher level, they learn to respond to all aspects, positively, effectively moving past these triggers. This is like skiing down a hill filled with many moguls or large mounds. You learn to maneuver around old negative associations and view yourself at your best. You simply see yourself maneuver towards positive outcomes and view how the negatives get bypassed and then do it!

With an overview map and value linkage together, new realms of self-development immediately become possible, despite our former conditioning. It is wonderful to be able to leave old conclusions behind with a flash of intuitive overview and move to valued choices. We open the door to the inner flow of generous and loving self-expression.

Imaginatively moving 'down the elevator' and overviewing detailed, situational challenges assists you to become more prepared. This works well, especially if you envision yourself handling them 'at your best.' You need to maintain an overview position, a Coach Position on your own inner energy.

Consider practicing both dissociatively and associatively for different projects, studying the needed levels of awareness. Use core elements of your own wider stream of vision and value thinking. You can open your inner vision capacity as you try out the diagrams and exercises both in this chapter and further on.

We humans can learn to shift in and out of all sensory systems, visual, auditory, and kinesthetic, even as we use a mapping system to move beyond and between various abstraction levels. With this skill you learn to feel, to sense, and to hold more awareness in all areas. You discover you can do this while soaring up to higher levels of abstract inner value awareness, or even while moving down into immediate sensory areas.

It is useful from time to time to move very high on your inner elevator. You can imaginatively look at your life from vision and value (10,000 to 15,000 meters) and overview your life's purpose.

What happens when you look from humanity's viewpoint? Notice how quickly the selfish concerns of private and personal 'wants' just vanish. At the highest levels of elevated awareness we overview the sacred opportunity that our amazing human mind design gives us. Our personal life is just a small stepping stone on Humanity's incredible journey of unfoldment.

Enjoy the following exercise to practice:

GPS System Exercise I: Project Pondering

With a strong connection to evolution's journey, we relax and face the tasks of our personal life. Use diagrams 7.1 and 7.2 to examine several specific life projects which are long term — 10 to 20 years or more perhaps — and which have challenged you along the way. Perhaps you might briefly overview personal health projects, creativity projects, legacy projects, family projects, or work projects to find areas that have challenged you. Moving down the 'elevator of thought' you can overview your twenty-year scope or ten-year scope for each life area. Notice the elements of most interest at each level.

Move gradually down the mind elevator from values to specific life elements, using Diagram 7.2 as a guide. For example, pause briefly at the 2,500-meter level, overviewing various key areas of your life development and study these projects in terms of your personal interests — then move down to 2,000 meters, separating them into distinctive aspects or learnings, like braids of meaning.

Move gradually down to the 1,000-meter level and start to explore your more recent projects from within a one-year scope or even a six-month scope, overviewing past, present and future together. Further down, you can scope by month and by week for your specific projects.

Eventually 'move down' to the 10-meter level to overview your day so far, ending up perhaps at the 3-meter level: See yourself in the next few hours 'at your best' doing the specifics of your projects with detailed activities you are committed to.

When overviewing, it is useful to move higher from time to time to survey areas of emotional development, value growth, and discernment of choice, finding key strands of your own development across time.

Now, use your elevator with each area to practice the process of diving down towards the one-meter level and learn to dance into the sensations of specific on-the-ground, action-oriented 'thought systems,' the way you want them to emerge.

From Coach Position, notice what this all looks like. You are creating an important *linkage system.* You are practicing to keep 'vast awareness,' and the specific areas of your life development together in your heart and mind as you work with all levels. Even as you review potential upcoming action steps allow your strongest vision of personal potentials to come with you so you gradually develop those areas of awareness as a closely linked system.

CHAPTER 8:

The Horizontal Dimension as a Source of Energy

Building Your Time Scope out of Intention

For every project, each of us naturally has a horizontal scope of intention as well as the vertical scope of attention. We work best when we learn to develop both these vertical and the horizontal scopes — attention and intention — as a set. We can do this in much the same way as if using the cross hairs on a huge compass. Our time model and time focusing habits are a subset of *intention*. When we set an *intention*, we naturally organize our idea of time around this. Similarly, as when we set our *attentional* focus, the space of our *attention* naturally opens up.

Humanity's legacy, as seen from 15,000 meters, is defined by our capacity to think forward on this timeline; our model of creative purpose. It is useful to set our intention as far as we can, even to our children's children's children. What if you imagined ahead, maybe 50 generations from now? Envision these future people also living a life of peace and serenity, enjoying the same sparkling oceans, vegetation, and natural beauty that you now enjoy.

How do you become effective at designing your future time scope around your intention? Set your timeline aim affirmatively to achieve what you aim for. What do you want to do with this one wild and wonderful life? To expand this, take visual overview from Coach Position setting the widest timescope for your life purpose that you can appreciate now.[15] If you want a compelling vision, you need to make it endearing, entertaining, and truly interesting, as well as practical.

We work well if we *first* comprehend our '*vertical levels*' as values from abstract to specific, then build equally clear '*horizontal*' dimensions or *time-planning distinctions* so that we manage our visions into our widest timeline scope of awareness. Eventually you learn to widen your now into various time-marked mindsets as if the warp and weave on a large loom from which you weave the fabric of your wider attention. The threads of intention now become included.

What compels your interest when you stretch your vision across time? Are we not fascinated by our historical step-by-step growth through the deep refinements of human perception over the last 100,000 years? For example, have you ever wondered thoughtfully into the 'past' exploring the history of the human soul? We revel in the paleolithic cave paintings of our ancestors such as those found in Lascaux, France or Cantabria, Spain. We love discovering how early humans expressed themselves, laughed, and played together. We are intrigued by examples such as Neolithic artistic development and the relics of handmade flutes and other musical instruments. We look for evidence of our life-building interests, and our appreciation of all music, art, mathematics, science, games, laughter, fun, joyful play, and human values themselves.

From overview, we can regard the whole human journey with interest, and recognize the gradual development of our current cultures and value systems stretching behind us. Watching humanity shifting shape, we can see how many positive aspects of our 'human nature' have gradually emerged. In this way, we can begin to envision moving past our challenges today as we develop our next steps in becoming a gentler, more principled human race. With this interest we can envision a future showing the ascension of a nobler, kinder humanity and start to create it.

The Horizontal Scope of Creative Life

Every creative project always has two aspects. We have said that to develop an effective intelligence system, we need to create a mind-matrix effectively holding attention and intention *together* as two key dimensions of the mind. *Attention*, of course, sets the vertical space, the *depth* of our project. *Intention* formulates the *span*. We look at span and depth together.

How does timeframe show up as a subset of intention? View Diagram 8.1. Do you not consciously set your most favourable time dimensions for each creative project that you do? For any project to be effective, our *timeline* is as important to us as the current 'height level' of vision and value that motivates us. We set the vibrational consistency for any future we envision on our 'loom' of consciousness.

How do you 'set' a timeline worth applying? First, we ask *why* the project is really important to us, do we not? We ponder what makes it truly worthwhile. We want to build liveliness, creativity, enjoyment, and fun into our future projects as we set these timeframes. What constitutes future joy potential for you? How far out are you willing to build?

Diagram 8.1: Overviewing the Mind-Matrix Potential of Your Goals

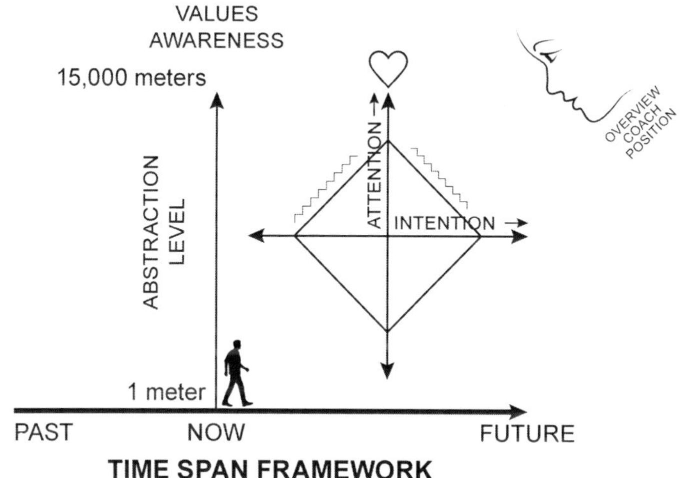

Evaluation and Intention — Energizing the Left and Right Staircases

As mentioned, the *evaluation* process is also like a bubble inside a larger bubble. You set the *evaluation* frame you use for thinking through a plan. This provides the womb for that embryonic plan to grow and flourish. It is wonderful to foresee a future of value, then to slowly build it. Evaluation is also a sub-part of intention. What is the dissatisfaction, and the difference you want to make that deepens your intention?

We need to appreciate our dreams and goals as part of this larger quest of life purpose. From Coach Position, our open questions allow us to creatively expand all choices. We discover both 'past' and 'future' as creative energy sources.

We may find our most valued timeline springboards by rummaging through 'past' memories. Or, we might find them by pondering and speculating about engaging future goals. With the *horizontal axis*, we can easily learn to move across, before, through, and beyond all old selections to link potential choices together into a high-energy vision. We explore the process of evaluating and comparing choices 'through time.'

Your inner *evaluation* capacities allow you to assess historical choices. When connected only to fear, your negative evaluations can contract your perception into a mental glitch — like a ditch — usually a repeating sentence with worry as the theme. Worries are the fingernails of the mind (useful for comparing and scratching at the details of each choice you have made in the past and might make in the future).

Overview practice moves us back to wider vision and to reviewing our choices from multiple perspectives. With Coach Position overview, your goals — as themes sparked by evaluations — assist you to maintain positive, personal reference to your 'timeline' as a learning line. You see how all evaluation can become positive evaluation. You learn to appreciate your aims to build a bright future and to keep your focus stable — beyond all glitches. Who we then become is the future that is calling us forth and, *as we build that future, it builds us!*

Harmony and Appreciation

Notice how your *intentional* focus is magnetized by time-scoped *futures.* You can gain power and fortitude when you extend this. Humans generally have a short 'future frame,' often extending only months and not more than a few years. With building this further, we generate our creative force.

Harmony and appreciation develop as you deepen and widen your future timeline as well as your coherent value-vision connection. We need our positive intentions to empower our timeline thinking. Call this life appreciation. Harmony and appreciation develop as you give yourself the freedom to both engage and disengage high-level goals. You learn to build your visions of creative purpose according to your own carefully set criteria. Our visions can then also assist us to develop *balance*, as we build the capacity to overview and choose key values for each step and stage in our development.

Balance comes with *discernment*. Four quadrant explorations naturally assist this. Discover what is important to you from the various elevator levels as you practice this, so that you discern your own harmony *triggers*. For example, particularly visualize the future elements of real joy on your timeline. Create small 'movies of purposeful value development' to view this. Perhaps also see yourself creating joy for others by developing various results — along the line. Try Timescope Exercise II, *Journaling Harmony*, at the end of this chapter.

Time Scope Your Future Dreams

You can *choose* to effectively engage or disengage, to contract or to expand your time scope with any goal. Whenever possible, whenever it truly expands your awareness — then build future value!

Our vibrational/resonance levels develop our empowerment capacities. We can move our value vibration forward 'horizontally' through a lens of vast future possibility, like a prayer! What forward reach do you currently engage? What typical forms of future dreaming do you extend outward far beyond your current reach? The power of this is the magnet you create by doing it. You *sense* the magnet's pull as soon as you attune to it.

Building balance between the vertical and horizontal dimensions is a great practice for developing creativity. What creative areas do you want to develop? With overview vision, you develop your project areas as a whole connected system, the fabric on the loom of possibility. This becomes a coherent playground for novelty to emerge. With your timelines you detail the actions and make it happen.

Experience and Relevance 'Times Ten'

Overview your current methods of building strong projects. Perhaps you think with a planning matrix or time organizer, using SWOT analysis (strengths, weaknesses, opportunities, threats) or tri-position planning in project design processes. *What would happen if you enlarged the time scope on each project,* ***times ten****, to see all the 'results beyond the results' for the efforts that you make? Would you find renewed energy to continue?*

As you explore your 'next step' intentions, your evaluations naturally combine experience and relevance, key aspects of the horizontal realm. You can quickly learn to build a scale from one to ten around any topic in terms of both the learnings from past experience and the visions for future relevance to determine the effectiveness of these evaluation processes.

We all find it valuable to build our next-step positive intentions in a systematic way. Habits of visualizing potential futures becomes particularly useful as you learn to overview 'across time' as a framework to implement a plan well. However, when we enlarge the scope — double, triple, quadruple, or raising to '10' the 'length' of our current timeline — then amazing new creative visions tend to appear. Negative emotions fall away and we find ourselves with new courage to build boldly. We build creative joy!

Use Four Quadrants For Viewing the Colors of Your Timescopes

What colors signify joy for you? Perceptually, from overview, you can always flow the colored appreciation into all moments and into every level of mind. Some people enjoy giving rainbow colors to their future intentions, then playing these pictures in mental videos. For example, to energize your purpose you might create various scenes from the future in colors that signify comedy and play. See yourself enjoying your life — in high-level detail with drama, movement, and color — and then see multiple generations after you also doing the same! How does this affect your 'weave' on the loom of life?

From Coach Position, you can notice that each 'past idea' is always colored by your perception *now*. This is because you can only notice them contained in your immediate thought system, and as part of your current '*now*' experience. Color signifies *value*. You know about wearing rose-colored glasses: If your rosy attention is on the sweetness of life, your perception is in rose color, from the momentary elements of any past details to the vast horizons of your hopes!

We need to be able to both stretch *out* effectively, with long term intentional goals, and focus in to the moment well, to appreciate our sensory joys now. We can add huge life potential and value expression as we build all these together in the colors that signify our deepest values.

Adding color to our future gives a quick renewal to our life purpose and energizes our capacity to focus in and to expand out. When we see ourselves in our vision enjoying colorful actions and projects we are making a promise to create that. If we give the same healing colorful vision to others around us, we are declaring harmony and peace. It is a form of declaration and has great power. In this way, we experience the vast potential of mind and body together.

We can also build pattern and texture into the fabric of the future. We can design for beauty, truth, care, and resilience. Were we link oneself to this with relevance times ten, we signify our intention to take real responsibility to make this future emerge.

Flying with Intention

Let us summarize the key ideas in this chapter at this point. What we are saying is that the metaphors of intention and time scope are highly relevant to the effective use of four quadrant visioning. They assist us to develop a powerful inner resonance and a flow of visions that feed our purpose. When we take control of our timeline vision — adding color and length for example — we also take ownership of timeless awareness. We enter the doorway of our deeper awareness and begin to build Coach Position consciousness on what that truly means.

To do effective planning, we need to keep all the planning 'levels' connected into 'wide-enough,' 'time scopes.' Clarity of choice requires vision and value coherence, and this requires positive questions and focused inner visions of multiple alternatives. We connect our *wider attention* with our long-term *positive intention*. See Diagram 8.2 for practice ideas.

Diagram 8.2: Widened Attention on Value and Meaning

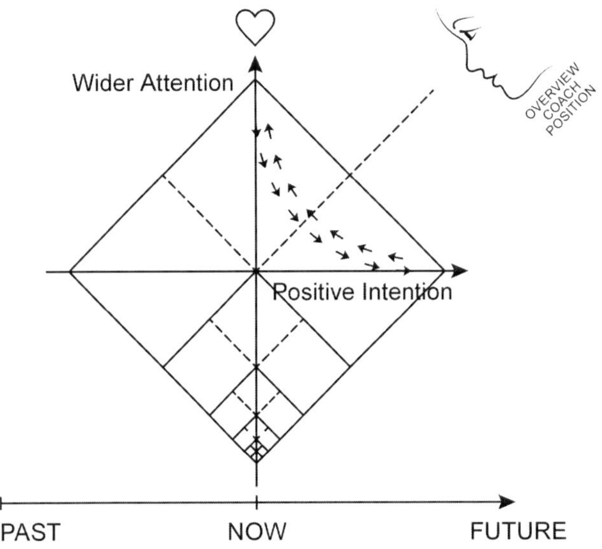

We have also pointed to the power of integrity overview. What engages our inner human attention on a day to day basis? I would like to suggest that we are often magnetized by four key areas:

- The 'vertical' informational specifics we build into our *perception* videos going *down* the elevator of mind.
- The expansive values we experience as our *wider attention* and vision going *up* the elevator of the mind.
- The 'horizontal' — on-the-ground — full spectrum *evaluation* of our intentions and goals, looking towards the past.
- The 'horizontal' flow of our *purpose* and our *intention* looking towards future results.

Diagram 8.3 summarizes these holographic attention/intention shift abilities.

Diagram 8.3: Focusing on What?

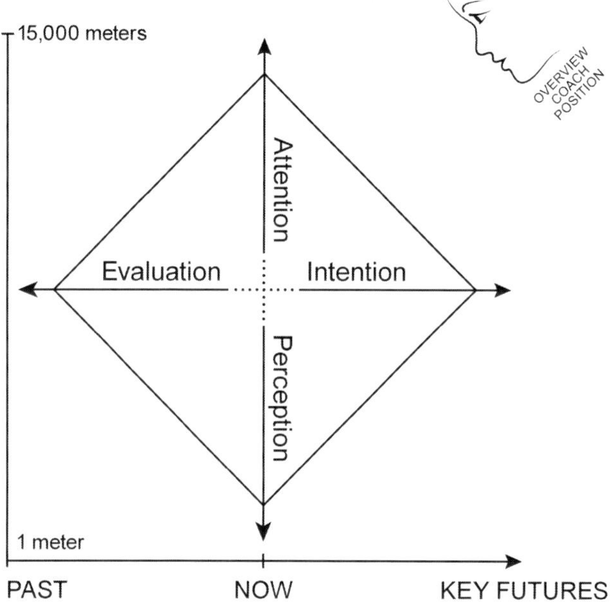

Here we see the four quadrant version of the mind-shift elevator and the loom of consciousness, which shows four key thinking habits that can magnetize — and polarize — the mind. These also generate visionary abilities when used systematically as a four-part skill set.

When used consciously, building each of these four as skill areas provides important capacities to assist with human mind-design. You can learn to sense, recognize, and create these different kinds of thinking as you come to know them, then systematically watch the various types of thought systems from high-level overview.

Difficulty arises when these skills get co-opted by our fears. For example, people often link their immediate perception to judgmental evaluations of what they perceive. Boxed in by the former judgments, they look through the glasses of pre-formed assumptions. Coach Position disappears. This may produce aches in the muscles of awareness because we must contract awareness to 'very tiny' to do this. Explore Diagram 8.4, Negative Evaluation and Perception.

Diagram 8.4: The Negative Evaluation of Perception and Subsequent Reliving of Past Fears

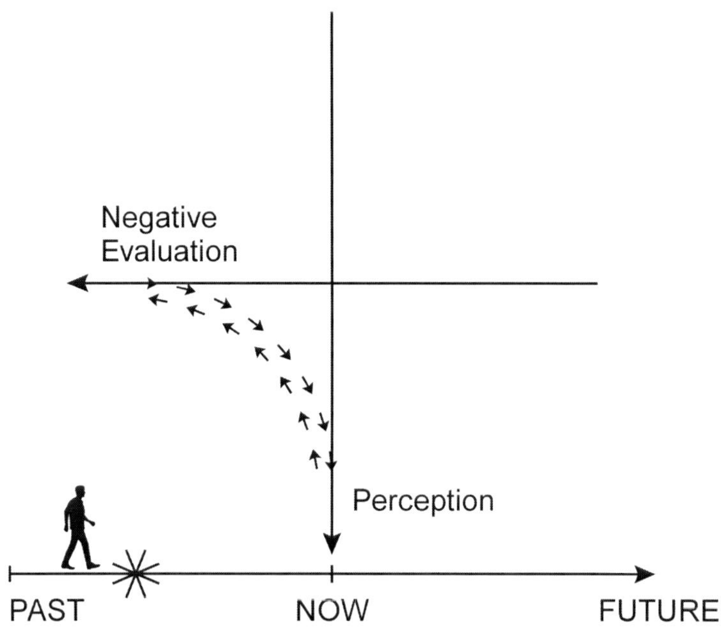

Only with practice, do we regain effective overview vision beyond the small thought systems owned by negative evaluation. Use these charts to ponder how to expand overview in your own life. When we survey our personal vision we can find a future that engages us. We then take responsibility to build it.

Expanding in All Directions to Move Beyond Negative

Expansion moves us up and out geometrically. Our loom builds the design of this larger vision. The opposite, contraction, simply means we tumble from 'all life' awareness to 'one event' awareness; to 'one concern' awareness, and even one 'fear-moment' awareness. Our 50 million year old limbic brain and emotional system does this naturally, but we do not need to follow its pull unless in immediate physical danger.

You can move from vast expanded awareness to 'just this moment' contraction in the blink of a moment. It is easy to 'crash' with all types of negative assessment, judgment commentary or personal self-concern. Yet, with a consciously set intention, a time scope and elevator practice, you can emerge quickly.

Notice you can move between both negative and positive viewpoints easily inside your own mind theatre. We can *expand* when we once again overview our wide intention and our deep life vision, scoping our vision point from the tiniest to the largest.

By charting our course, we can move up and out to high level non-local *attention* and *intention* and look through the vast filter of humanity's strongest potential. This produces a startling experience of expanded awareness. We can see who we have been and we can also see who we are becoming. Explore the value of this. Allow your own inner template of humanity's evolution and consciousness potential to guide your life discovery questions.

Intention and Long-term Purpose

The idea of *purpose* provides an inner power that assists us to envision beyond personal time. We all have this power but it often requires practice.[16]

When we overview our life purpose, our life responds meaningfully. We flow oxytocin, dopamine, and endorphins, the connectivity and learning chemicals of the brain and body, and we relax and attend to our intention. As you practice, you gradually learn to develop relaxation and happiness with whatever stage your project is at.

Practice flying with your true intention in the horizontal dimension by energizing positive purpose as your motivating awareness. Practice several of the exercises at the end of this chapter. The exercises work with energetic awareness and can be done even as you read them.

Expanding 'Reality': Experience the Oneness System

The Mind is constantly moving at all times, like wind through the trees. To 'mind' is to 'verb.' Consciousness is the ground of our Being and together, we experience our aliveness as a *whole*! The unconscious mind is in touch with this natural wholeness at all times. Yet, individually, and consciously, we constantly expand and contract our awareness of this, like breathing in and breathing out. In what ways have you noticed consciousness expand or contract as you explore the practices in this book?

Expansion and contraction also happens through your daily activities. Perhaps you have noticed how you can walk into a forest and your awareness of salient *presence* expands — almost like fingers moving out — to sense the aliveness of the forest. You immediately widen your perception, even experiencing awe. In contrast, regard the very different kind of thought system you require as you reach for your passport and follow instructions at an airport document inspection. You contract back into your specific, detailed, historical ideas of personal identity. As you strengthen Coach Position, you learn to watch these shifts as worthy observation practice, and enjoy the movement in and out. In the next chapter, you will learn how to "play your accordion of awareness," and find resonant music on all levels and in all areas.

When you orient to inner truth and set your *intention-time scope* together with your *vertical elevation* and *presence level*, you define the 'size' of your attention matrix. Effectively, this matrix designs your current '*Now*,' your attentional working system for choice and change, as in the Google Map™ diagram, Diagram 7.2. You define the size of 'now' so that you can operate the elevator of awareness *well. As you weave Coach Position into all aspects, you define the 'size' of your current awareness… as a matrix of meaning and purpose.*

With practice, your 'map' and your inner playground become as one, a context where you can truly expand and grow. You gradually replace the snarls of old, contractive, negative self-messages, and you rediscover your wide-screen, positive *value viewpoints... at every relevant level of awareness.* Love and joy become your natural context as you practice expanding them... through your mindful mapping process! Purpose and responsibility weave your future.

Diagram 8.5: Holographic Values Expansion

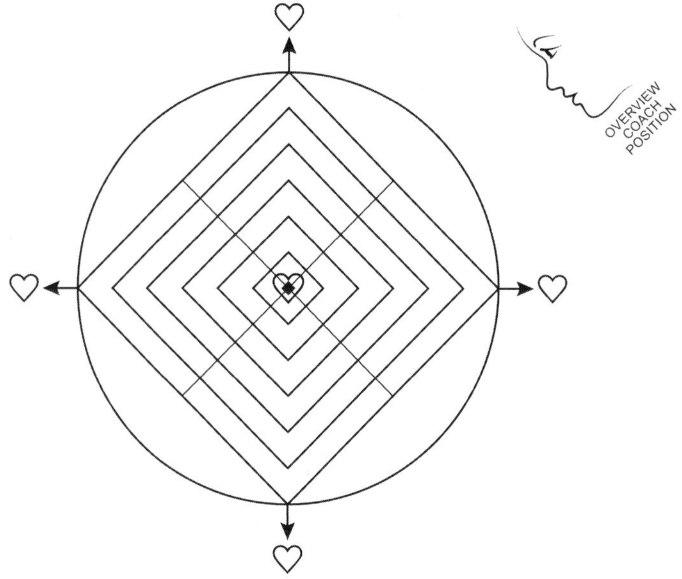

Timescope Exercise I: Creative Fun

If you choose one exercise to test this chapter, test this one: Set an intention for fun in your life and plan creative fun into one specific project you currently spend time with. Visualize creative fun emerging along the project timeline in various ways. See it vividly. Now, actually move this fun into your 'today' by giving yourself permission to expand it currently into special areas of your life — starting now.

Now, for fun, see the *attentional space* of fun as part of your four quadrant awareness system. Bring this into physical, relational, intentional, and meaningful awareness. Vizualize the many ways you can deepen this playful, creative dimension in every area you explore. How can you make fun valuable to your meaningful life?

Timescope Exercise II: Journaling Harmony

To maximize inner balance and harmony, it is useful to explore the attentional (vertical) and intentional (horizontal) axes together and very systematically learn to move between them.

To start this process, it is useful to keep a journal. Every evening for a week, write down three things that awakened you to feel real appreciation in that day. This is an exploration you may want to continue indefinitely, because just keeping these simple 'lists' assists you to develop this further. Call them your *harmony triggers.*

For the purpose of this exercise, select three 'harmony triggers' and explore them at different mind-meter levels and with various potential time frames. How do you sense the inner vibration that you associate with these moments? What do you discover when you do this? At some time during the day, or in the evening, take some time to actively reflect.

Practice with a joy trigger that you respond to immediately, such as a wonderful melody, a beautiful laugh, or an exquisite sunrise. You may want to add in color and light extending this quality around and beyond the body in all directions. Feel it as an on-the-ground, associative event. Try on both overview dissociated and centralized associated Coach Positions alternatively, so that you both *visualize* and *feel* the value of the expansion. Now move up to explore different mind-meters as expanded kinesthetic awareness. Notice the various ways you can join all areas together through working with your vision, your inner elevator, and your timescope. Finish the exercise by returning to your dissociated Coach Position overview of your 'harmony triggers,' exploring their quality in an extended form — in all directions at once!

Timescope Exercise III: Expanding Creative Value

Have you ever overviewed with your whole lifetime using a timeline? Lifetime timeline exploration is easy when you create a strong Coach Position overview. Coach Position always extends our mind dimensions as we see our maps from another dimension.

First build the full scope of your mind matrix. You simply need to float up, up, up... way up beyond your lifetime timeline to a warm overview awareness position of about 10,000 meters. Close your eyes and view this moment from high above. See a 'You' in the moment, a long way below you, and see the timeline stretching far before and far after this now. Notice you can view your lifetime timeline of events starting at birth and continuing out into your furthest future. Envision it as a small bright physical line or path in the wide, wide universe. Does it look like a line, a shimmering path, a glowing thread, or something else entirely?

Relax and observe from this open place of overview. Pause and really take in your full timeline below you. For the moment focus on your intentions for the future. Maintaining your altitude and relaxed curiosity, float further towards that future. Stay high above the timeline until you can look downward to envision possible value-focused 'future moments' below you and view them with relaxed appreciation.

Now, explore one creativity trigger that brings happiness to you: Maybe you enjoy writing, art, music, cooking, or other specific areas of deep interest. Pick one specific area of joy.

With this happiness in mind, and at a very high level, float again above your future timeline. First, wonder, then envision how this specific creativity system will continue forward. Find joyful ideas of active interest with this area and ponder them. See yourself building the *future* creative value of each area. Experience gratitude that this area is growing in your life and is available through your future.

Float back to a point above the present moment. With gratitude in heart, once again float down, down, and down into this moment, bringing this future happiness with you... to plan with, if you wish to review the full process and detail your visions even further.

GPS System Exercise II: Values Pondering

Use diagrams 7.1 and 7.2 for some exploratory high level visioning and pondering. Consciousness itself is evolution's gift, and also it's promise. Viewing the personal self, you can move to the 8,000-meter level to overview your lifetime on a time screen moving from birth on out to the furthest scope you wish to explore. Envision perhaps a glowing timeline filled with choice and change. Look at the development of your core values and the principles you build from these. Perhaps move down a bit further to explore some specific action values like adventure, learning, and fun. Explore how all value areas have inspired your life up to now.

You may wish to find some unique ways to envision these values expanding into your future, perhaps using flowing channels of color and light. You might visualize sparkling fields or shining atmospheres to surround and embrace the growth you see moving forward. Symbolize this growth for yourself.

Affirm your values personally and feel your inner commitment. Through your values move higher in your GPS elevator to envision your own unfolding life design. If possible, widen your design beyond personal arenas and appreciate these values for all humanity. Feel your inner commitment to this huge 'human opportunity' as it shows up in your own future. We start afresh each day!

CHAPTER 9:

The Accordion of Consciousness: Practicing Presence!

Turn off your mind, relax, and float down the stream.

— The Beatles

The 'Accordion of Consciousness' Idea

The Accordion of Consciousness idea is based on a version of a musical instrument called a Concertina. Have you ever watched an accordion player expand the scope of sound by widening out the accordion? It can go very wide with a **Concertina** accordion. This is much like how, with our accordion of consciousness, we are able to link the vertical and horizontal 'elevators' into a quickly expanding value-scope for developing our awareness beyond the 'personal identity only' framework. With the Concertina, we do the same thing horizontally.

Once visualized from Coach Position briefly, this can begin as an effective associative exploration where you quickly widen the sensing of your values across 'time and space.' You are discovering the process of widening your *Now* with speed and grace, by sweeping attention across your 'timescape' with deep Value Awareness present.

Consciousness expands into whatever frame we set, and it is possible to move any exploration beyond the 'individual identity' habit simply through dissociative and associative visualization and sensing together. It is useful to add speed into your ability to shift attention in this way. Speed is natural to the mind. 'Light speed' is a natural home for consciousness. We can easily shift into the timeless moments of value appreciation.

The 'Accordion of Consciousness' idea is important because everything changes *when you overview your own expansion possibilities from the context of universal value*. The evolution of consciousness, our larger context now permeates, invigorates, and links everything.

Diagram 9.1: Opening Your Inner Accordion

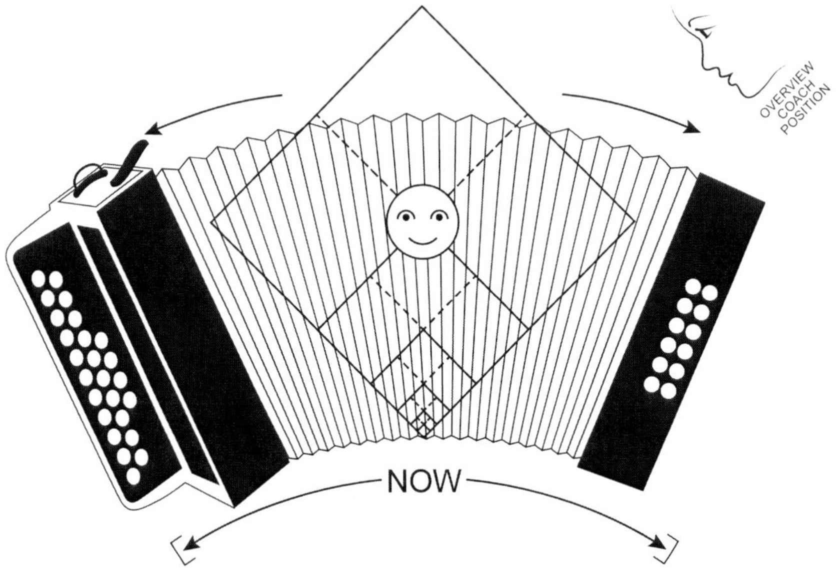

Start with value expansion. You expand consciousness powerfully when you see yourself doing it. In this chapter, you learn to observe value expansion visually from Coach Position. You can first watch a galaxy of value expanding with a color and light display. Second, you can step inside to deeply feel it, then, third, learn to expand it even further.

Expand the graceful yet simple music of living presence by expanding Four Quadrant Awareness in this way. Think of your Concertina as crossing all levels so that the music is able to form a comprehensive vibrational field. You become skilled with expansion speed when metaphorically, with your elevator, you move up to 20,000 meters to practice this. Now, practice expansion, moving in and out, yet again. Float 'your mind' on the vibrational field of that sound. Feel your 'musical' inner value to the core!

What might be beginning steps? Try the Accordion Exercise I at the end of the chapter. Then, after practicing Exercise I to learn to move from narrow to wide, use your Concertina to widen your awareness even further with the second exercise that follows.

Coach Position at Every Level

You can use four quadrant thinking to specify the types of attention and inner vision questions you want to develop. This begins to work smoothly when you maintain two kinds of Coach Position awareness at any — and all — levels of attention from one meter to 20,000 meters and for any size of time scope. Event by event, you can define your own simple practice and use it for self-designed self-exploration exercises. You can invite your beyond-conscious mind to assist you with goal-enabling dreams. You then discover the scope of value and vision you truly wish to expand.

You can expand each practice as a self-development framework so that your life becomes a living meditation. This appears complex, but is actually quite straightforward and doable, as are the exercises at the end of each chapter. What is important is to bring Coach Position into every level. Remember that *Intelligence*, metaphorically, means a vast, interlinked, yet accessible value-vision system — and that you are building this as you practice![17]

Diagram 9.2: Develop Coach Position at Every Level

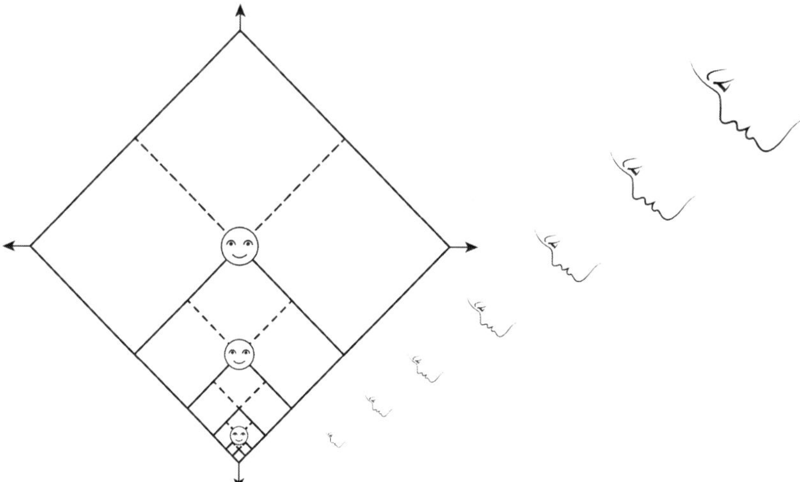

In the game of self-exploring, you may find yourself focusing back and forth: first, deeply associating into your *sensory awareness*, and then widely disassociating into resonant all-inclusive Coach Position overview. This means you move between Coach Position associated and Coach Position dissociated, experiencing value and vision together with full awareness in all areas. With both overview Coach Position and associated Coach Position as a linked system, you will find that you tend to sense, feel, and think — and to associate and dissociate — in a medley of dynamic experiences. The important thing here is that, you maintain inner presence with all. You can maintain full consciousness all the way. At any point, it is useful to link your experience to a two-dimensional drawing of four quadrants.

In many ways, this is like the entangled connection between 'particle' and 'wave' in systemic Quantum Physics descriptions. When we throw the pebble into the middle of the pond so that the wave expands from the center out, every molecule of H_2O on any moving edge stays connected (entangled) in the moving wave — no matter how far apart the wave moves. This is like the associative Coach Position we want to maintain — a vibrational essence we feel and that can expand as quickly as a Concertina can expand.

Making Music

With a four quadrant mapping system before you, you can try out a variety of value pondering questions as you link to the Concertina for overall expansion. You can learn to develop a personal 'system learning' practice that includes lacing back and forth between multiple areas and levels. Lacing means to link the various points of view together like laces in the shoes. We do this in the same way we link the notes together as we play a musical instrument from sheet music. You create internal neurological linkage systems as you do so. The neuroplasticity of your brain now becomes a key part of your leverage system.

Explore Consciousness with the Concertina image by using the four exercises that end this chapter. Always take a moment to notice and appreciate the *feeling* of expansion. What does expansion *feel* like for you? What do you sense vibrationally?

With your Concertina, begin briefly with dissociated Coach Position then associate into the expansion movement. How does associated Coach Position expand for you doing this? When you metaphorically learn to expand up and out, experiencing value all the way, you build a deep connection to the larger field of awareness that now becomes your natural home in perpetuity. Once entangled, we generally stay entangled!

Scope Definition

Scope definition gives you an event horizon overview to carefully choose your framework or context for each project. Are you experiencing your event horizon, your '*Now scope*,' as the next five minutes, the full day before you, the next week, or even the next year? Would you be willing — as an explorer — to expand your event horizon forward even beyond your individual life? You might explore even up to 100 generations and sense *this* human connection as part of your project's scope. You decide the scope of your stretch!

After some preliminary practice, imagine that your Concertina can stretch your event horizon far beyond your own lifetime, perhaps 1,000 generations in each direction. Now you can begin to expand your accordion of consciousness with the value/vision field of humanity as your center. With your music you expand into all aspects of human space and time — all the way up and all the way out.

Take a very practical goal and work with it. For example, perhaps you are an olive grower and, with your event horizon scope, you visualize the five years needed to grow your olive orchard to marketability. Or, perhaps your project's plan needs your event horizon, your '*now*' needs to be sized as a span of 'two hours' to catch a plane?

You extend your context and define your purpose. Immediately, you can expand your accordion of awareness to match. Hold, explore, sense, release. Next, take Coach Position on your expanded experience.

Maybe the project you are exploring needs an extended '*now*' to encompass a vast time frame. For example, perhaps it involves growing a family system over your lifetime. Or does your 'awareness project' extend hundreds of years? Envision how you can serve a community as it will develop. With your mind-compass, set your vision and value scope to match the inner resonant quality of being Alive — worthy of the range you select. Now step in, associate, and expand your accordion. Realize what you have set for yourself — as a vibrational viewing-sensing system. Overview this. Use the four exercises that end this chapter for situational practice.

Use The Accordion to Expand Inner Presence

What are we actually practicing with our accordion? What makes the Accordion experience different from how you widen and expand from ground level detail to high level abstraction on your simple vertical axis? I want to suggest to you that the accordion process is a strong way to practice presence.

The steps:

- Visualize the elevator matrix as part of your value expression. Explore this with an important life sensibility or value, and experience the value as you expand. Then open your accordion *quickly* to sense your widened value-as-vibration awareness of this.
- Pause, breathe, and allow your inner sensing to experience the widened frame. If possible, open your arms wide to sense it.
- Notice the vibrational quality. Also notice any accompanying visuals, sounds, or other sensations that go with this.
- From here, apprehend your purpose, and your inner declaration of purpose.
- Take Coach Position on all of this.

Who do you become when you *presence* awareness? Do you not naturally pause to become aware of deep appreciation? Do you create a colorful visualization — even briefly — in this field of value?

For example, you might expand to sense your scope of life awareness like a huge, widening gossamer balloon filled with lightness, peace, and warmth? Or, perhaps you envision your expansion like a shining white light? Notice your own inner metaphor to keep it strong.

Try a big one. Perhaps you are looking at an expanded '*Now scope*' to build a flexible consciousness system into a vast arena of awareness you wish to experience, and you are projecting out your accordion to match the span of your lifetime. Can you now open your Concertina *quickly* to encompass and empower the widest energetic awareness possible with this?

Explore and play with vast scopes to practice further. Tibetan Buddhists have some exercises where they presence themselves as huge, intercelestial Beings, floating in space, expanding that Beingness to encompass thousands of galaxies. Open your Concertina to explore — and feel that level and quality of Beingness.

Similarly, play your Concertina to move way beyond imaginable limits. For example, you might briefly consider expanding your awareness to the whole Universe as if you could. If you were to step into the context of unfolding the evolution of the Universe itself, what scope would you expand into? Do you find that you increase your 'dimensions' of awareness far beyond the usual four?

With your accordion it is useful to contract back each time into the frame of your normal range. However notice that each time you expand, your capacity for presence stretches and widens even further, and the next stretch becomes much easier, as with an expanding balloon. Expanding your Concertina with speed and grace also makes a difference. Notice how your appreciation of other human beings grows as well as you see them capable of such expansion.

Explore further. Set your compass scope to explore your inner truth awareness then open your accordion to its furthest reach! Then allow the depth and width of this scope to play your inner quality of truth awareness — like music — now.

The various Concertina exercises at the end of the chapter will give you more ideas because you can do these practices in so many ways. You may notice that some of these exercises are particularly compelling for you, empowering you to move you well beyond your normal range of awareness. Others may not.

In the next few weeks, notice each time you habitually contract again into a tightened 'personal identity structure.' Once noticed, all areas of personal rigidity now become your springboard to expansion. These processes will allow you to truthfully experience the ongoing deepening of value in your life.

With a little practice, you will discover that you stand on holy ground. We walk around in the trousers of God. Shifting from one inner practice to another, you can develop and widen inner truth awareness. From Coach Position, you can honour each process, perhaps noticing harmony, love, gratitude, and humour emerging with their own vibrational essence as you expand. You can also explore them dissociated, noticing the difference, like pulses of light.

What makes these exercises so humbling and joyous is that we can only experience our deepening awareness as *One*. All *One*: *Alone*. We can take vibrational Coach Position on star-spangled awareness at any time. And it is always — once again — now! We experience eternal presence.

Only you can consciously build the expansive quality of resonant, expanded awareness for yourself. You become skilled at value awareness whenever you notice that you can actually expand your mind *anytime.* Time vanishes and consciousness emerges as the underlying reality. Our interactive multilevel intelligence opens to all of us together.

Rumi, the poet, sang his reminders of deep awareness across the centuries. He continually roused people from their 'comings and their goings.' He used his poetry to call out his timeless request for all of us to meet each other in the holy field of inner Self-Awareness. He sang for Presence and Truth: "Come, come, and yet again come" he challenged: *"Even if you have broken your vow a thousand times — yet again come!"*

Here are four exercises for you:

Accordion Exercise I: Widening Context

Find an interesting goal to test your accordion abilities. Take a personal example for yourself. Pick one goal of real relevance to your life.

Notice with this goal that the vertical dimension of the goal defines all potential playing fields, value dimensions, and life development games that potentially surround this goal *right now.*

What values and inner truths do you determine this goal to encompass for you? You are overviewing your context, *the attentional awareness system*, as a visual declaration space.

What is the deepest *value* you can link into with this goal? What values *naturally* call you? This defines the height and depth you now open.

Notice with this goal that the horizontal dimension defines all potential playing fields and games that 'have been' or 'could become' part of this goal. What learnings do you want to weave into this evolutionary unfolding? This defines the sweep of your *intention* and the event horizon of your Concertina. It enhances your ability to make your goal deeply meaningful.

Briefly connect to this as a goal right now. Overview both your past path and your future potential. Now, with deep interest, open your Concertina quickly to this full mindscape and sense its truth on all levels — with all your heart!

Experience the widened, vibrational awareness, and notice the quality of inner declaration. How does this scope of awareness also expand your sense of inner trust?

Accordion Exercise II: Concertina Practice Using the Arms for All Humanity

- First, step into the timeless moment of *now.* Think of who you aspire to be as a person.
- Now — use one arm to 'open your Concertina' only on one side and looking out to the tip of your longest finger on this side.
- Start from now and begin to move your focus back through time. Now associate your life backward along the trail of human development as far as the earliest homo sapiens, even 1,000 generations past. Imagine Humanities stages out to this event horizon. Feel gratitude for 1,000 generations of human development and the opportunities it has brought to all of us, as if you can envision that whole span connected to your open arm, hand, and fingertip.
- With equal interest, now use your other arm to open your Concertina on the other side, associating with the future 1,000 generations as if you could. Envision forward out to your longest finger tip, and allow your imagination to leap along this timeline to this growing potential of all humanity becoming more alive, fulfilled, happy, and wise. If we survive the current planetary difficulties, who might we become in 1,000 generations?
- Now move your arms, very slowly towards each other, starting at their widest position. Inch by inch, move them back to center in a parallel way while centering solidly in the expanded *now* awareness that they provide. Clap your hands lightly together to close the Concertina and to feel the full impact of your expanded presence *now.*

- Do the exercise again, and once again open your arms up and out to open your Concertina so that you *deepen* your perspective even further. This means to experience upward on the vertical dimension to your fullest vision/value connectivity. Feel the depth of your life from 1 meter to 15,000 meters and experience your expanded awareness also from the 15,000 meter level of human value awareness. Again, close your arms slowly, experiencing expanded value presence on all levels — all focusing into this one moment of *deep presence now.*
- With both depth and height available through your Concertina, do the exercise one more time as before. This time, sense the expression of *Humanity's value development* in all directions at once. Feel specific core values such as love, peace, joy or appreciation, noticing their developmental energy through time. You can explore these one at a time as you wish. To do this you might also expand visually using color as well. Add in your heart awareness like a strong chord of appreciative vibrational certitude. Allow the color to intensify in brightness and brilliance into the gladdened Universe — like a jewel.
- A Concertina makes music with every movement! The next step, as you close your hands together, is to use your accordion to *integrate* your values deeply together into the central value core of inner *presence.* It is often useful to start to feel this like a tiny magnetic point in the center of your body. Become deeply present to the vibrational quality of this. Notice your life as a resonant doorway for human evolution to sense itself.
- Close your Concertina back to *now* — this timeless moment — and appreciate both widened and momentarily attention, all yours now yet available always.

Accordion Exercise III: Exploring Core Values

Here are some variations or practices to explore with all four quadrants of a specific core value in your life.

1. **The Widest Point**
   - First, choose a core value and appreciate it. Sense it through the body and give it a color. Associatively expand up on your elevator to 15,000 meters while feeling it, opening ***attention*** wide and high with your elevator.
   - Hold this deep scope of attention as you now widen your ***intention boundlessly*** forward and backward in space-time with your accordion value sense.
   - At the 'widest point' breathe into it and feel it deeply! Your unconscious mind will know how to do this even if your conscious mind simply follows the visual expansion plan and notices the expanded color and light.

2. **Wide x10**
   - Now, in your mind's eye, consciously expand your accordion even further, beyond the widest point you have opened so far. Move — x10 — beyond this widest point, even out to *universal* value. Once again, feel this expansion and again notice the light and color.
   - Open the accordion out wide once again and this time see all from Coach Position viewpoint. View how intention and value expansion work together and go much further than you dreamt into an expanded, connected vision.

3. **Universal Field — Full Potential**
   - Open your accordion again to the furthest reach of universal value — as-if you could — and now briefly feel this value through your body, breathing in the vision-value wholeness of the total scope.
   - *Pause*, *breathe*, and *experience* the full potential of this value to alter everything in this Universal field of value.
   - Hold with relaxed presence to honour and memorize this widened field of awareness.

Accordion Exercise IV: From Coach Position Defining Personal Identity as a Context from Coach Position

Explore several important 'reality systems' connected to life projects that you attend to on a daily basis. How 'big' are the time scopes you currently tend to develop with them?

Do a small exercise with each one, in which, for each project, you use your inner accordion from Coach Position to accelerate your ability to widen the size of your *Now*, and, at the same time, to deepen the awareness of vision and value. Explore also the specifics of this project to determine how this expands relevance and commitment. Use a scale and also note any shifts in your ability to *focus* on the importance of this project for you. Notice that for each project you are feeling the mindscape *Being* which attends the matrix of awareness that the project envelopes.

Take a moment to explore your own inner presence as an 'identity' inside your project. '*Who*' disappears and '*who*' emerges as you expand your Concertina? Does the *sense* of identity shift? Does the vibration of *Beingness* shift?

For the conscious mind, one focus will often transcend another, yet a Coach Position can be built on all.

Pause in Coach Position to overview your various aims and their unique contexts. Notice the various 'identities' that emerge at different levels. What is the evolutionary potential of this overview awareness for your life, long term? Can you create a simple word or 'identity phrase' for this?

When you now step inside your expanded aim, experience associative awareness of this wide potential as a coalescing 'I.' What is the context of this 'I'? Some of you may sense oceanic expansion, the wide inner space of expanded *presence*. What is your own name for this now? When you look from Coach Position, what do you see? When you step in, what do you sense and feel? This is the experience often found with truly effective meditation long term.

Finally, observe this 'I' from Coach Position. What possibilities do you notice?

Accordion Exercise V: Playing Your Values in All Systems At Once

- Set your accordion scope to 'play' deep value awareness — perhaps choosing one quality like the quality of inner peace or love — and experience expanding this vibration. Specifically include its color as a shining presence.
- Make this vibrational value — the immediate and all-compassing context of your widening presence. Open your arms to experience this.
- Now, use your accordion to pull together some expansive 'music' for this value (the sensing of such a peace) and integrate this into your central value core. Use this to deeply experience the value as a peaceful core awareness. Use your full body to deepen and feel this. How do you experience your inner connection to this deep value now? Link this to a chosen piece of special music if you find an anchor useful.
- Contract and expand once again using open arms to guide your Concertina! Step into your field of inner peace. Experience this deep vibration now surrounded by your own special music and color of peace. Deepen it even further as a physical sensing system. What does all-encompassing inner peace *feel* like?

CHAPTER 10:

Building Oneness Awareness as Stability

The present moment is a timeless moment.
A timeless moment is an eternal one.
It knows no past or future, no before or after,
no yesterday, no tomorrow.

— St. Augustine

Creating Value Coherence

We are creating the awareness of Oneness. To fully engage our awareness of Oneness, each of us, as an individual, is capable of building this as an awareness of inner value coherence and as our own life development system.

Like a great global positioning system, a GPS for humans, four quadrant thinking provides a dynamic 'aerial viewpoint' of multifaceted, ever-present value awareness. Values are the muscles and sinews of Oneness. Realizing them as a form of awareness allows us to build balance in four intertwined fields. Value awareness means that even as we are exploring our playground from our most relevant concerns and tying our insights to our clearest integrity questions, we constantly need to sense our wider field of inner knowing. Gradually the awareness of Oneness — or Wholeness — emerges naturally and easily. We experience the meaning of '*profound*.'

Overview Coach Position assists powerfully as you explore the mind-heart connection. You can playfully and metaphorically try out frames such as global positioning systems, staircases, elevators, compasses, timelines, and accordions, as you learn outside-inside thinking.

To build awareness of wholeness, we learn to focus beyond personal thought systems to the *field* of value, experiencing it like a vibrational presence. In this way, we stand on the timeless evolutionary bridge rather than becoming caught in the net of our time-thoughts. *The ability to shift inner levels consciously while staying aware of awareness is one of the first competencies needed for developing this skill.* For this purpose, the practices in this book work wonderfully.

Your exploration skills get stronger as you develop different kinds of inner purposes using four quadrant viewing. You move your attention to the inner quality of overview with value-based self-imaging. You enliven core-value thinking. You build your playground of *Being.*

We leverage overview capacity as we relate maps and diagrammed frameworks to genuine viability and vitality in practical situations. We need to be able to access high-level areas of inner knowledge, and at the same time, apply our practice in other more difficult yet personally relevant circumstances. We need to be able to use scientific inquiry and to perform research as we develop our relevant choices. At the very same time, we can experience a cornucopia of joyful living and discover the sacred inner doorway of Holy, Holy, Holy!

Diagrams and maps that define specific aims and levels can consistently assist with inner awareness, so that strong competencies can be built. We are like airline pilots learning how to use our value maps to move above weather systems so that we can find the easiest route for our journey. In this way, we learn to love flying.

Using your altitude map, from Chapter 7, you can gradually learn to remain aware from one meter to 15,000 meters. It is interesting to discover that negative internal dialogue, especially cynicism thoughts or self-attack thoughts are usually linked only to very specific atmospheric 'levels of mind' while other levels may remain entirely clear.

Some people have discovered levels of awareness that assault them with big winds of negative emotions or with mundane, yet pervasive self-protection thoughts, while other levels remain like a sunny day. For example, a physical pain at 'one meter,' may challenge some. For another, a relationship distraction, level 1,000, may bring fear and dismay. Interesting, isn't it?

As you check any former areas of entitlement, self-aggrandizement, self-belittling or other kinds of misery systems, label the 'levels of mind' that need your attention, and bring in the deep colors and feelings of your core values visually, like an atmospheric cleanse. You can also bring them in feeling-wise as an experience of deep life forgiveness. Bring the value color and feeling like a mist of coherence and wholeness through these key levels and in all four quadrants. In this way, you relink relaxed awareness to these levels.

With practice, you begin to experience more and more moments of your own natural joy and self-appreciation, no matter the old identity upheavals from the past. With small processes of inner alignment you learn to move out of a hurricane of old habits and emotional systems, and into the peaceful 'eye' at the center of the storm.

With four quadrant maps to stabilize your perception, you make discoveries that assist self-consistent and evolutionary overview. As you align your attention to your values, you naturally close old concerns and blind spots. When you magnetize to your values, your compass direction becomes easy and natural. As for an experienced pilot, the old storms become small and insignificant, and all levels of the mind become easier to navigate. You learn how to find the positive, warm 'updrafts' of value and vision with each task and choice so that flying becomes easy.

Let's review useful steps:

- First, set your intention for a vibrant purpose as a context for self-exploration. Link to the four quadrant system to expand this. For example, imagine your intention is like an arrow ready for the bow.
    - ◇ Firstly, quadrant 1 — pull your arrow on *intention*: Think of your best result with a project that you are committed to and are currently engaged with. What will be your strongest aim?

Diagram 10.1: Bow and Arrow of Intention

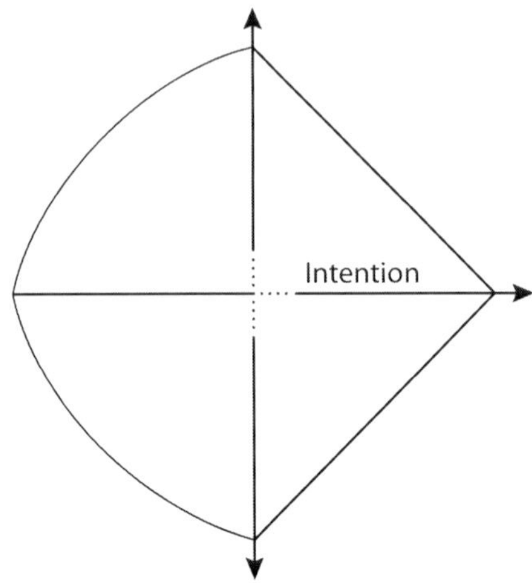

- ◇ Secondly, quadrant 2 — with *perception*: What will you do today to create widened perception with this project? What sights, sounds, and actions?
- ◇ Thirdly, quadrant 3 — *emotionally*: What will you plan to enjoy about this project?
- ◇ Fourthly, quadrant 4 — *meaningfully*: How can you deepen that enjoyment and make this both an intentional stretch and a great day in the life?

- Next, expand upward on your elevator, attending to the inner value awareness and connected to this four quadrant intention. Expand your timeframe appropriately as you do so.
- Third, envision yourself moving beyond all potential personal 'storms' or negative habits with ease and grace, and with a naturally wide value scope that continues to build around your purpose as a reality system. As you declare this inner purpose, step into warm awareness like a context, then create the color and brightness in your minds eye to expand your value and vision levels. Step in briefly to test the experience of this expansion.
- Fourth, as you take action with your aim, learn to use your inner four quadrant compass to steer your point of view between all levels, timeframes, and various quadrants of attention. You can

do this with practical daily exploration to develop four quadrant intelligence.

You will learn more methods in later chapters of these Volumes.

- Discover how to practice Coach Position with both dissociated and associated viewing, feeling, and listening. Use dissociated viewing — seeing yourself in action — to set your purpose. Use associated — experiencing — to step in briefly to test this and tune it to high-level congruence with your purpose.
- Practice positive viewing at all the different levels.
- Become curious about expanded self knowledge, especially exploring various difficult thought frames or reality systems that you want to develop in yourself. For example, perhaps you want more meaningful conversations with family members, or you want to experience physical exercise in an enjoyable way. What intentional stretch will allow you to develop these habits?
- Bring full attention and intention to your purpose, and 'settle in' once again to your four quadrant 'life frame.'

Mind as Verb: Creating Stability

We have been exploring methods to energize creative choice with whole system thinking. *The next step is to explore how to build stability.*

First, tune yourself to the *awareness* of *awareness*. The value of four quadrant thinking really becomes available when you learn to stabilize Coach Position at different levels because you simultaneously learn to stabilize wholeness awareness at the very same time. The jet pilot gets more agile as he learns to steer by viewing as if beyond *any* kind of weather system.

Four quadrant thinking needs to be a repetitive process. As such, it can simultaneously heal and cohere many layers of heart-mind dynamics. We work best when we do not try to dissect the mind like the brain, but rather create ways to actively explore, test, envision, and enjoy our dynamic, shifting system. With four quadrant systems, we metaphorically do this. The quality of exploration is curious, active questioning about the unfolding processes of your own inner learning and inner truth... at every level.

With practice — like a mountain climber who knows the trails from bottom to top — you will learn to map the terrain. Moving your attention to four quadrant 'values thinking' is different from exploring the specifics of 'ground-level ideas,' conceived at the one-meter level. It also differs from the detailed review of 100-meter-level thinking, making specific plans and steps so that you will do them tomorrow. In contrast, experiencing 'flashes of insight' connected to wholeness awareness may be very comprehensive, expanding your map of consciousness far beyond your wildest dreams. Yet, you will notice that *all levels are deeply connected!* As you expand with one level, you can gently bring the same value awareness to all the rest. Our **Being** holds **doing** which holds **having** a life of value awareness.

To develop our mind as a playground of purpose, developing the willingness for an ongoing stretch of the bow of intention, we need to gradually explore meaningful goals and aims at every level while we engage this overview. Your playground really is your playground. You alone can dynamically operate all your viewpoints, and create this integration.

Step by step, each one of us can build *stability*. You move this strongly forward as you link your deeply felt values to your inner field of evolutionary vision, each step allowing you to comprehend further. We become stable, not through halting growth but by stabilizing in our expansion abilities. We are like the Universe itself, always widening further and becoming stable in that capacity.

As you learn to move between areas and aspects, you develop your own kinds of creative 'minding processes' as a comprehensive skill set. You creatively integrate your own Mind system into one clear coherent presence. You gradually learn to navigate and to shape the 'byways' that link all areas and aspects of your fields of awareness together. It is especially useful to link curious, value-oriented creative thinking with physical, grounded, sensory awareness all the way down to your toes.

These might include simple check-in questions such as:

- Quadrant 1: What is my four quadrant purpose today?
- Quadrant 2: What am I experiencing in this moment?
- Quadrant 3: What do I love about being alive today?
- Quadrant 4: What is really meaningful here that I can strengthen?

Four quadrant questions then develop you towards what you might experience as 'quantum leaps' — sudden luminous insights into inner wholeness, which expand all awareness like a torch. Such insight is a form of vibrational seeing/sensing that includes the deep felt resonance of wholeness. The word 'quantum' actually means the tiniest shifts which totally change a whole system.

Michelangelo Thinking

Let me share a little about the history of this work as I, Marilyn, explored four quadrant thinking step by step. Early in my explorations, about 1985, I started using the great Michelangelo Man pictograph as a symbol to further assist self-discovery. I would imagine stepping inside and place four quadrants 'over-top' so I could sense them from inside.

For many years as I worked with four quadrant exploration, I drew various four quadrant 'thought vectors' on diamonds over this Michelangelo figure. My aim was to remind myself to 'step in' and explore each intention I had both with 'heart' (relational-physical thinking) and with 'mind' (intentional conceptual thinking).

Diagram 10.2: Original 'Michelangelo Man' Framework

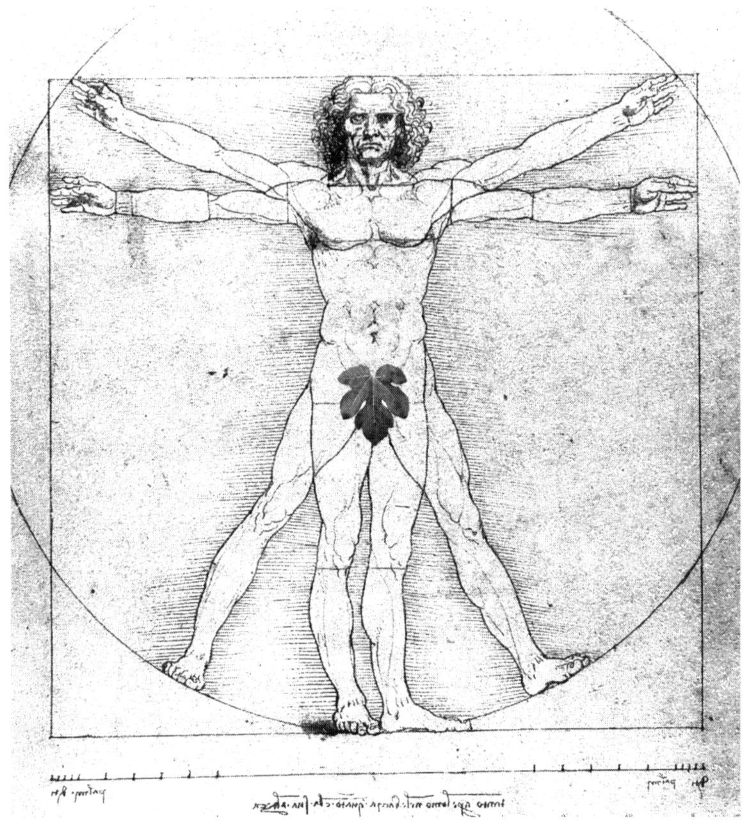

I began early in 1985, and by 1990, I had completed about 350 comprehensive 'Michelangelo Man' four quadrant drawings. Each was the base for a practice which assisted me to challenge myself with different kinds of inner explorations. I could step inside to test the 'thought and feel' of each arena. These particularly assisted me to expand my own relational capacity as I worked with others.

Leveraging the Michelangelo Man for morning explorations, I would — on a daily basis — overview the future connected system and then step into my positive assumptions about the steps to get there. Now I could learn to move in and out of these old assumptions by expanding time/space vectors and frames, and using four quadrant questions to aim much further into vast scope awareness. With elevator and accordion I could test my capacity to expand and deepen and to build quickly.

I also used the Michelangelo Man to encourage myself to slow down into presence or widen out into appreciation, to expand beyond old conclusions and to connect inwardly into the moment. My aim was always to see, to feel, and to sense for any larger truth emerging now. I would ask: What needs to become 'sense-able' and sensible today? I would explore in terms of the four specific dimensions: physical, emotional-relational, intentional, and meaningful, as shown in Diagram 10.3. I used my own emotional life as a testing ground to build my own next future with truly meaningful mind-matrices. Four intelligences merge step-by-step.

Diagram 10.3: A Michelangelo Man with Key Exploration Areas

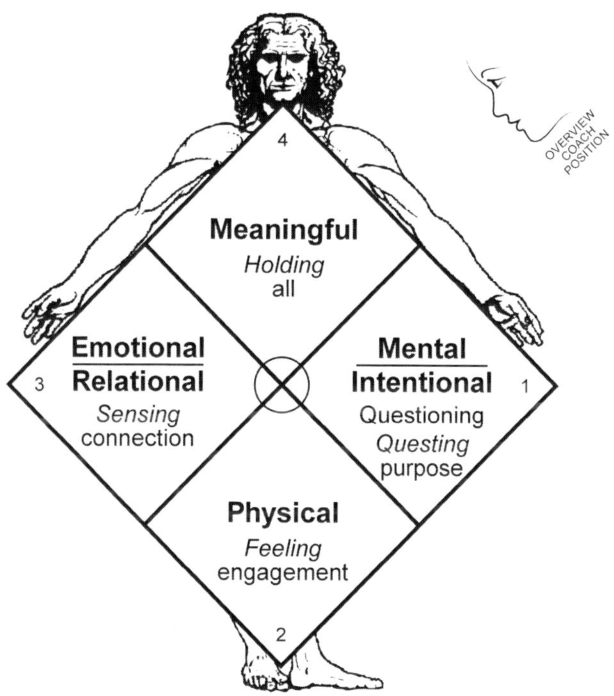

Body-feeling and relational-sensing are particularly useful using the four quadrants as a frame. You can test the various quadrants as a way to link into different inner learning processes: by feeling, sensing, questing, and holding the connection to core values. Bring all qualities together like vibrating harp strings so that they connect as a mind/brain system.

Holding the connection also means keeping at least three awareness systems operative at the same time, while lacing between them.

Using the Michelangelo Man, I gradually also learned how to widen out my timescope without re-associating to old mindsets. This enlarged my capacity to stay out of old history and to see useful patterns I could build with. *Holding connection*, you become stable. I discovered this connected to and deepened my capacity for Coach Position.

As a consulting psychologist, and as a speaker, I have heard so many 'time stories' that have constricted and twisted peoples lives. People say things like, "Time has got me by the throat," "I wasted ten years with that man!," I don't really have enough time for myself." These are sad declarations.

Let me once again urge you to practice Coach Position. With Coach Position, you can learn how to expand curiosity throughout and beyond the 'personal time' dimension. You begin to expand out to *vast*: timeless, eternal, and comprehensive. This provides a huge booster to expansion, because 'personal time' does not usually provide strong, strategic motivation for inner work. Connecting ourself to a purpose that can expand the lives of many others is much more compelling! To move beyond the heavy gravity of our old identity system — like a magnetic planet — truly requires such a 'booster rocket.'

This means you learn to sense the evolutionary value of your own life exploration on many levels and 'across time' as well. Two ways of working towards self-development becomes *three* ways as you view and sense them operating as a system. When you move to ongoing momentum, you learn to become a stable explorer, and the 'fourth way' appears.

Diagram 10.4: Key Process for Inner Learning

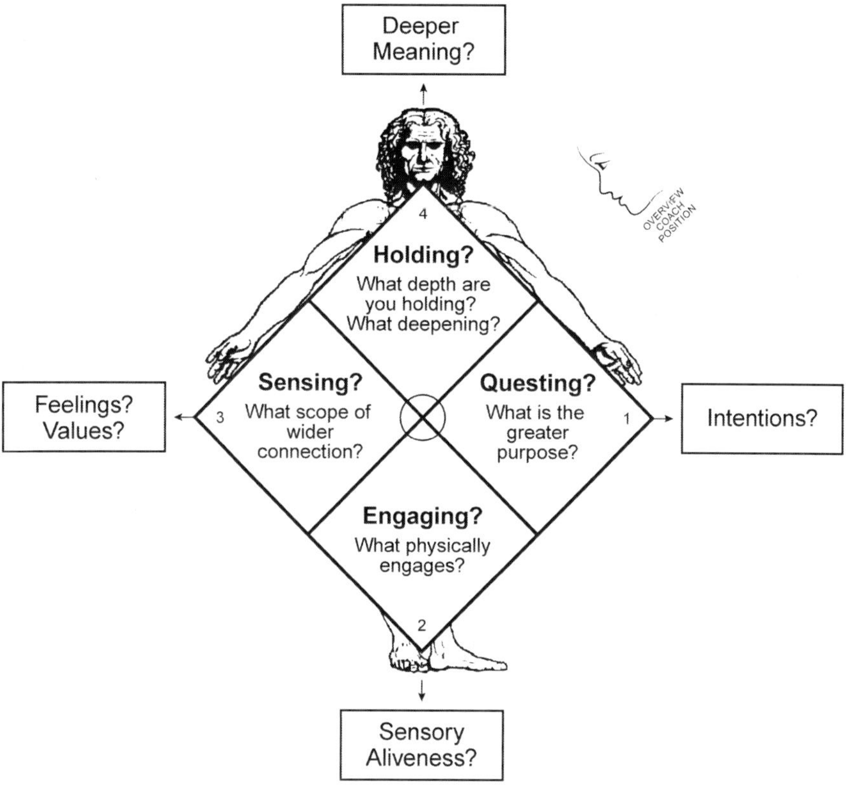

Deeper Meaning?

4 **Holding?** What depth are you holding? What deepening?

3 **Sensing?** What scope of wider connection?

Questing? What is the greater purpose? 1

Engaging? What physically engages?

2

Feelings? Values?

Intentions?

Sensory Aliveness?

OVERVIEW COACH POSITION

Creating Time for It

Use four quadrant thinking to expand and extend the metaphoric dimension of your larger intentions. Time and time again, you can watch your time ideas melt and re-emerge 'differently.' Let 'Time-Space' merge into a meaningful context for widened awareness.

If we take our old historical-emotional time ideas seriously, we do not take them seriously enough! Our old time beliefs (connected to negative emotions) are all made up, both personally and culturally! Learn to expand out beyond your 'serious' time afflictions and use the accordion and the timeline awareness scope to dive into the timeless moment! *Make this ability a stable one.*

The whole of life is a wondrous circus of 'melting watches' of different kinds, which you are able to pervade with humor and compassion when you become able to expand the realms of time and identity together. You alone can declare the realms of spacious timelessness as your now, and with that, determine all the contexts of purpose and value that you wish to set for the 'practicalities' of life. You set them instead of them '*setting*' you! Who you become is the quality of your emergent moment! You now convey the boundless infinity of non-local, comprehensive awareness, into one delicious timeless moment.

CHAPTER 11:

The Power of Declaration

It is important to understand the power and importance of declaration for developing four quadrant system awareness. Our declarations, both verbal and visual, create the mind. You may not have yet noticed, but you have always used declarations to establish your inner playground of mind and heart. Only through declarations do we create and cohere an identity system.

What is the quality of a declaration? It is important to understand the engagement you create inwardly with all declarative speech. A positive declaration connects you with inner vision. This means that a declaration is very integrative; a strong and immediate doorway to self-awareness.

A negative declaration, in contrast, can easily stop you in your tracks. It stops you, particularly when you make 'I am' verbal declarations that link you to negative states.

Look at how this works. When you say, "I am able" or "I am strong," you immediately stand in your ability and strength. When you say, "I am weak" or "I am sick," you begin to feel weakness or sickness in the moment of speaking. Whatever we pay attention to we get more of!

A four quadrant map, then, can be used powerfully, as a template for visual declaration, and assists us to have 'wholeness of mind' as the starting point for *all* self-inquiry. By using holistic maps to explore the nature of Being and Self, we expand our awareness to become holistic and inclusive. If we declare our map as a map of boundless awareness, we immediately expand the reach of consciousness, to taste this possibility.

A map, by its very nature, can be used as a powerful format for visual declaration. The power of any four quadrant visual declaration is that when we see it, say it, and step into it, we can build a congruent system. All 'overview mapping' such as we create with a four quadrant format, expands our insight. This moves even further as we overview our intention from an external Coach Position. To achieve effective overview, we use open-ended vision and exploration questions, but also inner requests, promises, and declarations. You will find an emphatic connection with creative intuition as you link these all together.

The Four Forms of Declaration

Within our speech, we can creatively work with four natural declarative forms. These are *declarations*, *requests*, *promises*, and *assertions*. Let us put these four forms on a four quadrant map since they form a clear overview system in terms of power. Again, we can view the levels from abstract to concrete. Within any conversation, we can declare, we can request, we can promise, and we can assert.

Diagram 11.1: The Russian Doll of Inner Power: To Declare, Request, Promise, and Assert

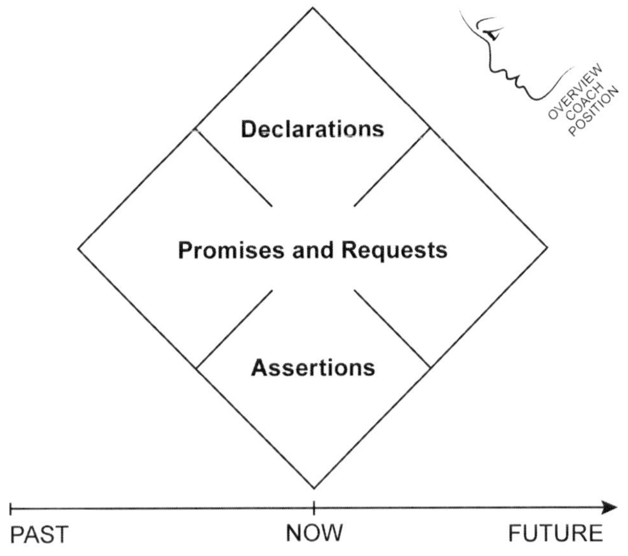

In the use of a four quadrant map for overview thinking, it is useful to get very clear about the nature of a *declaration*, the nature of a *promise*, and the nature of a *request*. These three are very different from the fourth linguistic function, the *assertion* function, which tend to rely on concrete, detailed, present to past-oriented description pegged to timed associations. In contrast, declarations, promises, and requests create a world.

Defining Identity and Roles

By definition, identity is forever. The word 'identity,' (*idem*), means sameness. If I asked you to notice your own 'identity thinking' you would begin recognizing typical thoughts, behaviors, feelings and emotions, would you not? When you explore your 'identity' you take Coach Position on your regular habits, and they may indeed seem like an 'inner you.'

Timelessness is the essence of identity speaking. This means declarations of identity tend to fix identity to be 'forever.' Notice how people tend to stick with old characterizations, even with many counter-examples. For example, people tend to label themselves; "I'm no genius," or to say "I'm the forgetful person in the family." They then live from this characterization.

People often make identity declarations inwardly and then forget them. These 'I am' statements stabilize and become a context for their life development moving forward. If we say "I am courageous, visionary, creative, curious, inventive" — you choose — we become more of that. Our internal dialogue now gets built from this to become the stepping stones that carry us forward.

When you understand the power of declaration as a mind creator, you learn to be very careful with any emphatic 'self' definitions or 'other' definitions. You especially learn to listen with care to identity declarations, because you realize the great power that they hold to fixate a point of view towards 'always the same.' See Appendix 7, *Characterization*, to explore this. Most people then live from 'same old, same old!'

What if you focused to indenitify only what is boundless in you — would you to start growing, changing, and becoming free to learn much more? Notice that we began to do this in Chapter 9 by working with the accordion practices. Our Concertina provided a 'visual declaration' of vast potential for choice and change.

Entangling with Enlightened Self

When you are clear about your own deep power to create visual, auditory, and kinesthetic declarations, you learn to tune yourself to them. You can now move beyond old, habitual, and limiting either-or identity verbalizations, as well as all noisy, internal dialogue filled with negative declarations. You start to notice them immediately!

When you have tested this you become very clear on what kind of internal declarations you determine to support in yourself. You hear and feel the level of your own inner congruence in the words you speak to yourself. As you choose your inner language you can effectively chart your pathway to further congruence. You can declare the old negative inner 'tape recordings' as just that — recordings. You can replace them with high-level *identity* declarations of dignity, value and purpose — and these new declarations ignite your energy.

Exploring identity ideas is actually wonderful work — once you develop a strong Coach Position on inner self talk. Remember that Coach Position is itself a declaration of the intention to create your own life from a larger context of learning and self-knowledge. There is power in this exploration because you can develop it to mirror and support your wider awareness. You then develop your ability to realize deep value states in accordance with your larger life.

We form identifications with family and team. We can declare these contexts as wider frames for learning, choice and vision. With focus, we can build this. We learn to request and declare value in others, and to declare appreciation, inclusion, and deep love for all.

Our link to others means we are part of something bigger than ourselves and we can palpably *sense* 'all of us together,' one family, one team, one whole life system. We can then learn to move this out to sense our vibrational attunement to each other. We can declare one resonant world! *'We!'*

Specific Kinds of Declarations

Notice the **form** of a declaration. It has a very specific format, very simple: *"I declare 'x'!"* We use this often in our lives in key moments. A good example is the naming of children. When you held your child in your arms for the first time and said: "Her name is Andrea" or "His name is Peter," you used a declaration to create a future, did you not? You created the future name for the child right on the spot. "I declare 'Andrea'!" *Any declaration powerfully shapes the future.*

Think of declarations in sports, for example. In some types of games, the umpire enforces the rules of the game through declaration. He is the one who declares, "You're SAFE" or "You're OUT!" This creates clarity and certainty, and the game moves on. If an umpire calls "Foul ball," his decision automatically *becomes 'the reality.'* It happens immediately, *by agreement*. The umpire, on the spot, is empowered to declare what's so. We have already *declared* this authority of his role.

Only we give the umpire the power to declare a reality. In the context of the game, what he says then becomes true for us. As natural owners of any system we have declared to be real, we give someone the authority to make a declaration, and then declare agreement to the form of decision-making we have authorized. We alone declare every 'reality' we inhabit!

Suppose you have created your own corporation. A corporate 'entity' becomes enacted through declaration when you apply for its name. Just like a new parent, you have birthed a corporate entity. A corporate mission statement can therefore be a very powerful declaration. When you build and declare your mission you create the context for your communal reality. You build the foundation for corporate and team values.

Creating Appreciation and Forgiveness

Declarations create the foundation for our life. One of the most basic declarations is a simple *"Thank you!"* The words "Thank You!" intoned with appreciation, shape a creative state of great power. Listen to the phrase "Thank you" while speaking. As soon as you say it, the person you speak to becomes thanked! It's done — and you get to *feel* this as well! "Thank you" is so enabling that this declaration forms the most fundamental building block of all our social networks. All relationships, all loving connections, are based on gratitude and appreciation... by declaration!

Similarly, look at the nature of forgiveness which is also a powerful form of declaration. As soon as we say, "I forgive you," we wholeheartedly shape our inner world with our words. All former negative thoughts are laid to rest and we declare peace. We perceive life differently because we now view our world from 'forgiven,' and we start to recreate this as an ongoing form of wholeness anew. Forgiving self and others creates a fresh world. To truly forgive means we can build vital, high-level energy states around this renewal.

Four Quadrant Maps as Declarative Integrity Systems

Declarations can be used to create the recognition of integrative awareness. We declare it and sameness awareness occurs. We enter the field of ethical oneness. We become 'entangled' with our ethics and our integrity! We move beyond the foreground of inner discussion to the wider recognition of field awareness. Yet, usefully, the experiential declaration itself remains in the foreground of the conscious mind, visually, verbally, and kinesthetically! We create a linkage system. For example, we can declare *Integrative Awareness* and begin to find it. When we then declare the inner quadrants as particular to this system, we find them as well.

We step into:

- Quadrant 1: requesting and calling forth our quest and purpose.
- Quadrant 2: declaring and standing for our presence.
- Quadrant 3: defining our core values.
- Quadrant 4: declaring the deeper meaning of all of it.

Diagram 11.2: The Four Declarations of Integrative Awareness

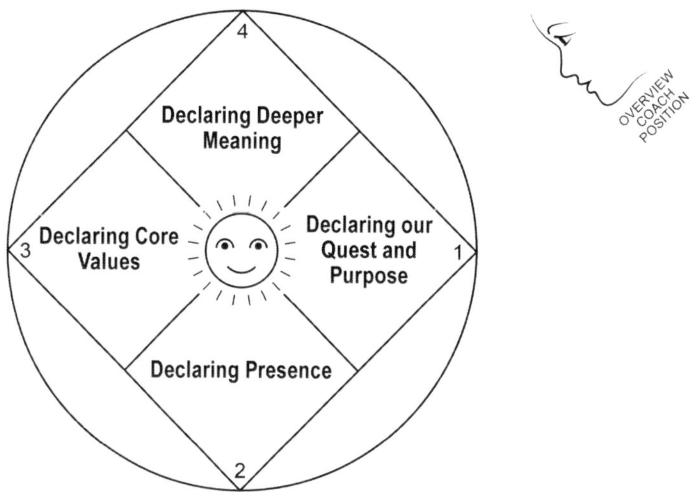

In other words, a declaration is not just verbal. Its resonance carries our life forward. Wonderfully, we can make our declarations through and with *any inner system* that we consciously declare to be valid for us. A declaration can include envisioning a truth, speaking our truth with words and tone, and expressing our truth kinesthetically with physical expression. We need only to focus strongly on intention and purpose to create clear magnetic realities! These then become the playgrounds we inhabit.

Special Declarations

This means that even by using a physical space as part of a visual-verbal declaration of wholeness, you can physically recreate a powerful purpose. For example, you can define a 'time line' as a three-meter stretch on the floor with markers defining past, present, and future. You can then step into this reality as a 'visionary timeline' to explore very specific choices you want to make in the next year. Or, you can use it to declare an identity of happiness and fulfillment for all the futures you can envision in a context of timeless truth!

You might also use such a physical timeline to rebuild your inner 'hologram' of forgiveness for others, using clear declarations, timelines, statelines, and four quadrant system-maps you can 'step into.' This is also available when you work with other balanced visual forms such as circles, wheels, pyramids, and isosceles or balanced triangles. (See Appendix 3, Symbols and Shapes.) Visual maps can easily be designed as templates for wholeness systems or holograms. They can then be used as symbolic declarations which can powerfully expand your awareness of integrity. Wholeness awareness begins to grow in you.

Think about the flow of value in your own inner system. Exploring your value priorities is core to your life development. Suppose you had some simple ways you could assist yourself and others to shift the mind stream of value awareness into a river of much wider value concurrence? Suppose you could easily *expand* and *deepen* your *experience* of love and gratitude? Would you not wish to step into and declare your deepening awareness, scaling it upward?

Once you truly understand the power of your own capacity for declaration, you can start to use integrative declaration to build your inner, intuitive life playground as a clear field of vibrational attunement. As you attune to vision and value, your resonance becomes a magnet to those around you. You accelerate both your capacity to coach others and your capacity to coach self.

Declarations Link to Our Larger System

It is useful to declare 100% commitment to any project you know is worth doing. It is useful to assist others to do the same. For example, if you ask any project owner, "What's the value for you in building this result?" You are requesting a declaration. Declaring our desired future allows us to visualize our specific choices and we start to make our commitments real.

To complete a project well, we need to declare a true beginning, visualizing a completion that calls us forward. In other words, we need to begin with the end in mind. We need to declare capability and the power to choose and decide to move forward, step by step. We also need to declare our ability to finish the job, to evaluate and assess our work, and to build abilities based on this. See Diagram 11.2 which charts these action steps as a journey.

Diagram 11.3: The Four Declarations of Project Ownership

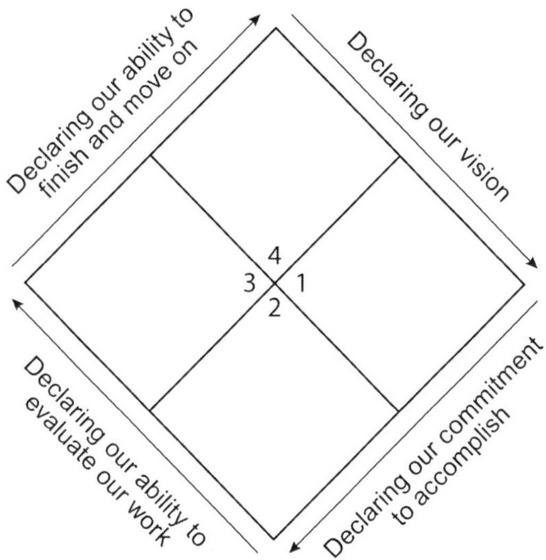

When we declare project ownership with a balanced visual diagram or chart in mind, we accelerate our capacity to think systemically. When we build a map to declare and chart any aim, the 'chart' will be created as a linkage system in the brain as well, and the reverberating circuits will hold, shape, and develop the inner template for completion. This means that as we work with any element going forward, *we now do so in the context of the larger system we have declared.*

Making a declaration, either verbally or visually (with the use of visual, symbolic forms), we quickly learn how to move towards an engaged flow of enlarged awareness. A declaration is a wonderful way to create this positive flow of enhanced meaning. Wholeness of mind can be explored and developed in any modality, and a visual map of wholeness — as a declaration — tunes this awareness. All declarative speaking, then, can be developed to hold the function of long-term appreciation, benediction, and value development.

We become the future that we create through vision and declaration! We can explore a four quadrant map and it assists us to declare powerfully by creating balanced, expansive, and palpable '*visual declarations.*' Holistically then, we truly notice to whom we are speaking. By it's very nature, a declaration is always for all. *We are speaking to all of us all of the time — both inwardly and outwardly.*

Coaching Towards the 'Promise Land'

What then are the inner qualities of promises and requests? With pondering we can notice that promises and requests are special forms of declarations, because declarations, promises, and requests move people towards present and future commitments. They all build futures. We're looking at the process of speaking into a creative 'next step.'

Promises particularly create futures. Assisting someone to promise is a key function of coaching. A promise makes a dream come alive for us. When we promise we see the future differently.

A *promise* is also an important kind of declaration linking us to *timelessness*. When we commit to our promise, we speak into the truth function. When we declare a personal truth or choice, we speak out to our 'next level' identity and declare our commitment to *act from that level. Our willingness to commit now becomes our identity.* Only with our promise to commit can we request inwardly to move further.

A promise is a kind of declaration that has a special quality: it leads us into a shining moment of personal commitment. This is because making a promise means we declare from a deep sense of capability. We are saying: *"I am capable to promise this!"*

Some really important promises for us as humans include the promise of an apology. To apologize means to 're-promise' commitment in an area of former difficulty. Apologies give us back our ability to promise new capacity to see what is needed. Another important promise is the promise to keep learning in any area of leadership or trust. We then become a beacon, assisting the courage of others to do the same.

The range of a promise becomes global because its resonance in the mind is *through time*, yet paradoxically, we create a future that is always spoken in *present tense*. We speak *now* for *forever*. Even as we speak our promise, we can listen through the wide horizontal range it encompasses as part of our natural global range of listening. We listen with Quantum ears into the timeless realm.

Notice that a promise necessarily moves us vertically upward towards the meaningful realm. It elevates us into value. When someone promises, we can listen to *who this person is becoming* through the promises they are making! Some promises go with role agreements, like Doctor, Teacher, or Coach. For example, for each *specific* situation that people bring to a coaching conversation the coach — through his or her role agreements — promises relationship and care.

When we listen for committed promises, and when we make powerful requests, our listening assists others to become *accountable*. With our listening they commit themselves and they know it. They naturally feel the inner joy that commitment brings. Their field of awareness expands accordingly, as an attractor field for future commitment.

The bigger our playground of request and promise, the more inner power each moment holds for us. As committed listeners, we agree to remind the promise-makers of their promised agreements. They are telling us their promise so that we **can** remind them!

Any map — such as a four quadrant matrix — that expands the range of our promise from verbal to visual and to multifaceted awareness assists this inner process. We move from old stories, a focus only on past 'stuff,' to the power of creating a visualized frame as an 'attractor field' to key potential futures. This truly expands our playground, with contextual possibility.

With any promise, all past, present, and future 'self-thoughts' now becomes unified into a holistic '*across-time*' frame for commitment and accountability. We step in.

Requesting

Requests are also a key form of declaration. A request holds power inwardly and outwardly because it asks for action. We either agree or disagree or to activate a potential or to take action when a request is made. We either accept or deny the request. It demands that we be clear on our specific response, and then either do it — or *not*. In other words, a request demands a clear response. For example, a request for competence — when they accepted — leads to strong expansion in willingness to learn. A request for effective decisions leads to evaluation refinement. A request for fairness or justice — when taken on — leads to deep interest in the realities and points of view being explored. We can also request inwardly for vision and value. Making our request *active* activates inner response!

All declarations, requests, and promises open awareness when spoken, affirmed, and listened to as a space of *commitment*. With the request, the person now has a map that holds enhanced action choices. They can affirm or deny. We have created a jewel box of wider possibility and now inside our creation we find our promised jewels of enhanced awareness.

Suppose there is a standing *request* for a person to commit to high level competence as a doctor or an engineer. Now the *promise* to do this and the *declaration* of ability leads to a vital new identity map.

Watch the shift in people at a professional 'confirmation meeting' when they are given professional degrees, perhaps as doctors, engineers, or lawyers. In one moment, they completely shift identity to step into the commitment level of the *newly confirmed identity*. The person accepting the degree is *becoming* a doctor or an Engineer because they, with their peers, declare it to be so. As observers, we hear who this person truly intends to *become*, through their promise to hold the profession *well*. This level of declared commitment now becomes the attractor field for their self-creation. The person now begins to live from the level of commitment that they have chosen and declared to the world. We can declare *Self* at any level.

Assertions

An *assertion* is a much more local and specific statement, quite different from the first three kinds of declarations, since it focuses on past to present descriptions and specific content. Assertions require or assume that evidence can be provided for what is spoken. With an assertion, we enter the land of 'because.' We test for evidence for our assertion. We demand proof of someone else's assertions.

Assertions are 'content-specific.' In contrast, promises, requests, and declarations tend to *expand* the mind towards the larger *context*. For this reason, four quadrant visual declarations where we request further awareness hold great 'promise.' They assist us to grow the *context* of our thinking both dissociatively and associatively through all the quadrants and levels we visualize.

It is highly appropriate to separate assertions — which require evidence — from declarative assessment. We become effective listeners when we require this clear distinction from others so they don't fall prey to their own inner characterizations and evaluations — as if they are accurate descriptions of some 'reality.'

Declarations of intelligence and value gently move us into our *wave* of intelligence, entangling us in vast fields of value. Assertive descriptions in contrast solidify a 'reality particle' — a particular conclusion linking us to the specifics of one time and one location. We create the different levels and kinds of identity. We are the ones who set them. The more we notice, the more we can reset and refine our access to mindful awareness.

When we notice our speaking power as a vehicle to create awareness we become strong assistants for those around us. We can use our coaching questions to provoke declarations, requests, and promises that deepen the meaning of our lives! We step off the platform of our descriptions and assertions and into the open vehicle of creation by making declarations, requests, and promises towards what we want to build. We create the inner power of our human template.

CHAPTER 12:

Expanding Out with Visual Declarations

Awareness: Listening for Beginners, Step Builders, and Completers

You may know some people who are great at starting things. You may also know others who are good at executing and moving things along. And, of course, there are some people who are good at ending things and amazingly strong with completion.

Who are those visionary people who are good at beginning things? These are people who are able to make strong declarations of *intention* and then inwardly move, step by step, towards designing the effective action choices that make them happen. To start something, we need to move beyond all fear of dreaming, and decide to create a meaningful vision.

The second arena of execution where we move our goals forward often requires grit, determination, and detailed steps — the operational zone of requesting and promising. To implement well, we need to focus on specific actions and promises to continue despite all setbacks. We often meet old gremlin fears such as the fears of failure, and of upsetting people as we carry our task forward.

And what does strong completion require? Often, we must develop the deepest determination and the widest promise of all: to forgive all inner or outer conflicts in our life and become able to finish despite all seeming contradictions. For example, you may need to step beyond some old assertion — requesting evidence that you will accomplish something a specific way — which you may indeed need to decline. We all need to give ourselves the power to decline old promises that are no longer appropriate. We may need to re-decide our commitments and renew our visions so that we are working with fresh, valid commitments. We move past the gremlin fear of inner conflict, and learn to complete what is valid for us — no matter what!

You have probably heard the joke about the man escaping to the roof of his house during a flood, with the river becoming more and more dangerous. He is waiting for a miracle and praying to God. He refuses a raft, a boat, and a helicopter rescue, maintaining, "God will assist me." Later, after drowning and facing St. Peter, he complains, "I declared my faith, so where were you when I needed you?" And the reply, "I sent you a raft, a boat, and a helicopter. It was your choice!"

The familiar joke is a reminder that a declaration only marks the beginning. We light the flame of our purpose with a declaration, a promise, or a request, and we need to continue taking committed and visionary *actions* to unfold our purpose. We then need to complete with strong action steps.

The 'Holding' Function: Accountability, Tracking and Self-Coaching

Suppose you are working as a coach, or you're in a conversation with a friend. You're supporting someone to keep going with a project and, over a period of time, you have been assisting and encouraging them to keep track of their accomplishments. This requires that — with each 'coaching conversation' or interaction — you are carefully listening to hear their next action steps. You are requesting that they keep their intentions alive, and move their actions forward, step by step.

Anyone who listens in this way is sharing an important process with a person; the process of *holding promised commitments as real.* This means that you are assisting them *through requests — to continue building energy with their intention*, even as each completion may become more difficult to fulfill.

To do this means, of course, that you are tracking declarations and promises. Before each coaching session, you ask: "What happened with the former promised action? And what about this other?" Perhaps, every month you build an overview map or wide-screen summary with the person, viewing their 'long term' timeline or wheel. Their aim is to examine and to scale how far they've moved towards satisfaction and completion with their commitments in various key areas. What movement has there been in *this* area? What about *that* one?

Every human being responds powerfully to this kind of assistance. By showing a promise *visually*, on paper, with quadrants, wheels, timelines, and scales, you assist the person to create the experience of *holding* both a visual and a tonal declaration and promise, so they start to strongly visualize and declare their next steps, and then to realize them! They leave behind the old assertions such as "I can't because...," and step into fresh mind-space. They declare their inner playground to be new, fresh, and positive, so that vital energy becomes available. They build the muscle of accountability.

Self-coaching means you do this with yourself. As you work with your own self-coaching journal using four quadrant maps and other such templates your own potential opens powerfully.

Diamond Diagrams and Open-Ended Questions

When we declare, request, or promise, and when we ask any question in an open-ended way, the mind becomes creative. The four quadrant diamond form can be used as a discovery system to support this, especially when we combine it with open-ended questions. We move from solid, 'squared-off' assertions, a balance sheet of reasons why we cannot accomplish something to the 'moving diamond' of discovery. We can use the visual form itself to stimulate creativity, so that we become more flexible and willing to receive and discover new ideas.

Creativity always needs an active probe, both outward and inward, and then a receptive curiosity as to what the inner intuitive system will bring to conscious awareness in return. Harboring that receptivity is a key function of any wisdom state. It is also one functional result of drawing visual diagrams. For example, in your journal beyond any quadrant outline of itself, you can designate your purpose with 'starred ideas.'

Any congruent *visual* diagram inspires meaningful inward exploration, especially when we use it associatively with open-ended questions. The diagram itself becomes a holographic template that assists you to declare and request purposefully. The intuitive system then responds.

Once we start to declare or request with our diagrams, the flow of awareness continues, continues, and continues through all the playgrounds of exploration that we build. Any strong geometric diagrams, four quadrant forms or mandala-type pictograms can assist this receptivity. The flow of value opens into the ocean of value.

Four Quadrant Systems as Visual Declarations

What we have been saying is that geometric templates can be used as visual declarations. This is the skill I request you build and to move with. All charts of potential movement within whole systems can be used to move us towards clear visual declarations. For example, if you first declare the system to represent Self, Mind, Awareness, or any whole system, you can then use it to discover, ponder, review, and realize powerful visual declarations. You now are able to explore your integrity, capability, action, satisfaction, and completion within and through that context.

Your four quadrant drawing declares your mindscape. Using a four quadrant diagram as an awareness system, you can formulate a visual diagram as a form of quest. This leads to exploratory self-declarations as recipes for self-awareness. You can then use such a diagram to develop strong visual flashes of the relevant futures you wish to create. Your mind expands to develop this playground. You might notice the article, *Nine Aspects of a Diagram* (see Appendix 5, The Secret Life of Diagrams), which details key aspects that can be used to build a rich self-discovery matrix.

Detailing makes a difference. Consider a four quadrant drawing being used to explore life satisfaction in key areas. Amazingly, the coding on your four quadrant drawings then has huge impact. A 'future-pointing' arrow can become an attractor that *powerfully asks your inner questions for you, as you ponder.*

You might show small arrows moving from the center, one out of ten, towards 'ten out of ten' satisfaction at each point. Those arrows are very important parts of that visual exploration because we use them to declare movement and further discovery. Each time we draw them, we naturally make an inner request, to which the intuitive system responds with a flow of visionary ideas and 'next step' conjectures.

Context is often the missing framework as we detail our lives. With our four quadrant drawings seen as movement system, every content gets powerfully linked to a declaration of context. We begin to move from a 'content' drawing to the wider contextual observation of our creative purpose. Next steps appear. We 'flash' on our insights, and surprising shifts occur.

In drawing four quadrant diagrams, it is important to make them as symmetrical as you can. When you use your diagram for observational thinking, you are in creative-question mode. What you experience externally is mirrored internally through the mirror neuron system, which works with all visuals. Once we create an internal 'mind visual' it is now ours to develop creatively. In contrast, if you treat your pictures as just taking notes, just writing down the past, the mind holds your pictures as only notes. Instead, use drawings as 'visual white-boards.' They now become a moving system that *prompts* to support deep value questions and future visions.

Call such templates 'white-board discovery systems' when used as tools and as prompts. By adding quadrants, arrows, wheels, and scales, you start the effective exploration of your own creative 'what ifs.' With such a whiteboard you can ponder productively, encouraging wide-ranging flashes of insight.

What is experienced externally is mirrored internally. The brain linkages naturally follow powerful drawings, as do the visualizations. You become able to develop and review your choices both dissociatively and associatively in terms of the wider context. The drawings provoke inner connection. Realizations happen.

Any four quadrant map of the mind offers a simple whiteboard for the development of courage and vision. We begin with questions and balanced drawings thus opening a 'wave' of self exploration. We find ourself opening further into fields of knowledge that gradually expand all aspects of our life. We jump-start powerful, dynamic, visual exploration zones, and create ongoing self-discovery.

If you stay in the *process* of exploration by using a balanced diamond diagram of potential futures, the inner process of self-discovery starts to become integral and coherent. The coherency becomes more and more visually available. Even our outward perception of the world around us shifts to become more balanced. As we proceed, the intuitive mind renews our outer perception creatively.

We observe that our own inner truth grows clearer and clearer, and it shows up in our comprehensive inner seeing as well as in our outer vision of the world. The wider the matrix system we have built — past, present, future — and the deeper the value base — the more powerfully we are attracted to complete what we have begun! Beauty appears outwardly, and commitment appears inwardly. As we link our map to multi-layered purpose and meaning it becomes more and more stable. It becomes a system of deep integrity, emerging into daily moments of gusto and joy.

Wholeness: What is it?

Our inner system is an energy system with the potential for huge connection power. With empowerment and all declarations (to ourselves or to anyone), *we are talking both to and from the All, all of the time.*

As we visualize wholeness, wholeness becomes the truthful context for all aspects of our life. This means that we begin to deeply understand the power of all inner declaration, both auditory and visual, and we also understand the deep responsibility of our choices. The inner field of knowledge and value becomes more and more connected to our purpose. When we *see* this movement in our four quadrant form, it naturally draws us forward.

When we are consciously aware of our life as a field of *becoming*, we get grounded in *Being*. We become *committed* because we realize (real eyes) that we are responsible. We develop response-ability. Our life becomes a prayer of service because we understand the vibrational nature of inner truth. We become resonant with this, a committed playground builder.

Prayer and 'Visual Declarations'

Notice that when we study the inner nature of declarations, promises, and requests, we are exploring a form of *prayer*. Prayer means that the 'value level' of our life has been made present at *every* level — a conscious matrix-of-mind that 'holds the value' so that we access it naturally. The value of all our awareness is speaking into All.

Why has prayer been so important through the generations? Prayer is by no means just a religious idea. True prayer means offering visual and verbal 'blessings' as positive, affirmative declarations into the vast fields of inner *Becoming*. Prayer means that we declare a 'generous' inner reach to others and to self: promising truth, intuition, gratitude, and generosity into life. We promise to share all aspects of fundamental awareness between self and others. We are promising our 'all' to the All.

As soon as we develop our capacity for prayer, we also develop the capacity to ask deep and important questions. Notice that — with any powerful declaration based on 'sensing' and 'holding' inner truth — we start to have a higher and wider reach towards strong commitment and inner flow. We get connected to a larger sense of '*we*,' multiple and inclusive. We get connected to the experience of being able to dissolve all our old fear-based assertions, and to forgive all our old fear-based habits. Paradoxically, inner movement begins through visualizing wholeness, and we hold our requests and promises as part of our very *Being*.

We have moved beyond the limits of negative or past-oriented assertions and built the capacity to trust the flow of value in our inner system. We access inner creativity and the generous quality of the generation of diversity.[18]

A strong four quadrant vision develops who we are. As we declare and affirm our values as the field of our life, the universe also changes. If we build our prayer auditorily and visually as well as in our feelings, any systemic vision we create assists us to move forward. We are developing the inner balance and flexibility to make our visions real.

Incremental Manifestation

Our visual declaration, our creation, is like a stone hitting a pond. With our templates of mind, and our whiteboard visuals, we can assist ourselves to see the ripples begin moving out, in gentle outward expansion. Through visual expansion, the ripples of awareness just keep growing incrementally. This means that through clear, visual declarations, you become the amazed owner of a vast, every-expanding awareness system. You can see the next steps before you and relish the ones you have already made. You, yourself now *become* the integrative quality of mindfulness in self-expression.

Here is a story from a friend, that demonstrates how this can work, even from a simple, strong tonal declaration.

"When I was 19 years old, years ago, I was a climber in a climbing club during the period when there was martial law in Poland. It was called the 'crackdown,' which meant we couldn't travel, even to the next town. At some point a climber from another club came to our climbers meeting and said, 'Who wants to go to Himalayas?' He went to each person and asked, 'Do you want to go to the Himalayas?' and they all replied, 'Not possible, it's martial law,' or 'I can't, I don't have money.' Near the end of the meeting, he came to me, and his words created visions. The visions drew me like a magnet. Somehow, from my innermost heart came the voice, 'I'm going!' And it took another nine months, but I made it happen. I found surprising ways to make lots of money and somehow it actually became possible. It happened. I found myself a member of a real Himalayan expedition when I was just 20 years old. This first expedition was organized by a student who lived in the same city as myself. And it just opened my life. And the next year, I organized my own expedition."

For us, as listeners, it's very useful to become really clear about how to listen to any person's visual and verbal declarations — as well as your own declarations — *as a form of manifestation.* We need to listen actively to hear the *manifestation* quality. Once we notice visualization and speech as manifestation, we clearly begin to experience it on all levels. *Through our declarations, we manifest our lives.*

We can listen to all declarations, from self or others, with *'empowerment ears'!* Again, this is similar with any committed prayer — visual, tonal, and with feeling!

What Assists Us to Manifest Powerfully?

Three aspects of commitment build a powerful 'attractor' field that formulate the next step in building our intelligence. We manifest this when we listen to declarations as a powerful formal commitment, like a prayer.

- First, we *manifest a clear and complete system.* Any balanced holistic map assists this.
- Second, we *promise* wholeness *at the action level.* We see our manifestation as reality in action.
- And, third, we *declare a Coach Position* on our promises. We declare a wide view on all our possibilities. We commit to keep committing.

This means, both visually and verbally, we learn to create both the *map* and the *territory* of the mind. The maps we create, the templates we use, and the prayers we wish to fulfill now expand our 'identity' to match the possibilities we commit to. Gradually they determine our wider territory of Mind. We request clear sight, and build clear *insight.* We build clear maps of inner integrity so that we can promise alignment to inner integrity.

A four quadrant map assists us to create a Coach Position on our inner world. Declarations, promises, requests, and prayers assist us to enter this creative process, a process of pondering and enlarging our committed life. We create a map of wholeness and therefore continuously think with and abide in our declaration of wholeness. We can then learn to manifest what we choose to envision through powerful inner requests and active promises.

And now a prayer for you.

May vast Intelligence become your native land. May expanded Mind-realization become your self-awareness system. May you find yourself at home in our inner dynamic wholeness; a star-spangled universe of all of us together. Hail!

Expanding Key Areas with Four Quadrant Exploration

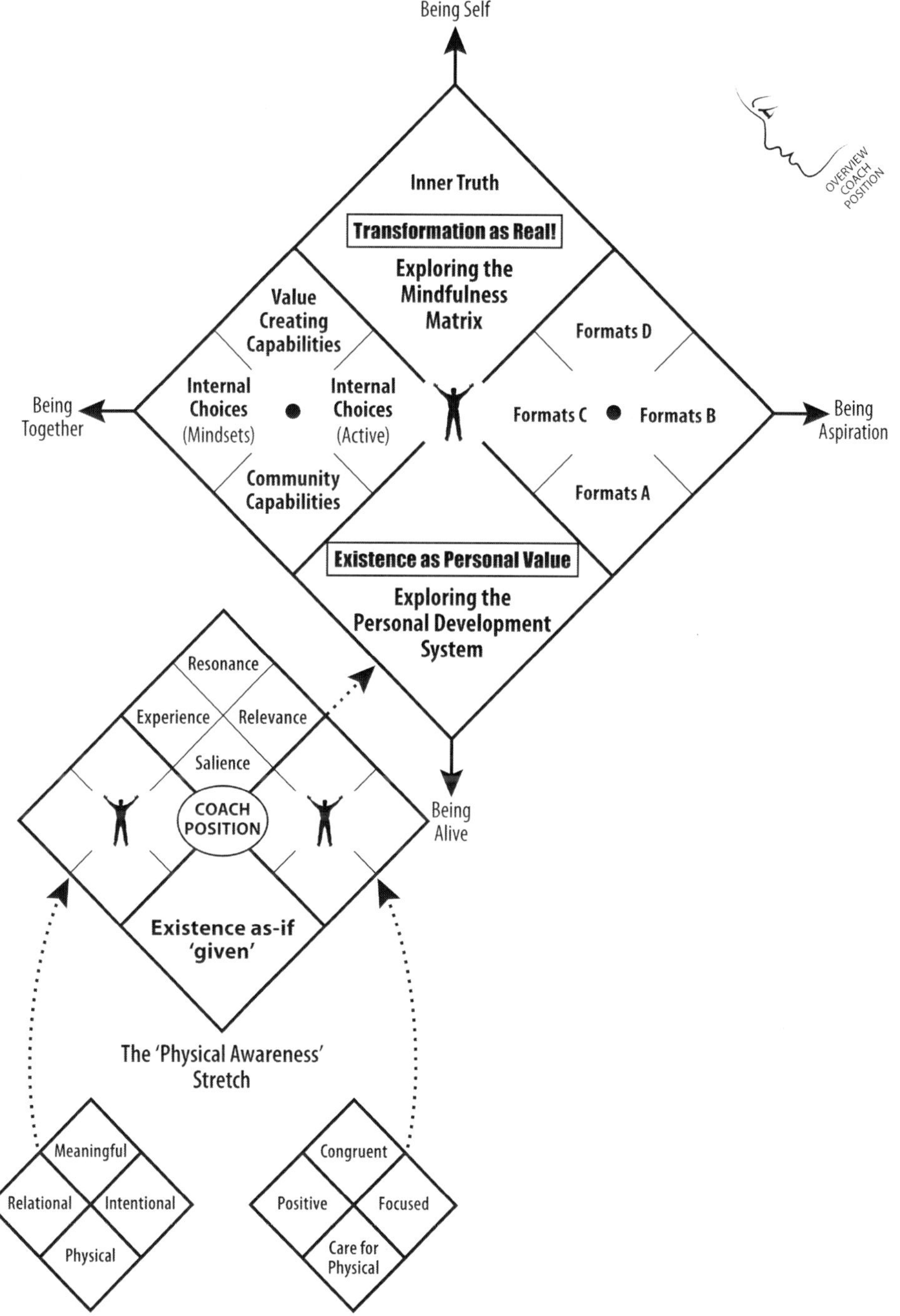

APPENDICES

APPENDICES

APPENDIX I:

Developing Coach Position

What is Coach Position?

Coach Position a neutral, detached, and non-judgmental observer viewpoint. We activate a perspective on a situation we are in as if from the outside looking in. This is probably useful when you need to step into an observational framework from which to relax and explore current awareness in its totality. In what you might call 'Zen-detached witness posture,' you can overview the elements of a whole system.

Before we can change anything, especially our thoughts or feelings, we need to be able to overview them. Holding Coach Position on your life also means *making sense of — and creating awareness from — the perspective of the whole system.* It means declaring inwardly your willingness to hold a wide-angled scope as well as a neutral, non-judgmental viewpoint on your life activities.

Coach Position might be described as the pivotal gear in an amazingly beautiful, complex, and precise instrument made up of many moving parts. The Coach Position 'point' is central to observing the mechanism in action. From the inside, it organizes the capacity for all parts and perspectives of the system to be beneficial and to work in harmony. From the outside, it offers a broadened perspective of all components and the overview awareness of the interconnectedness of the whole. From Coach Position, the coach sees the 'point' of life unfolding as much more than the sum of its parts. This is a creative viewpoint. We actively create what we are observing.

From the point of view of your working conscious mind, taking a neutral detached witness posture may seem less engaged and even boring. Yet the riches of developing a detached viewpoint bring true transformation.

The Flow of Truth

All points of view in a system are partially true and therefore, limiting. When a person is awakened to the fact that there is no one absolute right viewpoint in any situation, he or she becomes free to expand that awareness, and to start exploring many perspectives. As we lessen our attachment to our old habitual stance, our creativity naturally increases. We develop the freedom to relax and observe the flow of mind within the unfolding moment.

By definition, there is always an observational Coach Position one step beyond each more limited perspective. Consider that to support ourselves and others to understand our own aims deeply, to have rich relationships, reach goals, live a life we love, and so on, we need to provide ourselves a viewing platform to look *and* see our world from a variety of perspectives rather than being swallowed by only one viewpoint, often a limiting one. For example, suppose there is an amazing event that occurs and five people witness it, there will be five different viewpoints or personal truths, each representing a part of the whole truth. The flexibility of taking a more expansive outlook provides and allows for the capacity to change viewpoints, to shift beyond any one gear or any perceptual position to also see the other perspectives. We learn to temporarily move beyond our judgments, preferences, and reactions. With Coach Position awareness, people can organically become more resourceful and, therefore, more likely to get what they really want from the situation at hand.

Coach Position is always a moving perspective, central to seeing the whole landscape of your life, yet *wider* than that landscape. Taking Coach Position on your inner conversations means observing a range of thinking, perhaps the most expanded framework to explore your thought development, up to now, while simultaneously finding the deepest center of your own inner truth. With each position, you move to overview what is going on in your life.

The Expanded Perspective on Conversations

With a commitment to Coach Position, we develop a very subtle, yet powerful, flow of expanded awareness. In other words, you awaken to the flow of wide-frame observation. You open yourself to your more expanded self and thereby open that wider perspective to those you speak with as well. This makes it very important, especially for difficult conversations.

Entering Coach Position catalyzes the transformational power of any conversation. You naturally start building transformational awareness between yourself and the person you are speaking with. You develop trust with another by briefly stepping away from your own personal ideas to be truly curious about their discoveries. You ask open questions with genuine curiosity. This means you enter an expanse of relaxed awareness about this person's wider range of transformative aims, experiencing them here and now.

From Coach Position, you become able to hold a clear space for the person's exploration so he or she is free to also open up to their own range of useful viewpoints. As you do the same with yourself, a true dialogue can spark. From this expanded place, the flow of real conversation truly begins.

Visualizing Coach Position

There are many ways to enter Coach Position. It usually starts with an inward declaration and deep resolve. An effective step to learn is to enter Coach Position by *inner declaration*. An intentional and deliberate stance offers incredible value.

A strong way to strengthen Coach Position in difficult situations is to imaginatively look from at least '500 meters' above the situation you are viewing. Wayne Gretzky, the famous 20th-century Canadian hockey player developed this habit for difficult plays. In a competitive moment on the ice, and with the puck moving quickly between multiple players, he would look at the whole icefield as if from the stadium ceiling, viewing the trajectories of all the players, himself included. He would then quickly skate to where he visualized the puck would likely go several moves ahead. He was famous for being 'on the spot' in the right place at the right time, by 'pre-seeing' the plays.

An excellent analogy for Coach Position is the elevated viewing 'box' at major football stadiums that allows for multi-perspective viewing. If you are viewing a ball game, there are many high positions from which you might look.

Most 'close-at-hand' viewpoints tend to pull you inside, where you associate strongly with various players. Instead, try holding Coach Position from this skybox, the elevated viewpoint high above the field of action. Notice how this means we naturally enter a flow state of observational awareness. We see how all aspects work together and through time as well. This means *making sense or creating awareness from the perspective of the whole elastic system.* Coach Position can also include seeing the whole landscape of our life from the skybox and perhaps even the skybox beyond that.

In addition to the skybox metaphor, to do this well some people visualize sitting in a special overview chair; others visualize opening wide an awareness doorway or moving up an escalator into a higher viewing point, observing from a mountain peak or even imagine viewing from outer space or across time. What might work best for you? The key is expanded listening, sensing, and whole system viewing.

Reinforce the practice of Coach Position with a variety of visual metaphors just to try them:

- You might use your inner attention 'switch panel.' Specifically turn on the switches of curiosity and wide-level listening.
- You might move up the escalator floor by floor, always looking at the situation from an 'even higher' viewpoint.
- You might transform mind and attention with a colorful visualization of a 'magic wand touch,' seeing color development through time.

Our aim is to view our current 'position' from the widest possible lens. There are many different ways to build this muscle. We encourage you to develop your own playful way.

Move From Particle to Wave

Metaphorically, in mind-development terms, we start to move from 'part' or particle thinking (emphasizing only our own 'particular' perspective) to move into the 'wave' of development, seeing that wave of possibility as an ongoing movement. We playfully expand our dynamic viewpoint.

Make your wave of development a '*visual declaration*' by continuing to add visual elements that allow relaxed appreciation of what you are imagining.

Continue to maintain this overview as long as you can, as you ask open questions of yourself. You will soon learn how to instigate the flow of *spacious observational awareness and deep listening*.

Coach Position on Your Inner World

When taking Coach Position in your own life, the self that is holding Coach Position will take you into the heart of deep realization and awakened awareness. If you imagine yourself looking into a mirror, you soon learn to broaden your view to the landscape beyond. Your inner life promise assists all levels of self-awareness and perspective. This will naturally expand your consciousness and in turn expand your life.

The discipline required for this exploration won't always be easy. Taking an effective Coach Position in your own life involves genuine interest and dedication in the process of becoming more self-aware. This may mean thinking like a researcher or curious scientist: taking notes, detailing discoveries, and calibrating differences over time to see patterns and sequences. You view your life from a 'hero's journey' perspective, so that you dare to take the needed steps.

Coach Position on your own life involves consistent levels of self-observation. It requires the process of continuing to hone important open-ended questions and to send them inward. You learn to invite your own deeper knowing to view and think with you. This is valuable especially as we explore our own purpose to awaken to our larger life. An effective self-coach asks, "What do I receive as a core understanding, both from internal and external experiences now? What steps become right for me? What's next?"

Coach Position for oneself functions as an overview and witness position that makes it much easier to experiment with different points of view that may hold value for the inner project or conversation. Shifting points of view consciously from time to time to see, hear, and feel 'as others do.' We enlarge our capacities. To the extent that we look from our wise inner coach and from by as many points of view as possible, we collect various expansive ideas and concepts that we can then use to make informed choices. By taking Coach Position, especially on our idea of *self* and questioning from various perspectives, we create room for endless discovery.

Take Coach Position through daily 'expanded view' on your own projects checking *capabilities*, *tasks*, and *relationships*. This allows you to keep your boat of purpose afloat on the sea of life where there are multiple currents of attention. You are exploring your life goals to discover *true value.*

When we take Coach Position to overview our personal journey, we are able to build new maps. We light our inner fire and the passion for self-knowledge unfolds our creative life. We explore our life projects' as well as our own development from both inside and outside, enjoying the ideas and results without being attached to them.

Purposeful Overview Versus Contractive Dissociation

It is important to differentiate between relaxed, purposeful overview and the dissociation that children do automatically as a way to escape from fear and other negative emotions. Fear-based dissociation is organismic, a mechanism for quick 'emotional brain' regroup after trauma. It leads to habits of reactive dissociation that are one-pointed survival mechanisms, creating closure. Coach Position viewing is the opposite of this, widening choice and freedom. True Coach Position opens us so that we learn to overview our old internal dialogue, and witness old closure habits, while appreciating the younger person — ourself — who once built these necessary closure habits under pressure.

This assists us to notice we are free to experience emotions but also free to leave them alone. For example, I was once told about the death of a dear friend during a morning break in a course I was teaching. The program was complex and required my full attention. I took Coach Position on my grief and on the moment's strong emotions and moved high above them with appreciation and love for myself and my friend. I asked my unconscious mind to maintain this overview awareness for the rest of the day's program. Later, at home, I consciously released this, allowing the tears to fall.

Negative internal dialogue tends to accompany contractive dissociation. With Coach Position, we discover how to naturally view and then to forgive this negative internal dialogue learned for self-protection and emotional dissociation. We now can view our assembly of personal grievances and self-recriminations as simply a relevant stage in our own evolution. When we take Coach Position on the stages of our life, we can grow beyond that stage, even as all the old emotions remain available if we want them.

To grow, we need to appreciate these old emotions and understand their function. This means we let go of the old personal judgment and self-criticism and see ourself as evolution's gift, someone to love. We realize that our practice of Coach Position makes a difference to all who come after us. Viewing from outside gives us the possibility to design more freedom into our life. Through this we become able to create a field of shared consciousness which also includes more freedom for everyone around us.

In 1973, as a young psychologist, I participated for one year in a school of psychology that focused on "feeling and expressing the hidden negative feelings you find in yourself." We learned how to dig for them, then express them. "Take a pillow; turn it into Mummy. Show her how you really feel," were the typical instructions of the 'feeling therapy' senior psychologists. Observing the expression from myself and others, over that one-year period I found them basically harmful; because negative *expression* continues to reverberate. This can be replaced by simply watching feelings as they arise in the body, stepping in to note the intensity and feeling them free of a personal story.

All expression has resonance and gets recorded tonally when expressed, but *feeling an inward sensation without expressing it does not.* When we add Coach Position to each body response we now make Coach Position our true living platform, and the old feelings and beliefs gradually relax. This gives us renewed ability to live in the present in a position of choice. From the Quantum metaphor, we are staying with our larger wave of possibility invoking all of it including our future, rather than falling into and expressing one emotional part, or 'particle.'

We remain with the wave of Allness — and as it expands even more — all can be seen, felt, and acknowledged. You see your thoughts and feelings come and go with appreciation and compassion. You are expanding *as* awareness, experiencing the 'wave' of freedom.

Exercise: Your Inner Creative Lens: Building Wide-Frame Attention in Five Minutes

Do you have a special spot where you go occasionally to think through your plans?

For example, some of us may have a small bench in a special corner of the garden; others have a spot in a local park or at the end of a dock on the bay. Those in more rustic environments may choose overview points such as a mountaintop, hillside, or a high cliff above the ocean. Occasionally people create a special room filled with their meditation pictures and special music. Aldous Huxley, for example, had a private den with his special "creativity chair," where he simply would sit and open his "inner creativity lens." His best ideas would often come to him in that chair after this simple ritual.

Find such a spot in your mind's eye, connect with your heart so that ou sense the resonant inner expanse. Are you prepared? Here are the steps:

- Plan to remain in Coach Position, mindfully in this special spot, as you do a short, 5-minute life overview regarding your key purposes and plans.
- Set a timer for five minutes, if you have one handy.
- In your mind's eye, enter your special spot for yourself, and imaginatively settle yourself there. You can do this visually or with a genuine physical location. In other words, put yourself in your own personal version of your skybox.
- As you visualize your perfect 'expanding spot' for Coach Position, step in, relax, and breathe deeply and comfortably. Imaginatively turn on your inner camera. Do you see the switch?
- Now, deliberately start to witness your current life in a detached way. Settle into the flow of spacious awareness from Coach Position, and observe whatever shows up on your life observation screen.
- From time to time, breathe deeply, sense the aliveness of your body. Both metaphorically and physically, now perceive the current moment through all your senses — seeing, hearing, and feeling.
- Now ask yourself some basic future thinking questions that link strongly to your aim. For example, *"What do I truly want in my life right now?"* What do I want to give my strength to to energize this possibility?

Once you get a response, rest in this awareness and ask, "What do I want through having that, which is even more important?" Close your eyes and feel each response. Own the deeper meaning. You then might ask: "What values do I want to live and feel in my body each moment of each day?"

These questions keep opening Coach Position further. Now, from Coach Position, expand your viewing lens to the widest frame of purpose for your whole life. Look out, and — at the same time — into your inner world at the same time, over-viewing your purpose and its fulfillment through your whole life. Do not settle into or become intertwined into any specific areas that grab your attention. Allow yourself to expand your larger awareness. As you do, maintain the widest possible view on all ideas, aspirations, images, and thoughts that emerge in the context of your whole life and your larger purpose. Allow inspiration to be your context. Notice what comes up that you have never thought of before.

Remaining in Coach Position, notice this expanded position as a powerful context of meaning and purpose. You are awakening your life purpose even as you relax and observe. It may simply be a 'felt awareness' or something else that you recognize as your own inner home. Notice it as a crucible for development, and appreciate it!

Also notice that Coach Position continues to emerge and expand. There is always a Coach Position even more expansive than this one, and this next is always available as a viewpoint whenever we want to explore and try it on. All emergent awareness is a form of Coach Position.

Notice how your consciousness has expanded and how it feels. Enjoy this spacious awareness as long as you like.

Now, simply return to your special spot in your mind's eye and center yourself in Coach Position again. When ready, exit Coach Position and return back into your current location now. Then, open your eyes.

What was the value of the exercise for you?

Entering and exiting Coach Position can be a fulfilling process throughout the day. The best time to practice is when you find yourself in a mindless moment. This might be a specific old thought system where you are living out a dysfunctional pattern of some type. In these times, become aware. Stop. Enter Coach Position, explore awareness in its totality from this expanded perspective, and then respond to your true inner life.

Try it! See how heart-warming and expansive it can be. Abandon the wandering mind, hitchhiking on old emotions. Life emerges in brilliant awareness when you make your choices from an expanded Coach Position.

Multiple Viewpoints

Notice how valuable it is to explore the mind in various associated and dissociated ways. With any geometric shape that has a center point we easily learn to view our ideas from many positions. We can immediately start with two types of observer or Coach Position viewpoints: associative, heart-connected; and dissociative, vision-connected.

Diagram A1.1: Expanding Value, from the Center

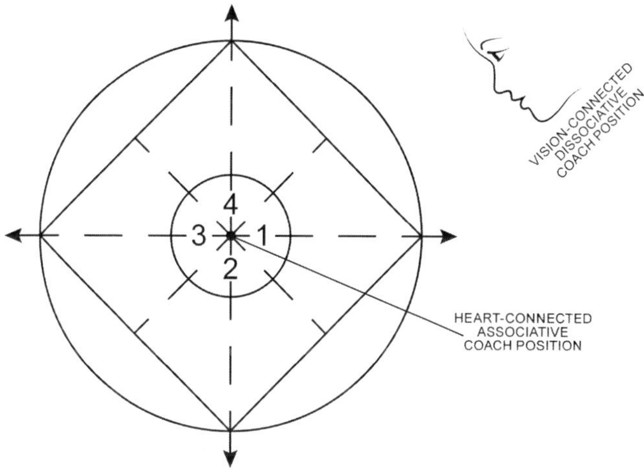

What is the basic principle here? *People expand self-knowledge when they explore any idea in ways that allow both associated and dissociated overview exploration.*

Maps are designed to be used as *process recipes*. The best ones are simple, but not simplistic. They are designed to promote self-discovery, both inward and outward. They allow us to remember to view a context even as we dive in. Use them to build your own mind-manifesting self-explorations.

We humans love balanced spaces with a center to orient from. We use them everywhere in life. Think of the old town squares throughout all the cities of Europe and Asia. We can look out across the square and sense the wholeness of the community. We can feel this value unification, even as we walk across the town square to the breakfast café. In the same way, we want to overview our mind system, yet to also move around in it with the ability to find the detailed areas of 'mindful inner exploration' that may interest us. At all times, we also want to *sense the whole:* the expansive space of awareness.

APPENDIX 2:

Definitions of Key Terms & Concepts

Four Quadrant Diagramming

Volume I discusses four quadrant diagramming and its purpose in Chapter 1, pages 5 to 9. Also see endnotes 4 and 6. Our rule is to keep all diagrams as simple as possible. Keeping the number of segments at 4 satisfies a whole host of conditions starting with the practicality of our conscious mind attention span (endnote 7), through the necessity to cover major areas/dimensions of the mind in order to create complete pictures of it. This includes the conditions of beauty and symmetry which run deep into the notions of symmetry and isomorphism of all the manifested phenomena in our Universe, as well as the dimensionality of space-time itself.

The four quadrant structured map covers the major dimensions of the mind and provides the space for full pictures of many mind processes to emerge with extraordinary precision. four quadrant diagramming provides a powerful aid to awareness because it allows us to quietly bring in fresh insight and intuitions through the visual power of the mind to explore itself. Self-exploration can then reach beyond preset habitual assumptions of perception.

Association and Dissociation

Associated Coach Position: Why do we need to study Coach Position associated as well as dissociated? The simple answer is that with Coach Position associated the mind is inside its own process and hence, in principle cannot see the whole of itself. It is like being inside a thumbnail on your cell phone, which you cannot click to open. On the positive side however, the person in associated Coach Position can sense the process itself, experiencing life itself with all VAK data input. The person is able to make free choices based on the data. This is a basis of internal

Truth. This is a first level process when a person directly senses the VAK of the situation/self at the moment NOW. Later, when dissociated Coach Position is added, we are able to learn effectively from the process. We are using four ways to designate Coach Position Associated: the central smiley face, a star shape, the little man in the middle with arms extended, and the words Coach Position in the middle of an oval. I vary them because I want people to try them on.

Dissociated Coach Position, *Overview Position*: is taking the aware point of view of self (the sensed seat of awareness) out of the situation/self by overviewing, as if from outside, with a full picture of the situation/self.

This is a second order process when the 'seat of awareness' transfers out of body and mainly sees the original situation including the original VAK. This second order process includes of course a second order full VAK exploration of meaning. In doing this, you can now map, "What I sense about my original situation and my sensing of that situation." Hence it is a meta state on the original state and as a meta state it has power over the original state. It can change/rearrange the components in order to achieve change. However, it does not allow for 'living' experience, full VAK in the moment of NOW. We 'see' our experience and feel our values about that, creating a new level of integration.

Coach Position associated and dissociated form a paradoxical complementary system. A paradox cannot be 'solved' by leaning towards one or the other aspect exclusively. The paradox needs to be managed by taking a both/and viewpoint rather than an either/or viewpoing and holding both positions alternatively. This will maximize the richness of discover and learning. This process strongly supports four quadrant Dynamic Intelligence.

Dynamic Intelligence

There is a definition of Dynamic Intelligence in Part 1, Chapter 1 on page 4: "What then is mindfulness?..." Another useful term for Dynamic Intelligence is mindfulness. Mindfulness starts as a "... process of simply observing unfolding intelligence as it opens before us. We might describe both intelligence development and mindfulness as the ability to accentuate and expand awareness through whole system attention. We notice our 'level' and 'kind' of consciousness. We become aware of awareness. A new level of intelligence or integration begins to form."

Dynamic Intelligence is very different from static intelligence. The combination of words "Dynamic" with "Intelligence" characterizes on one side the ability of the mind to self-develop and to reach a new level of self-overview as a result of conscious processes performed by the mind on the mind itself. This is best noticed with processes when the mind observes its own complete map, structured into four quadrants. Then that observation creates new awareness and adds new elements to the map. The mind grows with the growing map beyond its original boundaries. On the other side dynamic intelligence allows the mind to focus its attention down to minute details of the map and perform effective operations on some life project, leading to results with efficiency and ease.

Intelligence

We can define *Intelligence* as the coherent combination of our detailed, granular focus with our wider contextual overview built from many 'takes' on our perception. Intelligence means activating wholeness of vision and thought combined with feelings and inner states, and combining with the physical ability to act upon all of it.

Intelligence thereby, means the richness of united inner meaning manifesting on all levels. This is very different than simple intellect; which activates a collection of methodologies.

Metaphor of the Mind Compass and Time Dimension

The point here is as follows: The mind has a minimum of 8 fundamental dimensions. (Consider this as a working assumption — not confirmed by experiments.) These coalesce from our perception, evaluation, intention, and attention. Observing these four processes in action allows us to take effective Coach Position on the quality of our various thought processes.

Metaphors of Staircases as Steps of Development

This metaphor signifies the daily practice of exploring the mind and exercising mindful process, hence building new skills up to the point of unconscious execution. However, unconscious execution of a skill could lead to habit and no flexibility at all, so breakthrough explorations — as with the elevator and accordion — are also helpful.

For example, the elevator metaphor signifies quick movement up or down. Activating this metaphor, the mind's point of awareness moves up, acquiring a big overview, or down, zooming into the detailed elements. This ability allows the mind to keep track of the big picture, allows helicopter views on various realities.

The metaphors of the elevator and stairs comparatively and together form a paradox. Each provides a different 'thumbnail' for movement and developmental learning that needs to be opened separately. As a paradox this cannot be simply solved. The mind learns as it continues to generate both metaphors. We need to manage the paradox forward by making use of the positive value of both approaches — fast exploration with the elevator and the more gradual practice towards learning and integration as indicated by the stairs.

Mind Playground

A balanced — yet moving — relational network which can be explored as a holistic system of complimentary elements. (See Chapter 2, p.22.)

Thumbnail Agreements

Metaphorically, these are low resolution agreements or 'life metaphors' at all levels of content, structure, process, and form about the nature of identity, life, mind, and world.

Thumbnail Diagrams

Metaphorically, these are low resolution *diagrams* about how identity, life, mind, world, etc. are constructed.

The Time Exploration in Four Quadrant Work

Time is basically the change we notice in space when we perceive from one observation to the next one. That which is being observed, whether outside or inside, is brought in by VAK data, which are in principle 4-dimensional. We experience these perceptions timelessly. These show 3 space dimensions and 1 time dimension. We perceive space directly, but time only in a secondary fashion. This gives us a total of 8 dimensions, which can be mapped beautifully on a four quadrant map, (4 dimensions layered over it are formed by the observational process. There might be an additional dimension, dimension 9, related to the imaginary capacity since this is performed by our lack of conscious "handling capacity" with much more of the data being received by the unconscious areas of the mind.

Compare Your Experience of Space and Time.

For all humans, time, as an idea, is much less real than space. We draw a four quadrant map with the space-time data of what is observed, as well as the 4 axes of "process" over it. We then choose what the perception is related to, either space or time or both. We can include time as a larger frame using a timeline to represent this aspect, and this means we can toggle them around. If we tune in our attention to any specific focus NOW, then our perception naturally moves to a special focus first, say a picture or a tree or an inside vision. Our next awareness will then be time, as change. Notice that when our observation includes a timeline, it requires more skill, like floating above in space and focusing on changes within the space.

While exploring, it is useful to distinguish the diamond shape and frame of four quadrants as a holistic map of mind space. This becomes a visual declaration, allowing inner and outer exploration to proceed. Only then it becomes effective to draw the process of various four quadrant observations made individually and uniquely through the mind compass axes. The time element emerges as we do this.

APPENDIX 3:

The Content, Structure, Process, and Flow of Ideas

All ideas have a secret life. They are an evolutionary system, evolving through the continual adjustment of various specific contents, a structure of growth, a creative process, and a compelling inner form that flows. Together these four create an as-if 'entity' of thought. As idea creators, we dance in the experience of these four aspects. We focus on the unfolding.

Notice that all ideas contain these four aspects. They have a *form* of completion, the intentional meansings a formal quality. They have an as-if creative *process* of development, and processes for developing further. They have an as-if *structure* of antecedent thought and accomplished elements. The structure is like the record, the scaffolding of the idea's development that traces the steps in its emergence, simple or complex, elegant or awkward. And, all ideas have an as-if *content*, the part we all notice. When all other aspects are congruent, we can be content.

Content

First, let's notice content. Content is one of the easiest aspects of our thoughts to recognize. The content of an idea is like the plot line in a story. It provides detail and specifics. I am writing this page of ideas now — one specific bounded idea after another. We select and specify content. Yet to examine content well, we need to attend to various contextual aspects. We might summarize these by carefully examining the sentence components implied by the following sentence: *(I) (am) (saying) (this) (to you) (in this context)*. Notice that for every sentence, five aspects each require a separate examination for content components. Each and every one of these aspects makes a difference to the whole idea structure and its comprehensive meaning.

Structure

To examine structure, we ponder historical antecedents. With structure we are looking at the scaffoldings of thoughts and their emergence from earlier thoughts. To write this page shows the traces of many inherent, evolutionary structures; the earlier structures of thoughts, emotions and behavior that seemingly produce this set of ideas and underpin the capacity to refer to it.

Playfully, we can follow each structure all the way back to basics. For example, examine the techniques of *writing* in itself. Obviously, this provides a major structural development of our idea. For example, a previous attempts to write, or to correlate thoughts on a surface, are all rolled up into this one emergent event, a scaffolding of mind moments that can be traced backwards, event by prior event. They link together right up to this experience now. Along the structural scaffolding we can notice former landmarks moving backward, such as the development of writing as a communication mode, the development of alphabets, and even the development of language itself.

Creative Process

A creative process can be articulated in one moment as a forward movement now. It often includes open-ended questions, as-if formulations, and perceptive, compelling visions. The process of writing this page includes sparkling mind moments of sudden perception and creative evaluation. A process can be seen by noticing the interaction between the action elements and the intentional movement towards solutions. Our thought stream is developing through a process of perceiving distinctions. We evaluate them, reperceive them and re-evaluate them, moving towards greater opportunities or clearer formulations.

Form

Form is a kernel essence or ideal containing the fundamental aim. The formal communication from me to you holds a comprehensive vision, feeling, and aspirational inner logic, thereby producing an aesthetic experience of inner order. We experience this quality of "such-ness," we sense the flow of form, and we notice the core aesthetic, including the ongoing flow of awareness.

The Truth Function (Flow)

Together these four core aspects of idea production, the content, the structure, the process and the form constitute the truth function of any idea. As William Blake expressed it, "Truth is how the creation works."

To the extent that we understand and inter-relate form, process, structure and content we can create powerful and useful ideas. We can organize the function of the idea so that it demonstrates its own strong inherent order that is coherent, comprehensive, aspirational and whole. In searching for the inner order we learn to appreciate and add value to the deeper meaning. Truth gets revealed through our constant check for the inner inspirational self-consistency of all ideas that we examine.

Are we not always aiming our attention — and intention — to discover our own inner ordering system? We are encouraging our self and others to develop all aspects in our own lives, bringing in both system balance and cohereence unfolding next steps. We assist others as they examine the long-term *form* of a life well lived, build *structures* that support, and dive into the creative *process* of designing and appreciating wholeness. We become *content!*

APPENDIX 4:

Symbols and Shapes

The Symbols and Shapes Exploration Exercise

Let's explore further some aspects of our own abstracting process by studying visual symbols and our inner manifestation of meaning. This next exercise is a diagnostic tool that can deliver some interesting points of departure for self-exploration. It allows you to explore some fundamental forms. Because there are many different game boards to play with, internal and external, this type of exploration can open up your sensing.

Our use of fundamental forms is based on a metaphor, yet it is more than a metaphor. To start, find a piece of paper and quickly draw five common geometric symbols: The forms we will explore in our exercise will be an equidistant cross, an equilateral triangle, a square or diamond, a spiral, and a circle.

I invite you, on a fresh piece of paper, to draw these five forms: a circle, a square, an equal-sided triangle, an equal-sided cross, and a spiral. Each symbol provides a strong framework for developing three-dimensional spatial thinking and each can assist with mind organization and development, known as the geometric basics. (There are a lot of other geometric shapes we could use, but they usually contain these five.) No matter how you have drawn them, these are well-known geometric containers.

What I would like you to do is just notice your preferences as you draw these forms, and number them preferentially, one to five. As soon as you have them on a piece of paper, prioritize them: Put them in 1 to 5 order.

Once prioritized, study your preferences in the drawings you have made. What did you choose as your first, second, third, fourth, and fifth preference? If you are reading this, please try this exercise now.

A Brief History of Traditional Symbol Use

Anthropologically, we have contemplated these five shapes from generation to generation and made each of them culturally significant, both as two-dimensional and as three-dimensional forms. They are found in all human communities through recorded human history. They provide common visual ideas for clothing design, pottery design, and floor pattern design. Furthermore, each of them has been a symbolic central icon for some of the world's great religious systems. Notice also that they are important to mathematicians and are core to the study of geometry.

Diagram A4.1: Format C: The Formal Mind

Now, in all cultures what is interesting is that these shapes have a common meaning.

I have for many years travelled in various areas of the world home to antiquities: Roman, Greek, and others.

Ancient mosaic floors in old Roman homes are decorated with these shapes. Spiritual places all over the world use these basic designs; crosses, pyramids, and domes. You know them all well. What are the traditional values attached to these shapes? Notice that there are meanings that have been assigned for centuries in multiple cultures.

What Do the Symbols Mean?

As symbols what do these forms infer? What do they signify?

- In almost all cultures, a circle or sphere signifies *unity.*
- Similarly, in most cultures, an equal-sided cross symbolizes relationship.
- A triangle or pyramid often signifies 'a pointed effort' the 'hero's quest,' or 'breaking through.'
- A spiral signifies unfolding newness and difference.
- A square usually symbolizes strength, solidarity and foundation.

Preference Orders and Habitual Fixes

Let us examine these symbols in the light of these common meanings often attached to any preference ordering in itself.

The standard breakdown in assessing and ordering preferences is as follows:

As we sort through preferences, they generally are ordered according to the following criteria:

- Number one is what our attention is on; what we are dazzled by, what we think we want.
- Number two is always a choice that is easy for us. It's often so easy we don"t notice we can do it well.
- Number three is frequently what 'runs the show' in our lives; what we're really working with day by day in the key areas of attention.

- Number four is often where we get stuck. It causes us difficulty. It's a focal point where we need to do some strong exploratory development.
- Number five is frequently 'off the map' for us. We normally may not put much attention on it at all.

These orderings also tie to basic learning steps. Each time we learn anything valuable, we first begin our learning cycle with a new distinction that catches our attention and inspires us. Second, we then notice how it is the same as other previous distinctions. Third, we discover and hunt for the contrastive elements. And fourth, we integrate this with our larger picture or greater conception. All dissolves as five starts a new cycle.

In summary:

- First: What is new?
- Second: What is the same?
- Third: What is developing for us?
- Fourth: What is difficult?
- Fifth: What is invisible, still to emerge as another cycle with other elements?

How did these interpretations fit with your own preference ordering when you tried the exercise? Are any of these inferences relevant to yourself? Did they make sense to your own inner ordering of the symbols? Check them now:

- Number one: What's true for you?
- Number two: What's true for you?
- Number three: What's true for you?
- Number four: What's true for you?
- Number five: What's true for you?

For most people, there are some interesting correspondences between their preference orderings and assessments and the habits and personal meanings they attach to key areas of life.

Symbols, Colors, and Sounds

Let's do a little personal work with this map you have created so that you can explore it still further. For all five visual symbols, find a color just for that symbol, and add it to the symbol inwardly. And now, for all five, allow yourself to formulate a sound for each — listening for what sounds right. Proceed until each one has a color and a sound. Stop reading until this is complete. Return when you have a color and a sound for each one.

Now, for each symbol, add in a rhythm, vibration, or movement. In your mind's eye, see them expressing this movement. Each now has a color, a sound and a movement. View them each, one by one, with all of these characteristics as part of your inner representation.

Let's play with this for a moment. Explore our next exercise temporarily as a 'what would happen if' question. Later, you can decide to keep the result if you wish or 'put it back' the way it was.

Inwardly, give the color, sound, and rhythm that you have already assigned to number one to number three. See the number three with the color, sound, and rhythm of number one.

You are giving what you really want more of, what you are moving towards most strongly, but which hasn't yet become fully available to you to the area which is working strongly in your life and which you give the most attention to each day. What happens when you do that?

Now, in the same spirit of inquiry, give the color, sound, and rhythm of number two, the area that is easy for you, to number four, the area that is most difficult. What happens in your experience when you do that?

Finally, give the original qualities of number three — the specific color, sound, and rhythm, to number five. When you apply this color, sound, and rhythm of number three, the area that is occupying much of your daily attention to number five, the area that is not in your attention at all, what happens here?

With all these shifts, you perhaps will notice interesting visual, auditory and kinesthetic inner responses. Shifting these symbols, for some persons, produces real inner changes. It may produce deep feelings in the center of the body that you enjoy or maybe do not want. I have had people in my groups talk about feeling deep shifts when they start to add in different colors, sounds and vibrations to these very basic symbols. Some suddenly feel ecstasy and release. Others, some inward chaos to navigate. A new emergence.

For some of you making these shifts may add powerfully to your inner sense of harmony. It may produce an enhanced sense of harmony, balance, flexibility, and excitement about life. If this is the case, keep the color, sounds, feeling shifts and enjoy them.

A few of you may be finding this to be an unpleasant experience that challenges some kind of subjective feeling of harmony or coherence. Feel free to put all back the way it was before you started. This is simply an exploration and you are in charge of your preferences here.

Something really fundamental occurred, did it not? For example, often people have assessed their number five preference as less 'real' or even described it as a non-entity to the others. There may be inner differentiation in such areas as brightness, clarity and how close we see our inner image. If, for example, we give number five the color, sound and vibration of number three, it creates a whole different quality of experience. It leads to a new feeling and different value inferences. Explore the difference in each of the other meanings as well. Now think about your life anew in these areas.

Interesting, isn't it? Just continue to explore. These value linkages may be very useful to you, or may not be useful to you at all. Explore again a second time to test. Try the color and sound of number three with number five and of number two with number four. Now again, try the color and sound of number one with number three. Ask yourself: What experiences are valuable? What are not? And, how do you know?

Color, sound, and form hold deep meaning for us. Often people get brand new value insights, coherency, and joy with various inter-relationships and changes. The mandala of consciousness can open up into rich integrations.

The first 'word' of the logic system described by the Hebrew Bible starts with the phrase, "Let there be light." The second statement is about form. Balanced forms awaken us into our own sacred geometry of the mind.

Every phenomena can be distinguished this way. For example, light shows all aspects; form, profess, structure, and specific content. A beam of light is capable to particularize into one photon or 'particle' in the same way that our thought system can become totally reduced or totally expanded.

Who are we, as human map-makers, when our consciousness can be so profoundly affected by exploring our responses with basic geometric symbols? Explore this for yourself now and ask inwardly for some information about space shaping, coloring and diagramming. Ponder this! What produces the experience of inner coherence for you?

APPENDIX 5:

Russian Dolls of the Mind

With the diagram below, I also want to introduce the *Russian Doll* idea. You have probably seen stacking 'Matryoshka dolls,' one fitting inside the next until there are five to even eight or fifteen enclosed containers. The idea is important since we can examine 'levels' of inclusivity as we explore *Being*.

Diagram A5.1: The Russian Doll System as an Idea

The mind is an emergent system and a crucible for the development of inspired 'next level' self-discoveries. This means it is relevant to ask the types of questions that assist exploring and developing our emerging 'Russian Dolls of awareness.' This is a valuable source of effective four quadrant thinking.

With four quadrant systems, it is possible to discover how four aspects of a whole provide a beautiful complementary system. Between all the aspects, something even more integral often starts to emerge. I call this awareness of the deeper system *'Russian Doll Thinking,'* or emergent thinking. It provides a magnetic pathway to ask inner questions. The process of four quadrant visual pondering assists systems inside systems to emerge.

Russian Doll Thinking for Asking Inner Question

You can learn to notice *what's dissolving or being integrated in your ideas as well as what's emerging.* This means that all four quadrant diagrams can become useful for self-discovery if you consistently reference your creative questions with a relevant fouruadrant system. You will need to maintain an active Coach Position, or external observer position at the same time.

Diagram A5.2: The Vertical Dimension, The Resonance System

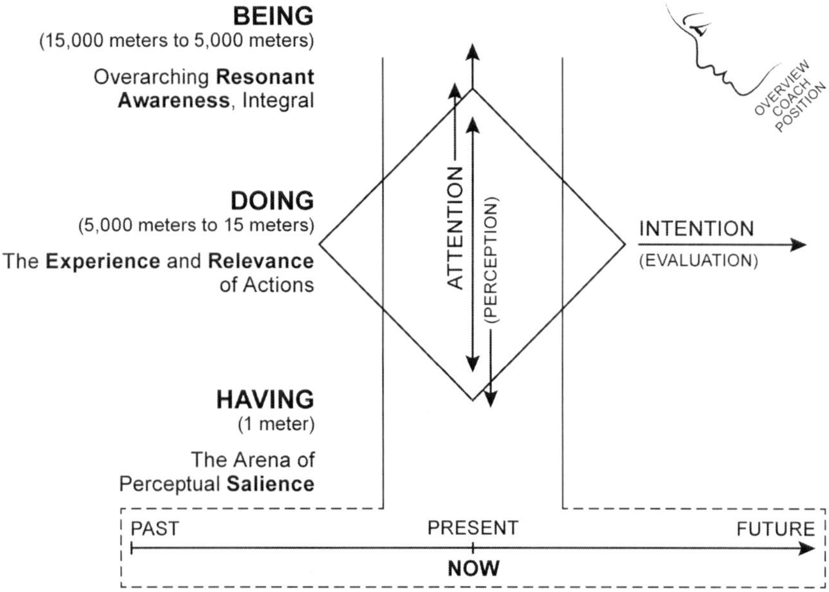

You can use integral pondering with any wholeness form (such as an even-sided geometric form). Aesthetic balance has provoked awareness since the time of Euclid. It's surprising, even paradoxical, when this occurs. We continually find deeper inner integrity, and a more finely tuned awareness through linking vision and value with purposeful questions.

Russian Doll Thinking: Notice the Aspects

- With the idea of the Russian Doll, we access a framework for asking questions based on the understanding that the mind is a multidimensional recording and integrated perception of every thought ever explored, including every sensory level and every abstract level of experience.
- Secondly, that every idea on the planet can be expressed at *any* level of abstraction.
- Thirdly, that every time we retrieve an idea or experience, we now surround it with a new, larger, multidimensional idea at a totally different level of integration and at a different logical level. This new level might hold our thoughts about our thoughts, our values about our values, or our feelings about our feelings.
- The corollary is that all ideas build in this way and each one, as it forms, gradually builds on the one before it and *now inside it*. We can see the progression of this growth inward to infinity so that we can explore the emotion inside the emotion, the memory inside the memory, and the idea inside the idea. Can you envision that?
- Thus, we can 'hold' an infinity of connected layers or levels of experience moving endlessly outward and endlessly inward.

  Once we make this idea *perceptible*, we can access any point or size of any idea and *perceive* the aspect we wish to explore. *Whatever we make perceptive and visual, we can reference as a comprehensive library. We can diagram it and use our map for further development. It can become usable and livable.*
- A key corollary of this: The larger the 'size' of the idea at formulation, the larger the base for flexible exploration. The more comprehensive the source idea at the start, the further we can build as we continue. When size is visualized, even metaphorically, we have access to all the inner ideas that build it to this point. Maps assist this process.

What does this actually mean? We can visualize the *vast*, and we can notice, metaphorically, the homeopathic-like 'solutions' found in every universe of thought. We find them as the tiniest and most essential quality of inner truth that sources the whole. We can see consciousness itself as containing a huge variety of Russian Dolls of such thought building. We can see our human mind as an inspired system of developmental emergence.

Invite one awareness source, the deep center, to occupy all thoughts in your universe of mind. Once invited, that source can unfold through the whole structure as an aspirational core. With this, you can explore the principal of the holographic, integrated capacity for conceptual and perceptual consciousness itself, on all logical levels.

- Any idea that brings order to a set of ideas lives at a higher logical level than the original set of ideas. It links all aspects. The idea of logical levels sits at a higher logical level than any particular set of logically connected ideas, or any idea or arrangement within that set. Notice: the idea of the idea is not a specific idea only: It contains the original idea and moves beyond it.
- Thus, the central idea of any logical levels *set* is a *process* idea that provides an infinite context for further development. It moves beyond the old structures and any of the old contents. It is an idea that holds expansive potential.
- There is always *a moving content, structure, process,* and *form* that inhabits every idea we can conceive of. With any idea, we can find the old contents and the old structures and, inside all that, notice a process of mind exploring itself that opens up to the deeper, living form of coherency itself.
- The common idea or belief that a single identity holds one perceptual position and one location at one time is one logical level below (and inside) a Coach Position that perceives all possible perceptions and moves one step beyond them, aspirationally, moment by moment.
- Our process of taking Coach Position on a thought system allows us to see all that is relevant, and to add new dimensions.

Yet we can never move beyond or see the Coach Position we inhabit until we take Coach Position on that one.

- This means that we need whole system thinking, which includes Coach Position, in order to think well and to build coherency of the Mind. Without that, our ideas do not move, grow, or change. Coach Position always allows us to move further and grow further.
- Because we grow all ideas like Russian Dolls, this signifies that our idea of time is naturally *timeless*, and that our common conception of choice belongs to a space that is, by its own inner nature, *choiceless*. The inner coherency develops all.
- It follows that abstraction in our ideas is generally about *order, the order beyond the order.* It is the order of in-form-ation. To move '*beyond the beyond*' — *the meta level* of any set of patterns—is to perceive the distinguishing patterns in the level within. Thus, by integrating ideas comprehensively in this way, we necessarily become capable to discern patterns of *order* that link and integrate what once seemed disordered.
- We perceive beauty when we continue to move attention throughout, while being aware of the order, wholeness and the coherency at the heart. Thus, 'double attention' awareness allows us to move to a 'third position,' a Coach Position on perception itself, and the capacity to continue asking the inner questions that takes us further into our own recognition of wholeness.
- Beauty, thus, is in the '*I*' of the beholder. The integrity of all patterns as contextually linked system emerges, beautiful, coherent and truthful to the core, as we recognize the self-consistency of all. We see an aspirational emergence in all phenomena.

Effective, moving process mind thus needs:

- *A conception of the whole.* Any diagram that holds a whole idea and a Coach Position will point us towards this.
- *At least three points of perception.* Three points allow Coach Position, yet tend to spin quickly. Four allow for more balance.

Five to seven points can be cogent. More than seven quickly become too difficult to view with 'process mind' and harden into a left-brain verbal system.

- A consciously chosen Coach Position outside to view the coherency.
- A consciously chosen Coach Position inside, to sense it, as-if.
- The *intention* to distinguish the order within.
- Questions that call forth distinctions. These are questions that request coherency. We need to aspire towards coherency and inner truth to find it.
- The realization that movement is always happening in the mind. Our aspiration towards beauty, truth and choice inspires a living truth that lies beyond, yet *within*, the observing point of view.
- Inner truth can be heard, felt, and seen. When we say the word, *"I,"* we can always hear, *to the core*, the resonance of our own inner truth. We can hear the inner tone of what rings true for us, and genuinely receive/perceive our felt truth. Inner awareness and vision align as we perceive.
- "All thinkable things are contained within the beauty that is unthinkable." *Coherency* has a life of its own, and emerges always just beyond the range of where we pause to look.

APPENDIX 6:

The Secret Life of a Diagram

Why Geometric Diagrams?

Four quadrant diagrams, wheel diagrams, equal-sided triangles and other geometric shapes are important tools to assist people to think dimensionally and to enlarge their visual intelligence. They allow us to visualize, organize, and explore core aspects of our key idea systems and to recognize complementary areas. As we do so, we build some observational principles that develop our capacity to think better. We begin to do effective, multifaceted overviewing, and move beyond the contractive verbal intellect.

Beyond our verbal mind with its separative, sequential thoughts, our capacity for geometric overview provides a strong framework for mosaic idea development. With a clear aim, Coach Position, and a multifaceted diagram, we can expand into high level contextual awareness with whatever task is at hand.

Learning to ponder using geometric forms is particularly relevant to all developmental learning as it directly maps to the important questions that stimulate our creative explorations. Notice what happens when you are creating a quadrant system, an exploration wheel, or other types of visual self-coaching frameworks? Even the simplest geometric ideas, such as those found in Diagram A5.1, 'change' the mind. Hail to inspired emergence and our humble aspirations to perceive this!

Nine Aspects of a Geometric Diagram

What happens when we link a geometric framework to well-designed diagrams or maps? We unconsciously engage nine different areas of differentiation within a model of wholeness. Like an iceberg with nine-tenth below the surface, this deeper knowing capacity moves us well below the surface of our questions into the depth of our intelligence system.

Nine aspects of a diagram give us nine different dimensions of *choice*. They create nine aspects of qualitative comprehension, and with this, our deeper intelligence creates effective perspectives for well-formed choices. We discover this as an inspired emergence of self-knowledge. We develop richness in our understanding so that our diagram and our game becomes valuable to us.

In quick summary these nine aspects include:

(one) the *purpose* of the diagram or game and the specific goals that accompany this. Our aspirational *intention* sets the framework for what we can discover

(two) the *edge lines* defining outside and inside

(three) the *rules*, principles, and policies for accurate play or use

(four) the *subdivisions* of the diagram or board to create the *particular parts* or gameboard *partitions* that support the purpose of the imagery

(five) the *current status*, often shown by a marker on the diagram or a 'piece' on the board

(six) the *prior measurements indicators*, defining the pathways explored and the momentum of change up to now

(seven) the *next steps or futures indicator*, often indicated by dotted lines, arrows, or color shifts

(eight) at least one outside observer position or Coach Position giving a view on the whole diagram or game from an external perspective

(nine) the *centerpoint* of the diagram. Most geometric diagrams shapes or boards have a *point* — usually a centerpoint, as a clear physical location

We outline these on a chart and follow with some example diagrams.

Nine Aspects of a Diagram: Setting a Gameboard

Element	Observation
1. Purpose Indicator	We declare the diagram as a unity framework to define the purpose. Our purpose defines the space inside. This also includes the goals of the diagram or game.
2. Edge Lines (Number of Edges)/ Border & Shape	The border allows us to define external and internal aspects. It creates a *shape* which has a natural meaning.
3. The Rules of the Game	Once purpose defines shape we can announce principles, rules, and policies for using the diagram or for playing the game.
4. Relational Spaces with Assigned Meanings/*Parts*	We set the meaningful relational spaces inside the whole to create a game board with inner boundaries, *partitions*, *parts* or special territories that match the relevant rules for using the diagram.
5. Current Status Indicators	We ask the question: "Where are we now?" This means we can set relational, movable status indications inside our various diagram territories.
6. 'Past' Indicators	We use the game board to measure movement completed and this also indicates the current status. If the rules and principles assist us to define our overall game, the prior measurements and 'past indicators' on the diagram define pathways once used which, when overviewed, assist us to move further. This also allows us to measure our momentum.
7. The Next Step Indicators	We use the diagram or gameboard to define potential future directions, according to the rules. We indicate future directions with symbols, (arrows, dotted lines, etc.) We now can 'play forward' with the gameboard using the assigned boundaries and territories to define next steps and potential futures.
8. Coach Positions Outside	We can overview our game as a totality with whole system viewing from the outside. We can also associate inside to be in the game, and view from an inner Coach Position that also includes *sensing*. There is always a Coach Position beyond the Coach Position, both inward and outward.
9. The Point	Every balanced diagram has a convergent point. We can sense relationships between all aspects when we focus from 'the point.' And, if we ask, "What is the point," we use the diagram to open up our creativity system. It is then easier to explore our diagram and game both outwardly and inwardly as a multifaceted, moving system since we take a pivotal 'learning point of view.'

Geometric Diagram Examples

Diagram A6.1: The Purpose

Set this clearly in your own mind as your main aim — your ultimate aim. Visualize your shape as holding the space for this aim.

Diagram A6.2: The Edge Lines

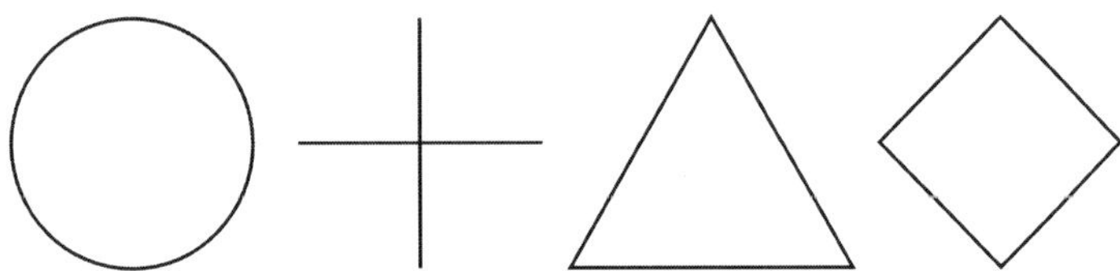

Diagram A6.3: The Rules

Rules are the area of inner discovery. Ask yourself: What is the most effective use of this tool for my exploration? How am I using it when I get both clear visions, inner congruence, and clear action steps? Follow those rules going forward.

Diagram A6.4: The Indicated Subdivisions of the Diagram

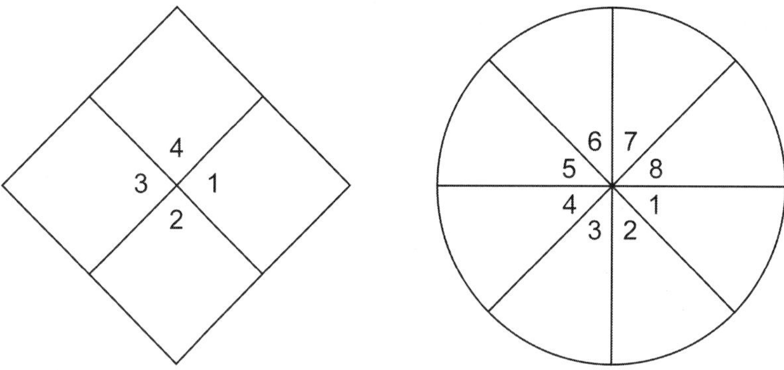

Diagram A6.5: The Current Status Indicator

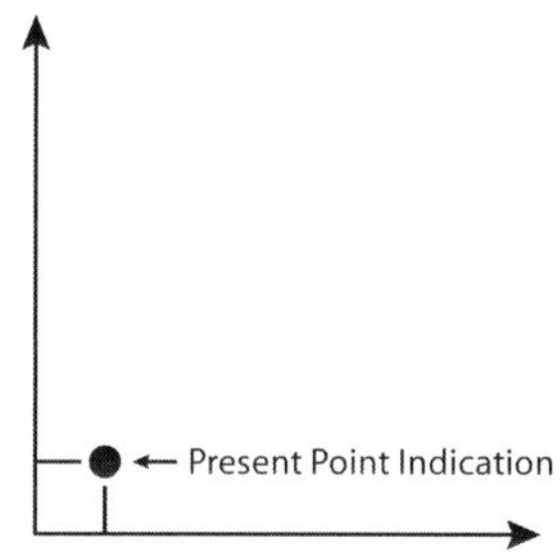

Diagram A6.6: Prior Measurements Indicators

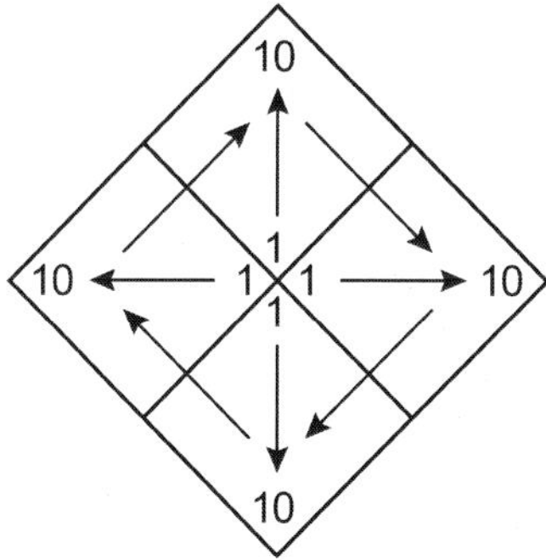

Diagram A6.7: The Next Step Indicator

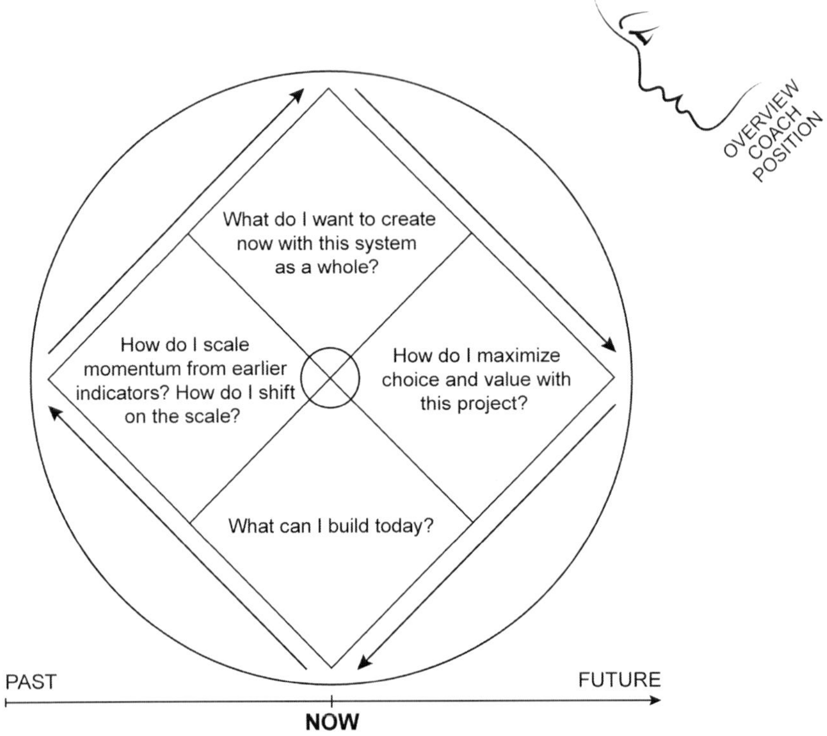

Diagram A6.8: Coach Position Indicators

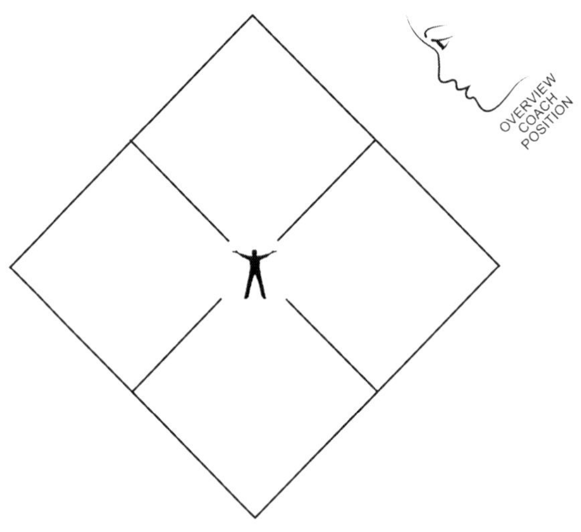

Diagram A6.9: The Point

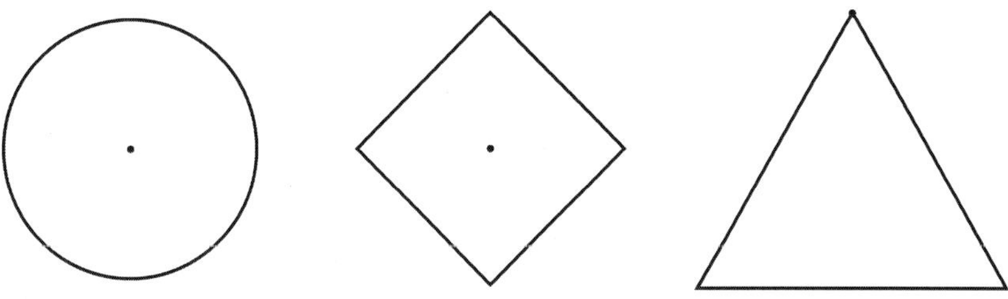

With visualization and a sensing tool like a diagram, we create a focus for inner questioning. We move below the surface of the verbal mind with our comprehensive 'viewing intelligence.' Conscious exploration assists this.

To use the metaphor of music, the inner music of a diagram is very thematic. The theme moves us back and forth, both inward to the central point and outward to the wider aspects. Moving inside (through our purpose) assists us in having an *associated* experience of these different aspects. Moving outside through Coach Position awareness allows us dissociated overview of all the elements.

We can engage any multifaceted diagram from both outside and inside and it is very useful to do so. We are exploring two kinds of Coach Position when we do this. We want to take external Coach Position to overview the whole system. We also can discover the value of associative Coach Position, from the inside. It allows us to get more internally balanced and flexible because we learn how to sense the balance point and to move into balance with all divergent aspects. We become like a small child exploring both the edge and the center of a children's playground wheel. If you are visualizing you see many more aspects when you move from inside to outside in this way. If you are communicating or trying to express big thoughts beyond words, these different viewpoints assist idea development.

The nine aspects of a diagram enrich all aspects of living experience. Our contextual awareness, naturally hologrammatic and richly patterned, is informed by our resonant perception. Our purpose becomes inspired. Enjoyment emerges naturally.

APPENDIX 7:

Characterization

What happens when we declare that someone has 'always been' a specifically labeled, characterized, or defined kind of person? To '*understand*' something means to '*stand under*,' to identify the 'meaning inside the meaning.' The word *identity* means 'the same,' so in this case the meaning inside the meaning starts with '*always the same*.' Our judgments can easily be taken on by those who we judge.

If we see someone as always the same then we are dividing the world into two kinds of people: those with *one* kind of identity, and those with another. Our linguistic brain hears 'sameness' and recreates 'self' by the sameness rules. We, ourselves, set these rules by declaring ourself to be a certain way — for example, on track or off track, a leader or a follower, fair or unfair, peaceful or angry, forgiving or unforgiving. Evaluations are declarations and people make them a lot!

The following is a key aspect of this: Suppose you say: *"I am confused,"* you put *self*, *(I am)*, on one side of a line. There are those in the world who are confused, like '*I*,' and also those others on the other side of the line who aren't confused. We have defined two types with this identity template, and they're now entirely and forever apart — by definition! In other words, '*who we are*' is, by definition, a '*forever state*.' This means that with an "I am confused" declaration, you create *confusion* as an identity! Any verbal evaluation of a negative kind must necessarily create constriction and rigidity: first, because it is a lie — since no-one has such a one-only kind of identity; and second, because it also puts you into the permanent role of outside evaluator.

Characterizations appear whenever we evaluate others. And here's the rub: Notice that on a deeper level we define ourself as 'human' and therefore the same for *all* of us. Our *context* is sameness. We have already declared our 'joint identity'! This means we apply all evaluations as 'the same' for self as we make for others.

The interesting part of this is that it doesn't matter who we are discussing, 'self' or 'other.' Inwardly, *'identity,' by definition, naturally includes us all.* Why? Because, with our emotional-relational system, which experiences from 'now is all,' we both feel, sense and 'know' the defined identity to be one and the same — despite our intellectual, verbal conclusions otherwise. Emotionally, we can only know any identity associatively by trying it on. That is what identity as 'idem' really enforces, linguistically.

This means that to understand any characterization we have given to ourself or to others, such as 'able' or 'unable,' 'smart' or 'stupid,' we first recognize it! And, we can only recognize from *inside* our '*self-definition.*' We notice the *resonance* that the definition creates in us. For example, if you were to define a person as 'mean-spirited,' you can only understand this through understanding mean-spiritedness in yourself. Now, through declaration, you 'fix' upon these features and declare them as 'permanent' in *that* person's 'identity' (and correspondingly in your own). It is as if completely separate and distinct from other features. *Whatever declaration we create for another, we must also resonate with within ourselves. We may see it in the 'other' but we are creating the vibrational level inside our own bodies!*

All role thinking is very simplistic. It diminishes your life choices. If you divide yourself or others into 'identities' in any 'permanent' way based on closure speaking your own life gets reduced to be the same. Describing someone, perhaps, as a 'penny pincher' or a 'philanderer' means we use criteria that doesn't relate to their inner world or their own self-discovery. This means we lose the opportunity to know them better or to influence them. You also now fix or hold in place any negative identity habit you have labeled in the other as a double and hidden identity for yourself, a 'twin' self that you cannot or must *not be* (and therefore *are*)! This gradually fixes and rigidifies the 'self.' In fact, we *then begin to harden the mirror of the identity we have defined as 'not self'* to be an alternate role we actually live from.

Consciousness is our ground of Being, and consciousness is always changing, growing, and developing, so we easily create both confusion and long-term sadness with this habit. We may become sad and only if we make rigidity a requirement to move away from this person or that and no longer allow ourselves to actually see them as growing and developing. We narrow our life.

Identity definitions easily become our blind spot because with them, we step outside of the 'inner meaning' of our life. It shifts our capacity to see the world since we *look* only to *see our own viewpoint*. We step out of the discovery of meaningful growth in both ourselves and others, and our life begins to rigidify — one judgment at a time. Some people live totally in declared evaluation roles for a lifetime and never notice that the role of external critic or 'know it all' allows no Coach Position for learning and for *self*-awareness.

The fallout is that everything we state about another person immediately visits our 'self' as a felt state. A blessing becomes a form of declaration that we then feel. In the same way we also feel any curse we deliver to another. They each visit us when we express them since in everything we say, the sameness framework maps across to include us. Since 'identity' means sameness, "I am" or "You are" as identity definitions only become useful when we generously declare possibility, opportunity, choice to change, learning, forgiveness, appreciation, and freedom for each person.

We can always expand our life as we expand beyond these judgemental identity beliefs since the identity idea is only a simple linguistic declaration that we can change — with *one outward verbalization* and determined follow through. Declare awareness and freedom as your fundamental identity, then step into *this* and live from it!

ENDNOTES: Volume I

1. (WHAT'S INSIDE PAGE)

See The Art & Science of Coaching, www.erickson.edu

In Volume II, **Part 3**, we focus on several great games, continuing what we call 'the three staircases' to higher level integrative thinking. Each is a staircase to what we call The Arrow's Tip — a point of integrative mastery and practical enlightenment. In Volume II, we explore the Right Staircase. You develop skills with formats A, B, C, and D.

With Volume II, you will learn how to ask the kind of questions that promote high-level inner response to your attention. The three staircases including Format D strongly assist you to dissolve old negative internal dialogue systems while accelerating the flow of value awareness, self-development and integration.

We explore how to build the deeper meaning of 'integrated mind' to unfold life's deeper meanings. We also move four quadrant thinking to the key questions of human development, particularly the nature of inner truth. You will discover exercises to explore mystic levels of realization.

Throughout Volume II, Part 4, we work with integrity development and 'inner truth' development. We test how to link to and accelerate this further. We unfold the nature of wholeness — even in the very moments we experience it. We develop the combined practices useful for integrative life development.

2. (PAGE F-4)

VAK is a common acronym for the combined label:
Visual-Auditory-Kinesthetic

3. (PAGE F-5)

Perceptual Positions:

1st Position – looking through your own eyes

2nd Position – looking though the eyes of significant others

– stepping into someone else's body and looking out of their eyes at you — as if you could!

3rd Position – looking from Outside Observer Position or 'Coach Position'

– looking from observer position or camera position

4th Position – looking from a 'through time' position

– seeing 'this' life through time; even as a thumbnail timeline

– seeing 'this group of people' through time

5th Position – inside 'we' position through time

4. **(PAGE 9)**

Notice also that Coach Position (Observer Position) inside the map creates a two-dimensional associative model of the Mind. The Mind is modeled on a four quadrant map with the third dimension created by Observer Position, which is outside of the system. Viewed from outside this creates a three-dimensional model of the Mind.

As you view a picture of a four quadrant map, you acquire a natural Coach Position on the content of the map. Hence, you can look at the map from a third dimension, so you get to move out of your own system and you can actually have a look at it. We model this in most of our diagrams with a small 'observer' in the upper right corner.

5. **(PAGE 11)**

Pre-hending defined: "To lay hold of; to seize."

6. **(PAGE 14)**

George Miller's original article postulated that the conscious mind could hold 7 (+ or - 2) 'bits' of information at one time, all gathered through different input channels. See *The Magical Number Seven, Plus or Minus Two: Some Limits on our Capacity for Processing Information*, George A Miller, The Psychological Review, 1956, vol 63, pp.81-97. There have been many further experiments that have gradually recoded the span of immediate memory (or working memory) reducing it to the generalization of 4 (+ or - 2). See particularly, Helen Pearson's research study for the November 6, 2002 Society of Neuroscience.

7. **(PAGE 15)**

We need to address the question of why we present the reader with a four quadrant model and not a three- or five-quadrant model of the Mind or any other kind. Our Mind, in principle, can mirror all possible states of our universe. However, our consciousness Mind can hold only a limited number of aspects at the same time. Hence, the answers are rooted in the symmetries of our space and the complex mathematics describing it. The upper limit for the model is the number of chunks of attention a conscious Mind can hold.

8. **(PAGE 24)**

Each 'thought shape' follows natural self-definitions. Structure and process frameworks follow rule structures you can discover. We intuitively create rules for the inner 'diagram system' we naturally develop inside each 'thought shape.' We can use this to create an integral system combining inner and outer. When the framework rules are well set, we are able to explore the associative aspects of our assumptions without being caught by old simplifications.

9. **(PAGE 35)**

The idea of the Triune Brain System, a model developed by Paul D. MacLean in the late 1960's is a model of the brain's evolution. It is supported in general by biology but is more expansive and diverse than originally thought. The inner system of life development shows other key areas of expansion. Many animals show some aspects of this. The 'Reptilian Structures,' the basal ganglia are also found in fish. Humans have a growing neocortex. This is also true for the other higher mammals, though differently.

Various capacities also seem to show up when the members of a species practice a new skill. For example, some species of parrots are becoming increasingly able to use language to think with. A major aspect in the brain systems of all species seems to be neuroplasticity. To put attention on something and to practice it eventually sees it stabilized as a skill.

The fundamental areas for human development, however, are seen in the diverse brain capacities. Our brain shows contrastive requirements that can collide. We flourish as we develop the emotional-relational dimension and the cognitive dimension both.

Understanding brain evolution makes a difference to mind evolution as we learn to develop beyond the linguistic-emotional constraints that impede and interrupt visioning abilities. Fear-based constraints can quickly become 'thought habits,' so that people may automatically impede the process of personal mind exploration. Practicing the exercises in this volume can move us past typical impediments.

10. **(PAGE 48)**

More information on the Great Yoga Systems is directly available from Wikipedia (www.wikipedia.com). See Hatha, Bhakti, Jnana, and Kriya Yoga.

11. (PAGE 50)

With Diagram 3.5, you view three 'empty' quadrants that will be gradually explored as we move through Volumes I and II.

12. (PAGE 59)

Wolfgang Amadeus Mozard, from a letter c. 1789. E. Holmes, THE LIFE OF MOZART INCLUDING HIS CORRESPONDENCE Chapman & Hall, 1878, pp. 211-13, It goes as follows:

"When I am, as it were, completely myself, entirely alone, and of good cheer — say traveling in a carriage, or walking after a good meal, or during the night when I cannot sleep — it is on such occasions that my ideas flow best and most abundantly. When and how they come, I know not, nor can I force them. Those pleasures that please me I retain in memory, and am accustomed, as I have been told, to hum them to myself. If I continue in this way, it soon occurs to me how I may turn this or that morsel to account, as to make a good dish of it, that is to say, agreeable to the rules of counterpoint, to the peculiarities of the various instruments, etc.

All this fires my soul, and, provided I am not disturbed, my subject enlarges itself, becomes methodized and defined, and the whole, though it belongs, to stand almost complete and finished in my Mind, so that I can survey it, like a fine picture or a beautiful statue, at a glance. Nor do I hear in my imagination the parts successively, but I hear them, as it were, all at once (gleich alles zusammen).

What a delight this I cannot tell! All this invention, this producing, takes place in a pleasing lively dream. Still the actual hearing of the tout ensemble is after all the best. What has thus been produced I do not easily forget, and this is perhaps the best gift I have my Divine Maker to thank for.

When I proceed to write down my ideas, I take out of the bag of memory, if I may use that phrase, what has preciously been collected into it in the way I have mentioned. For this reason the committing to paper is done quickly enough, for everything is, as I have said before, already finished: and it rarely differs on paper from what it was in my imagination.

At this occupation I can therefore suffer myself to be disturbed; for whatever may be going around me, I write, and even talk, but only of vegetables and geese, of Gretel or Barbel, or some such matter. But why my production takes from my hand that particular form and style that makes them Mozartish, and different from the works of other composers, is probably owing to some cause which renders my nose so large or so aquiline, or, in short, makes it Mozart's and different from those of other people. For I really do not study, or aim at any originality."

13. (PAGE 104)

Remember, the Google Maps metaphor can be used as a 'stepping stone' exploration; first dissociative, but immediately after, integrating in a kinesthetic experiential associative perception as we continue to build forward. We feel if it is right for us. This means it is a comprehensive metaphor first for Associative Coach Position, but then also for this integrative mapping process which involves 'sensing the value of the viewpoint.' For the Associative Coach Position, in this case, it is visually shown as located in the middle of the two-dimensional, four quadrant model. It is as if the Coach Position is moving along the vertical axis of the model. Diagram 7.1 would be superimposed on the four quadrant picture with the horizontal axis coinciding.

For the dissociative, three-dimensional viewing model, the viewing point of the metaphor is outside of the plane of the picture and it is moving closer or further relative to the picture. Diagram 7.1 and 7.2 become three-dimensional with a person walking on the four quadrant model.

We can always describe the dimensions of time, location, and value, all of which can be expanded with Coach Position on a fourth dimension. See the next Volume in this series.

14. (PAGE 108)

The vertical level can run along the vertical axis in a two-dimensional associative model and perpendicular to the piece of paper in a three-dimensional dissociative model.

15. (PAGE 115)

We seemingly live in a four-dimensional space-time. However, present physicists' theories require more dimensions to effectively describe all possible interactions of the Universe in a united way. Our Mind can be mapped on a four quadrant map, which is actually a four-dimensional model of our internal reality projected on a two-dimensional paper. We can project this additional dimension of time on a horizontal axis, building possible expansion into future or past within the model. Use the model to trigger your own Mind exploration, expanding 'past' and 'future.'

16. (PAGE 125)

Purpose is a quality of vision that we 'set' through declaration and request as described in Chapters 11 and 12 of this Volume. The dedication at the front of this Volume is an example of declaration and request.

17. (PAGE 133)

Let us start with two exploratory premises: 1) the Universe is being described by physics and mathematics but also by ourselves in a unique way, personally and metaphorically; and 2) Our Universe and our Mind show mirrored reflection. Our Mind constantly reflects our immediate idea of life, which seems like a three-dimensional reality we can describe. It then follows that the laws of physics and mathematics are also reflected in the Mind. Classical physics is, in principle, deterministic and there is no room for uncertainty. Given all starting positions and velocities of elements in a mathematically consistent system, the evolution of the system in time can be calculated in principle. A future is set. No surprises here.

Now, when we ask an open-ended question and we get a whole range of possible answers, we develop a whole set of possible futures 'as if' they were possible. The observer selects one by observing the whole range of options.

The idea of multiple levels of Coach Position, Diagram 9.2, has no analogy in classical physics! The only reasonable analogy is offered by quantum physics where the laws of Mind are reflected. This is the metaphoric context in which we refer to the word 'quantum.' Roger Penrose, one of the leading theoretician physicists and mathematicians of our time, offered a lengthy elaboration on the topic of quantum elements present in the functioning of our minds in his two books: *The Emperor's New Mind: Concerning Computers, Minds, and The Laws of Physics* and *Shadows of the Mind: A Search for the Missing Science of Consciousness.* Also see Henry P. Stapp's book, *Mindful Universe: Quantum Mechanics and the Participating Observer.*

18. (PAGE 177)

The 'Generation of Diversity' is usually known by the initials alone.

Suggested Reading

Almaas, A. H. *Diamond Heart, Book One: Elements of the Real in Man*. Berkeley, CA: Diamond Books, 1987

Bentov, Itzhak. *Stalking the Wild Pendulum: On the Mechanics of Consciousness*. Rochester, VT: Destiny Books, 1977.

Calleman, Carl Johan. *The Purposeful Universe: How Quantum Theory and Mayan Cosmology Explain the Origin and Evolution of Life*. Rochester, VT: Bear & Company, 2009.

Capra, Fritjof. *The Tao of Physics: An Exploration of the Parallels Between Modern Physics and Eastern Mysticism*. Boulder, CO: Shambhala Publications Inc., 2010.

Clark, Ronald W. *Einstein, The Life and Times*. New York: Avon Books, 1971.

Goleman, Daniel et al. *Measuring the Immeasurable*. Boulder, CO: Sounds True Inc., 2008.

Harris, Sam. *Waking Up: A Guide to Spirituality Without Religion*. New York: Simon & Schuster Paperbacks, 2014.

Jaynes, Julian. *The Origin of Consciousness in the Breakdown of the Bicameral Mind*. Boston, MA: Houghton Mifflin Company, 1976.

Jung, C. G. *Memories, Dreams, Reflections*. London: Collins & Routledge & Kegan Paul, 1963.

Jung, C. G. *The Archetypes and the Collective Unconscious: The Collected Works of C. G. Jung*. London: Routledge & Kegan Paul, 1968.

Jung, C. G. *The Symbolic Life, Miscellaneous Writings: The Collected Works of C. G. Jung*. London: Routledge & Kegan Paul, 1977.

Lowen, Walter. *Dichotomies of the Mind: A Systems Science Model of the Mind and Personality.* New York: Wiley-Interscience, 1982.

Lowen, Walter. *Personality Types: A Systems Science Explanation.* North Charleston, SC: Booksurge Publishing, 2007

Lynch, Dudley, & Kordis, Paul L. *Strategy of the Dolphin: Scoring a Win in a Chaotic World.* New York: William Morrow & Company Inc., 1990.

Macy, Joanna. *The Dharma of Natural Systems: Mutual Causality Buddhism and General Systems Theory.* Albany, NY: State University of New York Press, 1991.

Merrell-Wolff, Franklin. *The Philosophy of Consciousness Without an Object.* New York: The Julian Press, 1973.

Pearce, Joseph Chilton. *Evolution's End: Claiming the Potential of Our Intelligence.* San Francisco, CA: Harper, 1992.

Rosenblum, Bruce, & Kuttner, Fred. *Quantum Enigma: Physics Encounters Consciousness* (2nd edition). New York: Oxford University Press, 2011.

Sheldrake, Rupert. *Morphic Resonance: The Nature of Formative Causation.* Rochester, VT: Park Street Press, 2009.

Stapp, Henry P. *Mindful Universe: Quantum Mechanics and the Participating Observer* (2nd edition). London/New York: Springer Heidelberg Dordrecht, 2007.

Talbot, Michael. *The Holographic Universe.* New York: Harper Collins, 1991.

Tarnas, Richard. *Cosmos and Psyche.* New York: Penguin Group, 2007.

Tulki, Tarthang. *Time, Space and Knowledge: A New Vision of Reality.* Oakland, CA: Dharma Publishing, 1977.

Whitehead, Alfred N. *Process and Reality* (corrected edition by D. R. Griffin and D. W. Sherburne). New York: Free Press, originally published in 1929.

Wilber, Ken. *The Holographic Paradigm and Other Paradoxes.* Boston, MA: Shambhala, 1982.

Wilber, Ken. *No Boundary: Eastern and Western Approaches to Personal Growth.* Boulder/London: New Science Library, Shambhala, 1981.

Erickson Coaching International

Head Office:

201-2555 Commercial Drive	1 800 665 6949 (North America)
Vancouver	1 604 879 5600 (Vancouver, BC, Canada)
British Columbia	Fax: 1 604 879 7234
Canada	info@erickson.edu
V5N 4C1	www.erickson.edu

Erickson Coaching International has been expanding programs and courses into about five countries and language groups per year since 2007. In 2015, Erickson Training programs certified by the International Coach Federation were held in 44+ countries.

Courses are available on-site and online. Check for the country of your choice. You can also find us on Facebook and LinkedIn.

Contact www.erickson.edu to find out more. Look for programs either online or in the following countries:

Armenia
Australia
Austria
Barbados
Brazil
Bulgaria
Canada
Chile
China
Croatia
Cyprus
Czech Republic
England
Estonia
France
Georgia
Germany
Hungary
India
Indonesia
Italy
Jamaica
Kazakhstan
Kenya
Latvia
Lithuania
Macedonia
Moldova
Malaysia
Norway
Oman
Poland
Portugal
Romania
Russia
Saudi Arabia
Serbia
Singapore
Slovakia
Sweden
Switzerland
Thailand
Tobago
Trinidad
Tunisia
Turkey
Ukraine
USA
Vietnam

ISBN: 978-0-9953329-2-8

9 780995 332928 >